To Moira, who went through hell for this one

CONTENTS

Prologue – Begin with the Dream..6

Chapter One – Making it Happen...11

Chapter Two – The Space Girl..28

Chapter Three – Down the Rabbit Hole................................42

Chapter Four – Narrowboat Nomads.....................................59

Chapter Five – Guns and Roses..72

Chapter Six – Another Lovely Day in Paradise...................85

Chapter Seven – O, 'Tis Reading...102

Chapter Eight – Rowing Rows...118

Chapter Nine – Paints and Sinners......................................132

Chapter Ten – Of Queens and Castles.................................146

Chapter Eleven – Doing it Their Wey..................................159

Chapter Twelve – Into the Stranglers' Lair........................173

Chapter Thirteen – Carpe Diem...191

Chapter Fourteen – Capital Pains..205

Chapter Fifteen – Secret Worlds...220

Chapter Sixteen – Tunnel Vision...235

Chapter Seventeen – Westward Woe....................................249

Chapter Eighteen – Racing Uncertainty..............................264

Chapter Nineteen – Christmas Is Coming
(and the Geese Are Getting Out)..278

Chapter Twenty – Transnational, or Home from Home....295

Acknowledgements...312

PROLOGUE
Begin with the Dream

So there we were on Pangbourne Meadows on the River Thames on one of the hottest days of the year. I was splayed on the grass in the sunshine, messing about trying to repair something or other off the boat except that it was too hot to concentrate and I'd found myself dozing through the afternoon, disturbing my half-dreams only for long enough to get another beer from the fridge or to shift position to avoid the sun. I really should have put on suncream but I couldn't be bothered. It was that sort of day, the sort of day when you can't be fussed with anything.

Em, of course, *had* put on suncream – but then Em is much more sensible about this sort of thing. She was sitting motionless in a wicker chair on the front deck in her sunglasses, sheltered from the sun by a rainbow-coloured umbrella carefully positioned on the roof to provide maximum shade. She was reading some novel, probably, knowing her, by some in vogue feminista or other controversialist. The cat, Kit, was stretched out languorously on her lap and she was mindlessly toying with it, tickling it around its neck.

Meanwhile the river lapped against the bank, rocking the boat so gently that it barely pulled against its mooring lines. The current was slow and sluggish; there was hardly any flow on it at all.

Looking back on that time at Pangbourne it was, I suppose, the apotheosis of an ideal. It was the culmination of our long-planned project to leave home and live on a boat. And I guessed from the way they looked at us that many of the people who passed us on the towpath that day, walking their dogs or taking a stroll, might have seen us as a model for their own lives. We were, after all, the embodiment of a commonplace aspiration: we had escaped the rat race; we were living on the water. One or two of those surveying our brightly coloured boat *Justice*, its brasses glinting in the sunshine, might have been curious enough to want to know how we'd managed it and how this unremarkable couple had succeeded in pulling off the trick. Why were we the ones sunning themselves here, at this place, at this moment, during this long, blistering summer? Why was it us on the boat and not them? Why were they bystanders to this tranquil scene and not the central characters?

One couple let their curiosity get the better of them and struck up a conversation. This happens frequently all over the place. We used to do it ourselves decades ago when we were beginning to get interested in the waterways; we'd done it more recently too, just a couple of years before, in fact, when we'd been cruising on the River Stort in Hertfordshire and had come across a couple on their boat on a day as lovely as this and in a mooring equally idyllic. That brief, chance meeting had revived plans we'd been nurturing for nearly 40 years to live on our boat. It had been the reminder that we weren't getting any younger, and that dreams are OK in their own way, but that they'll never be more than dreams until you act on them.

'Beautiful day,' the woman said. 'Lovely boat,' the man added, addressing himself to me. 'You live on her, do you?'

Now, when we weren't living on the boat full time, this used to be a difficult one to answer because, strictly speaking, anyone who spends time afloat, even on holiday, is living on a boat. You sleep on it, you eat on it, you wash on it… the fact is that over just a few days you can do everything which comprises life, from the mundane to the magical. But that's not 'living' on a boat, is it? And people asking you the question know that. They're looking for something more from you, some measure of the commitment you've made to your lifestyle. They may not realise what they're doing, but the question they're asking is almost an abstract one in this context.

I used to blur the issue to conceal the truth. I'd explain that Em and I had owned various boats for decades, that we spent long periods on them, sometimes whole summers not to mention large parts of the autumn and winter too. But that wasn't the whole story and I knew it. Eventually I always felt constrained to add that, well, yes, we did have a house, in London as it happens. And finally I always had to admit that, well, no, we weren't actually living on the boat, not *properly* living on it because we could always go back to the house. Which meant, of course, that we hadn't completely committed to the waterways, that we always had a bolthole on the land, somewhere we could retreat to if the going got too tough.

Now, though, things were different, very different indeed.

Living on the boat? Yes, there was no doubt about it now; we were definitely living on the boat. Em had retired and we'd rented out the house. If the boat sunk we'd have nowhere to go. We'd be homeless and have to throw ourselves on friends and family and Premier Inn Ltd. OK, we might not lose all our worldly goods. But we'd lose a lot of them. Enough of them to hurt. Our toothbrushes and clean underwear for starters. Not to mention our bed, the only one we owned now after Em in a fit of generosity had given all the ones from the house to charity. And we'd lose tonight's dinner, don't forget that either – there'd be no salvaging that from the murky depths of the Thames. No, there was no need to shilly-shally this time, no need to vacillate or misrepresent the situation. We lived on the boat. Full stop.

I said as much to the couple.

They looked at me with eyes as wide as a cow's. It wasn't the first time this had happened. In fact cow-eyes were very much the order of the day whenever I told people, strangers or friends, what we'd done. It could have been a form of pity for the stupid people (i.e. us) who'd given up everything to embark upon this mad gypsy existence; though I like to think it was respect and admiration for the fact that we'd managed to get out of the rut and make a break for freedom.

'Leaving your house must have been a hard thing to do,' one of the pair said. 'Very hard indeed,' said the other.

I threw up my hands in derision. A hard thing to do? Pish! It was true, I didn't mind confessing, that there'd been one or two minor problems associated with our move to the water. One or two glitches, and snags along the way. But I didn't overplay it. It was no big deal. I didn't want to make too much of it – let alone to these new friends I'd just made, and in whose respect I liked to think I was still basking.

Put it out of your mind, it was nothing, I wanted to tell them. You can't dwell on the setbacks. Life is nothing without a challenge. What doesn't kill you makes you stronger, etc, etc. But I never got the chance to say anything because Em, who'd been sitting on the deck, apparently lost in her book, suddenly swept the cat off her lap, and stepped on to the bank where we were all standing. The look in her eye was murderous, like when she finds dental floss I've left on the side of the sink.

'No, it wasn't a *hard* thing to do; in fact, hard barely describes it,' she said, wrenching off her sunglasses. 'I'll tell you what it was; it was a bloody nightmare thing to do, a nightmare from start to finish. It was one of the most difficult things I've done in my life and even now I wonder if it was the right decision…'

CHAPTER ONE
Making it Happen

A bloke I used to work with told me once that more people commit suicide on a Monday than on any other day of the week. 'It's because they have a bad weekend and realise how unhappy they are at home,' he said. 'Then they go into work and realise they're even unhappier there.'

It was a Monday when he told me this; I'd only just got into the office and I hadn't even managed to grab a coffee. Why he brought up a topic like this when he did I can't imagine, but it couldn't have been to cheer me up, could it? I mean, you're not going to cheer anyone up by telling them something like that, are you? Especially at the beginning of the week? But perhaps that wasn't the idea. Perhaps he was after my job and trying to put notions into my head. I was his boss, you see. He could have seen this as a path to promotion. On the other hand, maybe he was just going through a bad spell and wanted to talk about it in that unfathomable way blokes do when the aim is not to talk about it at all. I can relate to that. I can relate to feeling bad about Mondays too. After all, none of us really like Mondays, do we? The least we can do is lend each other a bit of moral support as we struggle to get through them the best we can.

Em's approach was more direct. She'd had a dreadful Monday. She came home, threw her handbag on to the hatstand and announced with peremptory certainty, as if the date had been forever ordained in the stars, 'That's it. Decision taken. The thirtieth, that's my last day.'

'Your last day! What! You're thinking about topping yourself or something? It's that bad?'

She looked at me with incomprehension for a few moments. 'You know, Steve, you do say the oddest things sometimes; is it any wonder I worry about your mental health? I meant that I am packing in work, that's all. I've had it up to my back teeth. I just can't take another day on the treadmill, what with all these managers who haven't started shaving yet and all these new initiatives they're generating every ten minutes. And birdtable conferences – bird-table conferences! Whoever dreamed up that idea? Whoever dreamed up that name? Do they think the place is an aviary?'

This announcement, I have to confess, came as no great surprise. For months now – years, even – Em had been complaining about work. Not the actual work she did, which she'd always enjoyed and always thought worthwhile, but the people who ran the place. She worked for a charity, for heaven's sake. You know – care, compassion, kindness, that sort of stuff. The bosses treated it like a division of a FTSE 100 company. It had been clear to me for a while that this day was coming, and coming soon. And I suppose I felt I'd partly precipitated it myself by my own behaviour. Maybe knowing how it was with work I ought to have lent more husbandly support to her than I did. Maybe I should have been more solicitous and taken more interest in her interminable stories of office politics and departmental reorganisations. Maybe I should have turned into the male equivalent of a Stepford Wife, greeting her every night on the doorstep with a cocktail and a cheery exhortation that dinner was in the oven, honey.

Well, maybe…

What I certainly shouldn't have done is what I actually did, which was to abandon her for a canal narrowboat we'd owned for years. Even now I don't know how it happened, or why she allowed it, but I began embarking on long solo cruises around the country, using as an excuse the fact I wanted to write books about the waterways. Eventually we were only meeting up at weekends, sustaining our relationship the rest of the time with mobiles, which we spent so much time on I wondered sometimes if we shouldn't have married them rather than each other.

'Well, I can come with you on your trips now,' she announced brightly that night at the end of a celebratory bottle of something bubbly. 'There's nothing stopping us. We can rent out the house and go and live on the boat full time. Do you remember that couple we met on the River Stort a while back? They'd both retired and were living on the boat; now it's our turn. We've talked about doing it for long enough…' And it's true, we had. It was an idea we'd nurtured for almost as long as we'd known each other, from the time we'd first rented a narrowboat for a holiday to the time we first bought one, from the time we'd dreamed of having a boat purpose-built for us, to the time we sat down and designed it together. True, the idea had lain dormant for long periods. Life had got in the way of our plans, as life often does. We had family and the responsibilities that come with it; we both had careers too. But the idea never went away. It was like one of those wretched winter viruses that, once it's got its claws into you, hangs on forever. Somewhere in the back of our minds was always the idea that one day we would live on a boat together.

So why was I so unhappy at Em deciding that now was the time to do it? Why did I lie in bed that night tossing and turning with worry? Could it have been something to do with the fact that even at that early stage in the proceedings I'd begun to realise that maybe this wasn't going to be quite as easy as we thought?

Take the idea of renting out the house. This was key to the project; we couldn't afford to fund our plans any other way without selling the house and living off the proceeds, which we didn't want to do. OK, we were lucky enough to have some savings, but they weren't lavish. We hadn't got fortunes stashed away in tax havens, or massive share portfolios we could realise at the drop of a hat. True, we both had pensions, but we weren't at official retirement age. And even if we had been, after the financial crash they were nowhere near as valuable as they'd once been.

Financially, renting out the house was our only option; at least we could console ourselves with the knowledge that we were in an area where it was feasible to do it. We lived in London, in leafy Blackheath, close to the City and a step or two away from Canary Wharf. The housing market here was what the experts call 'buoyant'. This means that after the crash it didn't collapse as badly as it did in the rest of the country. But that's no surprise, given that the crash originated through the antics of bankers working in the City and Canary Wharf, many of whom lived in Blackheath. Blimey, if anywhere was going to be buoyant it was Blackheath.

So I wasn't concerned we'd get tenants. Nor was I much bothered what sort of tenants they'd be and what they might do to the house. No, what kept me awake at nights was something more fundamental than this, something which was gnawing at me in a way that didn't affect Em, who was caught up in the excitement of the moment and the decision she'd taken about work.

It was simply that it had dawned on me that we were going to be leaving home.

Now, you'd have thought I might have realised this much before we got this far. After all, I've got A-Levels and a university degree. Not that this counts for much. The human brain doesn't always make the connections it should; it doesn't always recognise the full implications of the actions it pursues. It was only when faced with the real prospect of leaving the house that the full significance of what we were doing dawned on me. What it meant was that we were renouncing our lives, jacking them in for something new. And we had very pleasant lives. The house was spacious and comfortable, warm and welcoming. We had lots of friends and we liked to socialise. We liked going to the pictures too, and to the theatre and even the opera from time to time. We liked the occasional meal out and a pint in pubs where people were friendly and everyone knew our names. We were waving goodbye to this, saying arrivederci to it all. This was the bottom line of the choice we'd made.

If you've been happy living somewhere – and we had been happy in Blackheath – uprooting is a raw process: it's a sort of death-like disconnection in which you shed bits of yourself before you make your final exit. The enormity of this struck me a couple of days later after I'd made a few phone calls and the first of a series of estate agents I'd contacted knocked on the door.

She was a woman, an attractive woman, as it happened – and that threw me. Really, I should have had the word sucker tattooed on my forehead. It made me forget she was an estate agent. Not that I have anything against estate agents. It's easy enough to diss them, but they do a job and if we didn't want that job doing we wouldn't use them. It's just that dealing with them you have to keep reminding yourself what the rules are. You can't afford to be naïve. Or blinded by your own sexual prejudice.

When she knocked on the door, wreathed in smiles, I took her to be a warm and caring individual who understood my needs and aspirations and wanted to satisfy them. In reality she was a hunting lioness licking her lips as she planned to strip my bones bare. I invited her inside and we sat drinking tea. The financial bit of our interchange I could stomach: the fees she'd take for this, the charges she'd exact for that, the payments she'd need for the other. This much I'd expected. What I wasn't prepared for, though, was her manner. Without ever once being rude, or even impolite, she later took me on a tour of my own house, telling me what was wrong with it, what needed doing to it and why, as it stood, it wouldn't be satisfactory for one of her 'clients'. (God, how I came to hate that word 'client' over the time I was dealing with estate agents. It was months before I came to terms with it, and then only because I was having a quiet pint on my own one night when I realised that I was a client too – a revelation which, I can tell you, nearly made me choke on my beer.)

But I suppose I can't complain. What she said about the state of the house, unpalatable though it was, was something that needed saying, and others told me the same later, except with more charm and subtlety. It was no use burying my head in the sand. The fact was that the crumbling old pile we'd lived in contentedly for years was actually a bit of a wreck which would need a serious injection of cash to bring it up to any sort of standard.

'How much of an injection of cash?' Em asked. This was a week or two later after she'd given in her notice and was coming to terms with the fact that she'd just packed in the best job she'd had in the middle of the worst depression since 1929.

'Roof work, replastering, complete redecoration from top to bottom, new carpet... Think of a figure,' I said, 'then double it.'

I paused while she took a sharp intake of breath. 'And that's just the house,' I went on. 'We need to start thinking about the boat too...'

She came up for more air. 'The boat? What's wrong with the boat? The boat's OK, isn't it?'

'Well, it's OK as long as you ignore the stove that's falling apart, the fire which is a serious health risk, the leaking side-hatches and the floor underneath them which has rotted as a result. And then there's the electrics. And the engine. And the... '

'All right, all right, I hear what you're saying. So how much then?'

'You know that figure I asked you to think of? The one I asked you to double? Well, double it again – then add a couple of thousand more just to be on the safe side.'

I could see her brow furrow as the scale of the project dawned on her. But then she brightened and when she spoke there was a note of the devil-may-care in her voice. 'I don't suppose we've got much choice now, have we?' she said. 'We've stepped off the cliff, we can't go back now. I suppose we'll just have to roll up our sleeves and do as much as we can ourselves to keep the costs down.'

And so it was that as Em worked out her notice, I was commuting between London and Banbury in Oxfordshire where the boat is moored, arranging to have work done, and doing a bit myself when I could find time. Meanwhile, the house was overrun by builders, who clad it in scaffolding before proceeding to pull it apart, wrenching off bits of roof and stripping back walls to bare brickwork. They made some vague promise that they'd put everything back together again at some indeterminate point in the future. Frankly, the early signs weren't encouraging, though. To add to the growing sense of chaos overwhelming our lives like a tsunami, the boat was soon in the same sort of mess as the house. My mate John who'd built it 22 years earlier had taken it into dry dock and had ripped out the hatch surrounds along with insulation and internal lining in an attempt to stop the leaks. At the same time I'd pulled up the rotting floor below so that you could see the slabs of concrete ballast below and the steel base-plate of the boat beneath that.

'It looks to me like it's been dripping since you built it,' I grumbled.

'Well it's not covered by a bloody guarantee after all this time if that's what you're thinking,' he said.

Whatever spare time Em and I had during this period of manic disarray seemed to be filled with so much work we never had a moment to ourselves. Even when I wasn't in Banbury actually working on the boat, the boat and what needed doing to it was never far from my mind. And in Blackheath there were those hundreds of little jobs on the house which had been put aside over the years and now needed doing.

You know the sort of thing: the jobs you tell yourself you'll do sometime when you get around to them – except that you never do get around to them. Now, with the reproaches of the estate agents still ringing in our ears, we had to knuckle down and do the lot – everything from that tap which had been dripping to that wobbly light fitting, from that dodgy shelf that had been on the verge of collapse to that rattling door handle that sooner or later would come off in someone's hand. In addition, in case anything that hadn't already gone wrong were to go wrong in the future, everything had to be checked over: gas, electrics, water, central heating, windows, doors, locks… the list was endless. Every day it seemed there was another man in a blue boiler suit at the door charging us 60-odd quid appearance money before he'd even opened his toolbag.

We consoled ourselves that if we could do nothing else we could at least do the decorating ourselves. We'd done enough of that in the past, so surely that wasn't beyond us. The problem, however, was that this was decoration on a scale we'd not had to face before. It wasn't just a room or two which needed freshening up: the whole place needed painting – all three storeys of it. If it had been a question of just emulsioning the walls and ceilings it would have been easy. But the state of the woodwork was a completely different story. A horror story. Most of the doors and windows in the house hadn't been stripped back since the place was built 150 years ago or whatever. New paint had just been layered on over the years, coat after coat of it, until it had the texture of a Braille history. There was nothing for it but to take it back to bare wood. We had some experience doing this using hot air blowers in other houses we'd lived in, but this didn't make us any more efficient at the job, or faster at it – just better at kidding ourselves how long it would take. I worked at it every day; Em joined me at weekends. But even with two of us on the case progress was painfully slow. Stripping a sash window as an amateur takes a couple of days, sometimes more. Soon we graduated to working two or three hours in the evenings as well, after the builders had knocked off, eating late with the acrid smell of burnt paint in our nostrils.

It took more out of us than we could have imagined. We're pen-pushers, remember, not used to hard graft. And we're not spring chickens either. Physically, the work was punishing – but it was punishing psychologically too, for the message from the estate agency we'd finally chosen to represent us was that everything, from the skirting boards upwards, had to be painted a pristine, unblemished white. This, we soon realised, was a process of obliterating ourselves from the house. Taking ourselves out of it. There had to be no sign we'd ever lived there.

Decorating like this was a slow and painful process, like having a limb gradually sawn off. But it was also like being trapped in some surreal alternative cosmos where things weren't as they should be. It was decorating, but not as we understand it, Jim. It wasn't beautifying the place or embellishing it; it wasn't enhancing or adorning it. It was painting it to reduce it to an inoffensive norm, and to eradicate any sign of our personal taste in case a potential tenant found it objectionable. Part of the process was clearing the house completely, moving our furniture either into a storage facility or into the attic. Essentially what we were doing was creating a three-dimensional blank canvas against which other people could play out their lives.

Meanwhile, these other people were beginning to arrive on the doorstep for viewings. Most of the potential tenants were charming and seemed to love the house – or at least they said they did, which is probably a very different thing. There were exceptions, though. A Danish couple seemed well mannered on the surface but their pursed lips and clipped manner couldn't conceal the fact that they really didn't like the place, and weren't much impressed by us either – especially when we didn't know whether the radiator covers came off for cleaning.

At least they didn't hang around long wasting our time. By contrast, an Australian couple were in the house half the morning. They must have been accustomed to living in expansive mansions in the outback. It wasn't that they didn't like the place. It was just that you could see from their faces they couldn't comprehend how anyone could live in somewhere no bigger than a sheep dip. For some reason they insisted on scrutinising the cellar, examining every dark corner of it as if they expected there to be more house hidden away down there. But perhaps I got that wrong. Perhaps they just wanted to check if it was an escape route back home. Either way, we never heard from them again.

I made another trip to Banbury. In my absence, work on the boat had advanced significantly. The hatches had been repaired, and John had installed a new wood-burning stove, and a high-tech battery charger/inverter system which was so expensive it makes my eyes water to think about it even now. Inspired by the progress, I rolled up my sleeves and finally got around to replacing the rotten floor. Afterwards John was scheduled to service the engine, and another old friend, Jez, was booked to paint our tired-looking livery. While he was doing his professional arty stuff along the side, relaying unrepeatable gossip to me about other painters as he worked, I slapped a very amateurish layer of non-slip across the roof and blacked the hull. A week later with no ceremony at all *Justice* was relaunched, resplendent in new paint job and with new signwriting.

'She looks better than she's done for years, like a new boat,' I said to Em over the phone. 'John's still got to rebuild the galley, which means we're going to have to decide very quickly about a new cooker and work surfaces and stuff. But the job's all but finished now. If we had to, we could just about live on her as she is.'

I was expecting Em to be excited at this news. I thought she'd be happy that at least we now had somewhere we could call home. But she didn't react to it at all. It took me a moment or two to realise that this was because she hadn't listened to a word I'd said. She was lost in a world of her own and everything I said had gone careering over her head.

The reason suddenly came spilling out. 'I woke up last night in a cold sweat,' she explained. 'I was terrified. It was like a nightmare, but it wasn't a nightmare, it was real. It IS real. It's the attic, don't you realise? It's going to collapse with all the stuff we're putting up there. And the tenants' children will be sleeping underneath. It's going to collapse on them...'

I went silent. What did she mean, collapse? Collapse, as in suddenly give way? The house was built like the proverbial brick outhouse. It had joists that could have supported a tank, walls that could have resisted bombs – and probably did during the Blitz. Did she really believe a house constructed to this spec was going to fold like cardboard under the weight of a few boxes of knick-knacks and an IKEA desk?

So worried was she, though, that eventually, when I got back to London, I had to take her round to neighbours who had recently had their attic converted to a second lounge; and they explained to her how, with architects' advice, they'd had joists taken out to open up the place, and how this hadn't altered the structural strength of the house at all because these old houses were always so over-engineered.

This explanation put her mind at rest for a while, but fundamentally there was to be no reassuring her rationally, because her logic wasn't rational. This was par for the course with her: she had form for it. Years before, on the verge of leaving a previous house, she'd reacted in a similarly peculiar way. At the eleventh hour she'd wanted to call off the whole move even though she was aware that we'd exchanged contracts and were committed to it legally.

'Oh yes, I know all that,' she'd said brightly. 'But if we just went back to the purchasers and asked them nicely...'

Em's final day at work arrived. She had decided to have her leaving party near the office at a pub called, appropriately enough, *The Narrowboat*. The celebration was exclusively for work colleagues and, as instructed, I kept out of the way, arriving only as the fun was finishing, just in time to pour her into the back of the car with her leaving presents. She was drunk and tearful. Part of it was the emotion at finishing her working life; but part of it too was her mounting uncertainty at what the future held. It was the same stress that was making her worried about the attic collapsing. I felt it too, though in a different way. It would have been impossible not to have felt it. The house barely seemed ours now; we felt like interlopers. We had a box of crockery and a few pots and pans, but apart from that the only personal stuff remaining were a few items of furniture which would go to a charity for the homeless when we left.

A new carpet had been laid, which added to the sense of unfamiliarity. It smelt like dead chrysanthemums. Even the cat was getting restless and anxious at the disruption. She'd taken to wandering incessantly round the house, padding from room to room, bewildered at how her territory had changed and little suspecting how soon it would be before she lost it completely. From time to time she'd search us out as we were tidying up odds and ends, or maybe she'd catch us at the end of the day having a takeaway pizza on the only two remaining chairs in the house at the only remaining table. She'd look at us and start meowing as if demanding some explanation of what was happening and what was going to happen next.

How did she expect us to know, for God's sake? We hadn't got the first idea. We had finally decided on our tenants and a date had been set for the handover. All we knew was that we were on a countdown to departure.

We had planned meticulously for the endgame: all the things that needed doing, the order in which they needed doing and how we would do them had all been logged by Em on an enormous multicoloured flow chart with so many arrows it looked like an early design for the Bayeux Tapestry. In theory this schedule should have ensured that there wasn't a hitch and that things worked like clockwork. But you can't prepare for the unexpected. Everything went smoothly until the last day. Then it fell apart.

It started with the burglar alarm company who hadn't been able to give us a maintenance appointment until this, the very last moment. Of course – Sods' Law being what it is – no sooner did the engineer start work than he discovered a major fault. If it had showed up earlier we'd have been inclined to ignore it and rent out the damned house without an alarm. But it was too late for that now: we'd signed a contract guaranteeing a working system so there was no choice but to let him get on with repairing it – despite the fact that the work involved ripping up wires from under our fresh paintwork and pulling components out of our newly decorated walls.

We were still desperately trying to rectify the damage when Olga rang the doorbell. Maybe she wasn't called Olga. Maybe she was called Nastya or Kasia or Agnieszka. At that stage it didn't seem to matter. Neither did it matter where she was from. I think she said Bulgaria but it could just as easily have been Romania or the Ukraine. She was our inventory clerk – the person whose job it was to prepare the definitive record of the state of the house for when we came to reoccupy it in the future. It was a big task for anyone – let alone someone standing only about 5 foot tall, 7 inches of which were accounted for by a pair of preposterous high heels she wore, which made her gait troublingly unsteady. She wore fishnet tights and carried a large notebook and a camera around her neck, her tiny eyes constantly darting from one side to the other as if looking for the next shot. Soon after arriving she disappeared into the bowels of the house, jotting down memos to herself and snapping away at everything she encountered, including the cat, which shamelessly posed for her every opportunity it got.

Meanwhile, the cleaners had arrived. Cleaners, I hear you say, cleaners? Couldn't you have done the cleaning yourselves? Well, yes, we could have. It was what we intended to do until the estate agents had warned us against it, gravely shaking their heads and cautioning us that if we did an amateur job for our tenants, our tenants would be perfectly within their rights to do an amateur job for us when they came to return the house. Since most of the work would have devolved on Em she was quite happy to get shot of it.

'But it's a scam,' I said to her, 'I'm sure it is. The estate agents probably own the cleaning company. Or they're on a percentage, or they...'

'I couldn't care less,' Em interrupted, showing me the palm of her hand. 'I've got enough on my plate as it is without having to worry about cleaning too. Now talk to me again about the attic: why are you so confident about the strength of that floor? Remember, there'll be children sleeping in those bedrooms underneath...'

The cleaners, a man and a woman, were Ghanaian and they immediately disappeared in the house, along with Olga and the burglar alarm man, and set to work. They couldn't have been at it for more than ten minutes when I heard a dreadful banshee screech. At first I thought the cat had caught its tail in a door; but when I'd identified the noise as human I could only conclude it was an expression of despair on the cleaners' part at how squalid the place was.

Actually, the cry was a serious howl of anguish and I shouldn't make light of it. It was a matter of life and death, a genuine matter of life and death. The man had taken a call telling him that his mother in Ghana had died of a heart attack.

What do you do when something like this happens? Actually there's only one thing you can do, and that is to try to act with a level of basic humanity. I expressed what condolences I could, given that I'd only just met him and didn't even know his mother existed until moments before. I reassured him that I could get something else arranged if he needed to leave. But it didn't take long for me to realise that the option of abandoning a job when your mother dies is one you don't have if you're poor. Most poor people have to do what this guy did. They have to knuckle down and keep working.

During the afternoon I heard him making long tearful calls to members of the family about those hundreds of arrangements that death precipitates. The word funeral was used a lot. There were raised voices too at one stage, some argument about a church. As a result the cleaning on the house dropped further and further behind schedule, the morning becoming afternoon, the afternoon evening and the evening night. The burglar alarm man had long since gone. Olga had departed many hours before. Em and I were supposed to be staying with friends nearby. There had been talk of us all going out for a meal, a sort of celebration. But our tenants were arriving first thing in the morning and so much still remained to be done. Em was on her last legs with exhaustion; she couldn't stop talking about the attic now, it was her only subject of conversation. I sent her to our friends in a taxi, reassuring her that I'd drive over as soon as I was finished.

But I never did. When, in the early hours, the cleaners left and I finally completed everything that needed doing, the car, damn it, wouldn't start. And because there wasn't a bed in the place, I spent the last night in the house which had been our home for so long sleeping on the floor covered by an old pair of curtains.

CHAPTER TWO
The Space Girl

The rain was pelting down the afternoon we drove to Banbury to begin our new life on the boat. No change there then. It had rained the whole night I'd been trying to sleep on the floor in Blackheath, and it was raining when I woke the next morning, and raining when the new tenants had arrived for the handover. It was raining when the AA man came to get the car going, and raining too when I drove over to pick up Em at our friends' house where she'd at least had a comfortable bed.

By the afternoon when we set off up the M40 it was raining even more heavily. The boot and back seats of the car were so chock-a-block with boxes and bags and cases that I couldn't see out of the rear window and had to drive by side mirrors. This didn't make it easy. And conditions worsened during the drive. Even though the wipers were on full, thudding like a metronome on amphetamines, the sheer volume of rain made it hard to see through the windscreen. And if that wasn't bad enough, somewhere in the back of the car, buried among the clutter, was Kit, who hadn't stopped meowing since we'd started and was now beginning to irritate me to the point where I was considering violence as a quick solution to the problem of how to shut her up.

'If that creature doesn't be quiet, I'm just going to have to throttle it,' I said as we passed Beaconsfield.

Now, to be fair, this may not have been the first time I'd complained about the cat since getting on to the motorway. It may not even have been the second or the third, or even the tenth or the twentieth. Indeed, it may have been true, as Em maintained, that I hadn't stopped moaning about the cat since I'd got in the bloody car. Even so, she could have been more sympathetic to me.

Instead she took the cat's side. She said, 'If you don't stop complaining about the cat I'm going to throttle *you*. The cat's just frightened, poor thing; she's not being irritating for the sake of it. You're just bad-tempered because of the rain. It'll clear up soon though, bound to. It can't go on forever...'

But in Banbury there didn't seem to be much sign of it stopping. If anything, it was lashing down worse than it had been on the motorway. And it was getting dark now. We'd left London later than planned and predictably there'd been a series of traffic hold-ups along the way so we'd arrived later than expected. We parked the car temporarily on the forecourt of a garage at the end of a disused arm of the canal where we moor. Knowing that it would be unsafe to leave the car overnight with all our worldly goods inside, there was nothing for it but to unload it there and then, carting everything by torchlight through the deluge to the boat.

We piled it on the front deck, threw a tarpaulin over it and left it. What else could we have done at that time of night in those conditions? What was the use of worrying?

Inside, the boat was exactly as you'd imagine anywhere to be that had just had a new kitchen fitted. Every surface was covered with sawdust and wood shavings, and the bath was littered with offcuts of work surface, spent silicon cartridges and empty screw boxes. It was bitterly cold too, chilled with that permeating dampness which soon envelops an uninhabited boat. It gets into your bones, that cold, it saps your spirit. I lit the fire while Em connected the gas and put on the kettle. Afterwards we sat sipping tea, looking forlornly into the flames without a word passing between us. There was nothing to be said. This was what we'd wanted; this was what we'd been working towards all these weeks and dreaming of all those years. Neither of us thought it would be like this though; neither of us had imagined it this way. Our lives suddenly seemed impoverished, reduced to bare existence, jammed into a cigar tube with everything we owned heaped outside like so much junk.

We went to bed that night clutching each other as much for reassurance as warmth, the cat nestled between us, silent at last.

***

So, like, how is this supposed to work? Perhaps someone could enlighten me? Is there any way of embarking on a dream effortlessly, so that everything falls into place in the way it's supposed to? Without the setbacks? Without the angst? Or is it just in the nature of dreams that this is what it *does* involve? Because to make dreams real requires change, doesn't it? It means letting go of one life and taking up another; and maybe the setbacks and the angst are part and parcel of the uncertainty that accompanies change. Perhaps when it comes down to it we're all a bit more like cats than we like to admit? Perhaps we're all hiding in the clutter whinging as we hurtle towards our new future.

Restructuring your life is an agonising process however you do it. Well, that's my conclusion. After all, why were we so het up about what we were doing? What had we got to worry about? We weren't even leaving our house, not properly leaving it. We weren't selling up and moving to a different part of the world. We were just renting it out and moving to a boat – a boat which was like a second home to us anyhow. What's to make us anxious doing that? What's to make us so fearful?

Yet we did feel anxious and fearful. It was a real feeling. And a painful one too.

Em was up early the next morning for a heavy cleaning session – a process which she persisted in referring to as 'bottoming out the boat' – presumably because the result of it was that neither I nor the cat could rest our bottoms anywhere without getting moved by a brush or a vacuum cleaner. I rolled up my sleeves and lent a hand, and gradually the place began to look more presentable. Little by little over the course of the day the weather improved so that during a break in the rain Em felt confident enough to dart outside and randomly grab at something from under the dripping tarpaulin on deck. It turned out to be a box of bathroom paraphernalia; toothbrushes, soap, shampoo and the like. It seemed to me a lot of stuff for just two people. OK, I could appreciate that Em might have bought some spare supplies from the supermarket to tide us over for our first few weeks on the boat. But all the same, this huge boxful seemed too much. Where had it all come from? And more relevant to our present predicament, where was it all going to go?

'Is this the stuff from the bathroom cabinet at Blackheath?' I asked.

'It's the stuff from one shelf of the bathroom cabinet at Blackheath,' she corrected me.

'Oh? Really? There's a lot of it, isn't there? Are you going to be able to fit it all in?'

Half an hour later she emerged from the bathroom with the box empty. She glanced at me triumphantly before disappearing on to the deck again and returning a moment or two later with another full one. This too contained more bits and pieces from the bathroom.

'In this box,' she explained, 'are the contents of the second shelf of the bathroom cabinet at Blackheath.'

'The *second* shelf? What could there possibly be on the second shelf that you haven't unloaded already?'

'How about all your lotions, ointments and unguents, for a start? And then there's your balms, potions, salves, creams and embrocations, not to mention various poultices, elixirs, unctions and medicines of yours, most of them at least two years beyond their best-by date...'

And in the twinkling of an eye, she had unpacked them too, finding space where I wouldn't have believed space existed, conjuring it as if from nowhere. This was a talent I'd not seen in her before, one that verged on genius, if not out-and-out sorcery. I could only gaze in admiration. This was a woman whom I had known for more years than I cared to remember, a woman whose body I could map and whose clothes sizes were etched on my memory after one Christmas when I'd bought her a dress which was too large for her. This was someone I'd have said I knew, really *knew*. And yet she had, before my eyes, turned into a Mistress of the

Fifth Dimension. She had become a Space Queen, a Density Defier, a Witch of the Third Age who could manipulate for her own ends the very laws of physics on which the universe was built.

She demonstrated this magic a lot over the coming days and it never ceased to astonish me. After all, let's be clear about this, I'm the bloke around here, right? I'm the one who's supposed to have the spatial awareness, the one who's supposed to be able to drive the car up narrow streets without smashing the wing mirrors and read a map without turning it upside down. Yet she could be faced with a box of cooking pans (or sweaters – or books – you name it) and with the sort of effortlessness you associate with magicians doing vanishing tricks with rabbits, she could make it disappear into the boat.

What was even more wondrous to me was that she could always find a stored item again days afterwards, when I'd even forgotten it *had* been put away. She had compiled a mysterious book of lists, you see. Spells, more like, if you ask me. So I'd be cooking something and ask her if we had any thyme, say. And quick as a flash out would come the book and then, very soon afterwards, out would come the thyme too.

'Don't exaggerate, it's nothing mystical,' she tried telling me one day. 'I've just made notes.'

I wasn't having any of that nonsense. I make notes too. In fact I make notes all the time. It's just that I keep losing them. Or I can't read them. Or when I look at them they seem, perversely, to be not what I expect them to be. I make a shopping list for the supermarket, for instance. But when I get there it turns out to be the instructions for loading new software on to the computer. Or if I'm looking for the instructions for loading new software on to the computer, what I'll have in my hand will be a list of the wood I bought months before on some long-forgotten DIY project.

Eventually, between rainstorms, we cleared the deck, box by box. Well, more accurately, Em cleared the deck, because an old boating injury to my knee, which I've nursed for years, suddenly flared up again. I could scarcely move and was about as useful as a scrubbing brush without bristles. I did what I could, though: I made tea for her, and tuned the radio into *Woman's Hour*, and I kept coming up with suggestions about where she could put things, which I could see made her feel much better about herself because it allowed her to ignore me and treat me like an idiot.

My main job was keeping the fire going. This is my uncontested responsibility on the boat, my unique role. Me Man, Me Make Fire: it's my given function in life. I am an expert in tending fire. This could be because I have a knack for it, because it is instinctive with me. On the other hand, it could be because it's a messy, unpleasant job which Em's never wanted to do, so I've had to learn how to do it whether I've wanted to or not. One way or another, and though I say it myself, I am pretty damned good with fires. Other men may fool around satisfying their inner warrior by blackening a few sausages on a barbecue, but I am Iron Steve and that sort of flippant weekend entertainment is mere child's play compared to the duty I have keeping the boat fire burning day and night when it's cold and chucking it down outside, and when not just warmth, but our health, happiness and spiritual well-being are at stake.

Most narrowboats have a solid fuel stove; it's a key piece of equipment – though you wouldn't know it reading the boating press. Any amount of overly complicated technical rubbish is written in canal magazines about the skills of controlling canal boats. I should know, I've written a lot of it myself. Articles about steering them, reversing them, getting them through locks, that sort of stuff. But nobody ever writes anything about keeping in a fire overnight. This is ridiculous, because everything else about canals is a doddle. People try to make out that locks are complicated, but you can master them in the time it takes to go through your first one. And steering's a piece of cake too, of course it is. Do you think they'd let hirers out on their own after half an hour's tuition otherwise? They'd be killing themselves by their thousands if steering was that complicated.

Tending a fire though – knowing exactly how much coal, coke or wood to put on it to keep it burning until the morning – that's a real talent. Being aware of how much air to feed it so as not to either asphyxiate it or burn it away too quickly; appreciating how to keep it glowing steadily during the day at a constant temperature, and then knowing how to get it blazing in the evenings when the temperature falls and the mists rise – well, this is the ultimate narrowboat skill. Get it wrong and you'll either be freezing with no fire at all; or worse, you'll be crawling across the cabin floor gasping for air in the first stage of heat exhaustion.

***

The disused arm where we moor just outside Banbury is under the satanic smoking chimneys of what used to be General Foods until it changed its name recently to Mondelez, a PR tactic which may have softened the way we view this US-owned multinational, but which – take it from me – hasn't done much for the emissions which bellow out from the place day and night, like a dragon with heartburn, burping out its dinner of flaxen-haired maidens.

Once we'd negotiated our way out – never an easy task because there are always boats jammed higgledy-piggledy into every available space – we headed to the town centre where we needed to stock up on provisions before setting off in earnest. When we washed up in Banbury for the first time 30-odd years ago the canal was grim and forsaken, and the guidebooks advised you not to moor there because of the dangers of vandalism. The canal then was shallow, the towpath muddy, and in the centre of town, overlooking the water, was the back of the bus station. This had been built on the filled-in basin which in the eighteenth century had been the temporary terminus of the canal after the builders had run out of money trying to reach Oxford, and it was a filthy place with all the exhaust fumes that collected there.

The one saving grace in those days was Tooley's boatyard, and its Grade I listed dry dock, which was as old as the waterway itself. Even then Tooley's was an icon of the waterways, for it was from here that the author Tom Rolt started his cruise around the Midlands, which he immortalised in his 1944 book *Narrow Boat*. This archaic but strangely compelling elegy to a lost England raised the curtain for the first time on the secret world of the waterways, which were then in such serious decline many of them had already become derelict. It's no exaggeration to say the book was the single most influential element in the restoration of Britain's waterways, and that without it there'd be no canal system today worth talking about. The book changed the way people thought about canals, and it led to the formation of the Inland

Waterways Association, which fought a long and radical battle for their preservation when intransigent governments and obdurate local authorities would have filled in the lot given half the chance.

The boatyard was a sad sight long past its best. Bert Tooley, who had been involved in preparing Rolt's boat for its cruise, still lived on site in a dilapidated caravan; he must have been in his eighties himself then and you'd see him pottering about making himself useful. Some work was being done on leisure craft, but the commercial traffic for which the yard had been built had by then completely dried up. It looked shabby and run-down, and even after Bert's death British Waterways, who ran the canals then, couldn't decide what to do with it. It was allowed to deteriorate even further under a succession of tenants who struggled to keep it functioning without the benefit of a long-term lease which would have justified them investing money in the place.

Rising land values as much as a change in previously hidebound bureaucratic attitudes altered things. For years Banbury Council had treated its canal like a malodorous squatter who had set up home in the garden shed. As other larger cities like Birmingham, Manchester and Bristol took the lead developing their water frontages, Banbury finally woke up to the potential of its own canal.

Today the canal's a key feature of the town centre; and although Tooley's is much reduced in size and sits under what seems to be an ugly suburban greenhouse, at least it still exists as a working boatyard, literally connected to its history by a glass-sided walkway which leads to Banbury Museum. The development could have been better designed, and the faux-warehouse style of Castle Quay shopping centre, which backs on to the towpath, still grates with me. But it could have turned out a good deal worse, and all things considered, it's a far more pleasant place to visit as a tourist than the town's better-known cross which stands on a busy road and is a Victorian confection built as a concession to the popular nursery rhyme after the original cross had been pulled down by the Puritans in 1600.

We moored a little beyond Tooley's, between a small lift bridge and a lock, and while Em disappeared into Marks & Spencer I set about filling our water tank, which is a huge one under our front deck and takes about half an hour. It was still raining as heavily as ever, and I probably wasn't paying enough attention to what I was doing because the hose worked itself loose under the pressure of the water and it suddenly went snaking across the towpath, catching me full blast two or three times as it passed backwards and forwards. It was probably hilarious to anyone who happened to be in the shopping centre looking out, like a gag from a silent movie. If I'd been watching myself from the warmth and shelter of an arcade, I'd probably have found it comical too. Who wouldn't? This old bloke (me) standing there, dripping wet and looking like thunder while the hose danced a merry jig around him. From my perspective things were anything but amusing. It wasn't just getting wet. Getting wet was the half of it: I was already wet enough from the rain, getting even wetter from the hose was neither here nor there. More serious was that, as the first jet had hit me, I'd reared instinctively to avoid it and wrenched my troublesome knee in the process. I don't know how but I found myself splayed on the ground, a pain creeping through my body, increasing in intensity all the time. Before long I was retching in agony, heaving as if I'd had too much to drink or had eaten a dodgy burger. Somehow I managed to struggle back on to the boat where Em found me.

'What shall we do now then?' she asked after I'd explained what had happened. 'Go back to the mooring? Stop here? You're going to have to see a doctor.'

'Why? A doctor will only refer me to a specialist and I can arrange to see my own specialist as soon as I can get an appointment. We've still got an NHS, you know.'

'What about the pain?'

'Oh, I can handle that,' I said cheerfully, stripping off my saturated clothes. 'Just feed me ibuprofen and whisky and I'll be fine.' Even to me my voice seemed rather too chirpy to be entirely credible.

'Not a good way to start a couple of years living afloat though, is it?'

I didn't answer but instead dropped into a chair, wincing as I tried to pull off my socks. 'I need to get under the shower,' I said. 'And then I've got to go for a walk. However painful it is, I need to exercise this knee before it seizes up on me. If that happens I'll never get it working again...'

***

Two or three hours later we finally got underway; the light by now was beginning to fail and the rain was still relentless. We passed under the new fixed bridge, built at the time of the shopping centre redevelopment to replace a lethal lift bridge where a youngster lost his legs larking around a few years before. We were heading south towards Oxford, but we didn't get far. At Grant's Lock – the first lock outside Banbury – our progress was brought to an abrupt halt by a queue of boats moored either side while their crews prodded around in the water with bargepoles and boathooks. Something was blocking one of the gates and it wouldn't open. This sort of thing can happen at locks, and sometimes you can be lucky shifting the obstruction yourself. Some years earlier at Kidlington – just a few miles south of here – we'd hauled five or six sodden bundles of free newspapers from the water late one night in the dark when we'd rather have been tucked up in bed.

No one was having as much luck here though, and eventually someone called the Canal & River Trust, the charity which since 2012 has run the waterways in England and Wales. It was impressively efficient getting a two-man emergency team on site and, despite the fact one of them was missing his daughter's school play, they set about their task cheerfully and soon fished out the object which was causing the hold-up. It turned out to be a fender – a vulcanised rubber tube an inch or two in diameter and a couple of feet long which boaters use to protect the hulls of their boats when they moor.

Sadly – despite the fact it's dangerous and bad boating practice – a significant number of inexperienced boaters have taken to using them when they're cruising too. They think it protects their hull – though what on earth they imagine the rubbing strakes built into their boats are for I've no idea. You'd have assumed the name 'rubbing strake' might have given them a clue. Unlike fenders, they don't get ripped off in locks. And they don't get jammed behind lock gates either, preventing you from opening them.

We moored that night in darkness as soon as we could find a length of decent towpath to get in close enough. It wasn't a perfect place to stop. We could hear the interminable drone of the M40 in the distance, and to add to our discomfort the already filthy weather conditions had deteriorated, with a wind blowing up which buffeted us around all night like a cork.

'We're not off to a great start, are we?' Em said.

I suddenly felt very protective towards her. 'Oh, it's not been perfect, I agree. It's bound to get better though. You see if I'm not right.'

But I wasn't right. The next morning the rain continued unabated and the wind turned into a gale. To add to our catalogue of woe, my knee had seized up overnight and was barely functioning. We cruised a mile or two, but lost the will to go further and eventually, somewhere beyond the water meadow at Somerton where the canal borders the River Cherwell, we called it a day. It was spring and only afternoon, but it was so stormy and dark it could have been a winter's evening. We stoked up the fire, battened down the hatches and poured ourselves large whiskies. Soon we were in bed, snuggled into the duvet listening to the wind playing in the trees and hearing occasional twigs falling on to the roof above our heads until we fell asleep rocked by the wind.

Then a miracle occurred.

Totally without warning, without the weather forecasters having a clue it would happen, we woke the next day to find the rain had stopped and the sun was blazing.

And it didn't stop blazing for three glorious months.

CHAPTER THREE
Down the Rabbit Hole

*P*eople kept asking why we were doing it. To many of our friends, our decision to abandon home for the waterways seemed incomprehensible. What on earth were we thinking of? We had a lovely house in a nice part of London, we had family and a busy social life, and we had interests we shared together. We had each other, for heaven's sake. Why would we jeopardise all this for... well, for what, they kept asking us.

It wasn't an easy one to answer and even after we'd upped sticks and done it I don't think either of us was ever entirely clear about what had been our motivation. We never asked ourselves at any point why we were doing it. Not in those blunt terms. Not in any sort of way that might have opened the possibility of us *not* doing it. Whenever we discussed the future it was in the context that the decision had already been taken, and that *we* knew why it had been taken even if no one else did, and now it was just a matter of getting on with the pragmatics of it.

Part of it, of course, was that we'd always loved the waterways. The prospect of living on them and exploring them at our own pace, without the need to get back at the end of a weekend or a holiday was something we'd dreamed about for so long it had built up an unstoppable momentum of its own. But what sort of answer is that? People harbour all manner of dreams. We'd dreamed about learning to play musical instruments, about living in Florence and studying Italian, about spending a year or two in a house swap in California. There surely has to be something more to make you pursue one dream rather than another?

We wanted to reacquaint ourselves with this country of ours: that was important to us. We'd lived in the city-state which is London for so long that we realised if we didn't break free of it now, even for a short period, then we never would. It was a part of a yearning we both had to be shot of restriction after a lifetime of work. It was a chance to experience life differently. Yet there was more to it than this.

There was something about our life in London which had started to make us feel uncomfortable over recent years, something to do with the excesses of the place. London is one of the richest cities in the world, so rich that if it were a country in its own right it would be one of the richest countries too. But there's also widespread poverty. This makes it an unsettling place to live. Even if you're of modest means, if you have any sort of conscience worth talking about, then you can't ignore the privation that you see around you on a day-to-day basis. And you can't ignore the intemperance of the affluent either. The restaurants charging for one meal what a normal family spends on food for a month; the luxury cars worth more than an average house in most parts of the country; and the houses themselves, rising inexorably in price year on year so that they're now totally out of reach of the young.

It gets to you, this sort of shameless materialism. Either you react against it or you go along with it and everything it involves. We have friends who ripped out their two-year-old granite kitchen for something more fashionable, others who never bother turning off their lights or their computers, not because they have no sense of global warming but because they don't have any sense of the bills they pay and wouldn't care if they did. There's a wastefulness about London, a selfish profligacy which seems to have worked its way into the core of the city. It throws away more food than anywhere else in England. It throws away more of everything.

We just wanted something simpler. We weren't out to save the world. We were just fed up living in a place that was constantly trashing it.

Perhaps what it ultimately came down to was that we needed to challenge the value of all those things our friends thought were vital to our lives. We needed to test ourselves. Could we manage without the lovely house or was our identity so inescapably tied up with it that without it we were nothing? And the family and the busy social life, we had to discover how important they were to us. Most of all we had to discover how important we were to each other. It wasn't a question of jeopardising anything; just getting a fix on life.

As it was, we couldn't even get a fix on where we were taking the boat. Don't ask me why we started heading south when we left Banbury. We'd only gone into town to get stocked up for the trip. I thought we were going to turn round afterwards and head for the Fens. Em had been mumbling about going north to the Pennines, which would have also meant turning around. But we didn't turn round. For some reason when we started the engine, the boat just kept going the way she was pointing and neither of us could find it in our hearts to stop her. So the River Thames became our destination. Without it ever really being decided, we were going back to London, which we'd only just left. I don't know how it happened.

But narrowboats are like that: they have minds of their own. I've lost count of the amount of trips we've made when the boat's decided things more than we have. We had a period with one boat where it was constantly breaking down in places we didn't want to be, but where, with the benefit of hindsight, we'd have hated to miss.

Boats decide things for themselves even when you're manoeuvring them. They can promise one thing and do another and sometimes it's no use pretending you've got any control over them. In the wind they'll be blown into the bank. Unless they don't want to be blown into the bank. Then they won't be, and you'll make yourself look an idiot steering them as if they were going to be. In reverse, they're even worse. You steer one direction and they'll go the other until you change course – at which point it's a toss-up which way they'll go except it won't be anywhere you want them to.

The best thing with narrowboats, I find, is to let them do what they want – then look as if that's what you intended doing all along. This way people will think you're an expert.

***

There are two routes to get on to the Thames from the Oxford Canal. The first is to head straight into Oxford where Isis Lock branches off to the river just before the southern end of the canal. It's not a particularly scenic route though. True, if you're nosy like Em and I, you get to see into the back gardens of the

45

lovely houses which sweep down to the water's edge in Jericho; but the downside is that you have to pass some scuzzy-looking floating communities around Wolvercote, where many of the boats seem to be at their final resting place, sinking where they stand; and where the soundtrack to your passage will be dogs snarling at you from the bank, desperate to make acquaintance with your throat.

Going this way the canal peters out in a rubbish-strewn dead end opposite a car park – an unsightly finish that would shame a South American shanty town let alone an ancient and world-famous seat of learning like this. There's a proposal to rebuild the canal basin which once stood here, but I don't hold out much hope. The land belongs to Nuffield College and the car park's been a nice little earner for too long.

Since we'd now, apparently, decided by default to cruise down the Thames it seemed sensible to get on to the river as soon as we could by the most direct means possible. This involved us leaving the canal before Wolvercote at Duke's Cut, the first link built to the river in 1789 and named after the Duke of Marlborough, who lived at nearby Blenheim Palace and so had an interest in the new waterway to carry goods to and from his extensive farmlands. Going this way you make a wide sweep around the flat water meadows east of Oxford, eventually arriving in the city at Osney Lock just behind the railway station.

Mind you, even taking this route the outlook's not immediately promising. From the canal you turn a hard right back on yourself and pass under a low railway bridge and through a gloomy lock so that the effect is like descending into a dark and unwelcoming hole. Emerging at the other side, however, there's an immediate transformation. You suddenly find yourself in the wide, willow-lined channel of a meandering waterway so unlike the one you've been on you could be forgiven for thinking you'd arrived in an entirely different world. This sense of having unexpectedly stumbled into new and unfamiliar territory is compounded half a mile on when you reach the junction of the river itself.

Here there's another startling change. We turned left to go downstream and, attuned as we were to the slow progress of canals, the width and flow of the Thames caught us unawares. *Justice* surged forward in response to the depth of the water beneath her, her propeller suddenly liberated from the cloying muddiness of the cut. The channel suddenly widens and on an expanse of water like this even a gentle afternoon breeze seems like a gale. It buffeted *Justice*, making her unfamiliar to handle. Above us the equally unfamiliar sunshine was a distraction too. It hit us not just from above but from below too, reflecting from the dazzling water so brightly that without sunglasses it was no easy job to see where we were going.

We moored that night at Godstow Lock, at the side of the meadow adjacent to the ruins of the former Benedictine nunnery of Godstow Abbey. Here, in a tomb in front of the main altar, was once buried 'The Fair Rosamund' – Rosamund Clifford – celebrated as Henry II's mistress. According to legend he met her walking along the riverbank hereabouts and carried her off to his palace at Woodstock. There he hid her inside an intricate maze, which Henry's understandably resentful Queen Eleanor only managed to penetrate by following a snagged silk thread from Rosamund's dress. After that, the story goes, she was forced into Godstow on pain of death.

Whatever the truth of all this, it is the case that she died in the abbey and her tomb became a popular local shrine always resplendent with flowers which, it was said, her lover Henry arranged to have put there. However, since the flowers continued after Henry's death, I'm more inclined to think it was local women putting them there – celebrating not Rosamund's beauty but the power she wielded and the sexual freedom she enjoyed, both of which were denied to them. The patriarchal church authorities thought so too. Visiting the abbey in 1181, a couple of years after Henry's death, and seeing candles burning and the flowers on her tomb as usual, Bishop Hugh of Lincoln ordered what he called 'that Harlot's body' to be moved outside the church so that 'other women, warned by her example, may refrain from unlawful love'.

Despite the proximity of the noisy Oxford bypass, the ruins of Godstow Abbey still have a certain haunting appeal which it's difficult not to feel drawn to in the fading twilight of a balmy summer's day. We brought our cabin table up on to deck and had dinner sipping wine and watching wild rabbits feeding as the shadows lengthened across the meadow. Godstow ruins stir in me the same sensations of melancholy I feel looking at those etchings of Ancient Rome which Grand Tour travellers in the seventeenth and eighteenth centuries brought back with them in lieu of snapshots. It's something to do with the transitory nature of grandeur, the feeling that judged against the passage of time the affairs of kings and commoners alike are just fleeting moments in an eternity from which we're all only separated by a heartbeat.

It's no surprise the abbey ruins are popular as a day trip from Oxford. It's been that way for centuries, and passing through nearby Godstow Lock early the following morning we were delighted to find the lock-keeper had scrawled a message on a blackboard outside his cottage announcing that it was exactly

151 years ago to the day since the Reverend Charles Dodgson had rowed upriver on an excursion to Godstow. Dodgson was with a friend and in the company of the three daughters of the Dean of Christ Church College where he worked as a mathematics tutor. They took with them a 'large basket of cakes' and had tea on the bank; and Dodgson entertained the girls by telling them bizarre and surreal stories. One of the girls, ten-year-old Alice, later asked him to write these down for her and in due course they were published under Dodgson's pseudonym Lewis Carroll as *Alice's Adventures in Wonderland*.

The fluke of us passing on the anniversary was total coincidence, but all the same it encapsulated something of how we were feeling at that time. For both of us were aware of a dreamlike quality to the start of our trip. There was something far-fetched about it, something out of this world; but though we didn't know it, this was to be the way of things that extraordinary summer when sunny day succeeded sunny day for months on end, and when we seriously began to think that in going through Duke's Cut we'd gone down a rabbit hole of our own to a Wonderland as enchanted as Alice's. I couldn't help idly speculating whether one of the rabbits we'd watched at the abbey as we'd sat having dinner had been white. Maybe it had a pocket watch too. After all, it had been late, very late...

It was another scorching day and we cruised past the green expanse of Port Meadow, which at one time afforded the most famous view of Oxford's 'dreaming spires', though recently it's been badly spoiled by the construction of some ugly student halls of residence along its edge. It was still early, before 7 a.m., but even at that hour swimmers were out in force; and along the shallow bank cattle stood chewing the cud knee-deep in the water, already cooling themselves in anticipation of the day ahead. As we made the short journey into central Oxford, our bow gently rippling the glass surface of the water, we were accompanied by shimmering swarms of iridescent demoiselle damselflies hanging above the boat in that poignant mating position that leaves their bodies con torted as one, head to tail, in the unmistakeable shape of a heart. Some, still at their business, flew alongside, leaving me to marvel at the speed they could travel even as engaged as they were.

My musings were disturbed by Em, who was on the tiller. At first I didn't register her at all. When I finally did, I became aware that she was screaming at me hysterically for reasons that weren't immediately obvious until I turned to see the looming arch of Osney Bridge bearing down on me. At only 7.5 feet at its centre point, Osney Bridge has the lowest clearance of any bridge on the Thames. It is a single-span structure which serves a vital purpose in blocking off the upper river from the towering plastic gin palaces which would otherwise pollute the environment by the noisy chatter of their garrulous owners crowing about annual bonuses and rising world stock markets.

For this reason – a little coarsely, you might think – some boaters refer to it as a 'wanker filter'.

Whatever you call it, it's not a bridge you'd want to mix with, this bridge. It was built on the site of another, which collapsed in 1885, killing an 11-year-old, and it has the same sort of attitude as its predecessor, exuding a quiet hostility in its passive-aggressive way. You're best advised going through the very middle of it where it's highest, because at the sides it lowers significantly and despite the wooden rubbing strakes there to protect you, it can easily have your head off if you don't watch it. It nearly decapitated me as *Justice* scraped through.

For some reason Em seemed to find this highly amusing. Perhaps she was thinking about all the fun she'd have once she got her hands on my pension. 'That'll teach you to pay attention,' she chuckled. And before I could reply she pulled into a convenient mooring she'd just spotted.

***

Oxford is built on an island. Actually it's built on a series of islands and if you look at it on a map you'll see it's laced not just by the canal and the Thames but by the River Cherwell too, not to mention a whole series of channels, streams and backwaters, which gives the place the pattern of a steamy window after the condensation's been running. Unwittingly, Em brought the boat into the bank on one of the most celebrated islands of the city – Osney Island. And if any proof were needed that the designation 'island' was a meaningful one, recognised by local people as an important factor in the geography of their lives, the evidence was there to see the next morning when we woke to the sight of teams of men balancing on top of precarious ladders hanging bunting from any surface they could knot a string to. It was, we discovered, the day of the Osney Island Neighbourhood Festival.

Although it only encompasses about a dozen terraced streets and a couple of hundred houses, Osney Island has a strong sense of neighbourhood. It also has a history dating back to the Middle Ages. Chaucer's miller in the *Canterbury Tales* was the miller at Osney, though most of the tiny terraced cottages in the place were built more recently for railway workers based at the nearby station. Today it's home to an eclectic mix of people, some of them traditional working-class residents, but increasingly there are academics, artists, writers and the like.

It wasn't long before music struck up. Something a bit funky, I seem to remember, something a bit modern jazzy – but perhaps I'm inventing that. Crowds began to gather. Soon the place was teeming with people, *The Punter* on the corner doing particularly good business as crowds spilled outside from its bar into the sunshine and on to the pavement and the grass verge, which is the only thing that separates the street from the waterway. The men were all in standard summer wear: shorts, chinos, faded T-shirts sporting the name of some half-forgotten band from the eighties; the women were mostly bare-legged in sandals and summer skirts dug out from the back of the wardrobe.

The kids though... phew! They were something else. For while the adults had effectively abandoned fashion and everything that went with it, paradoxically embracing a sort of shabby anti-fashion as their style, anyone under the age of 14 – babies included – looked as if they'd just walked (or crawled or toddled) off a junior catwalk. Girls and boys alike were dressed in the most spectacular array of designs, all of them flamboyantly colourful: dresses, patched denims, T-shirts, romper suits, blouses – a rainbow mishmash that couldn't but make me feel like some kind of Edwardian throwback. But kids were just dowdier in my day. You went out in your school uniform for best. The rest of the time you wore old shirts over a pair of old grey flannels.

The festival at Osney Island wasn't a big one. Indeed, I'm hard-pressed to say what it consisted of apart from some face painting, a lot of drinking and a bit of tug of war, which for a while inconvenienced us since it took place on the towpath next to us, stopping us getting on and off the boat. Even so, there was something about it that I found reassuringly familiar, although at first I couldn't understand what. Later it struck me that the festival had an unmistakeable rural feel to it, which, once I'd recognised it, I related to instinctively as a kid brought up in the countryside in a real village. But Osney Island has this rural feel about it too. It's a self-consciously urban village, saved from having to call itself one (as so many places in London do) by the water surrounding it.

By comparison, the Cowley Festival which we went to the following day had an uncompromising urban feel to it, like a smaller version of London's Notting Hill Carnival – though it was no worse for that in my opinion. Cowley, to the south-east of central Oxford, is the industrial bit of town. In 1912 William Morris located his car production lines there and it's still manufacturing cars today under German ownership, its most famous marque the new, misnamed and monstrous Mini which has swollen so grossly in recent years I swear you could fit an original into its boot.

Its industrial past has bequeathed Cowley a certain brash self-assurance. They were always a bit bolshie on the factory floor, and there's this same belligerence about the place today. But maybe that's because it's in your face: contemporary, creative and multicultural. It seems by its very presence to challenge the status quo of the rest of Oxford, which is nothing if not establishment to its core. Cowley's almost a separate city in itself, but a more modern city and one which, like it or not, is far more representative of contemporary Britain than the manicured lawns and quads of the ivy-covered colleges. Of course it's an arrogant overstatement, but there's more than a grain of truth in Cowley's confident contention that it is the *real* Oxford and that the university part is its cultural Left Bank.

Despite my knee playing me up something cruel we walked to Cowley for lunch with friends, passing Iffley Road running track where in 1954 Roger Bannister ran the world's first 4-minute mile. Afterwards we sauntered around the packed streets in sunshine which was uncomfortably hot. The wine I'd drunk with lunch and the beer I was still drinking from the many official and unofficial outlets along the way added to the sense of drugged unreality I'd been feeling since passing through Duke's Cut. There was thudding reggae and hip-hop music coming at me from all sides, and there was the smell of exotic cooking in the air: jerk chicken and Thai curry sauce, Spanish chorizo and Filipino noodles. The streets were again a catwalk and people were out to be seen, a kaleidoscope of divergent style. There were women in extravagant African dresses and tiny Japanese women dressed like 12-year-olds. One divine creature of indeterminate gender was wearing a white wedding dress. There were men in garish Hawaiian shirts, others with waist-length dreadlocks threaded with vibrantly coloured beads. One was in a white linen suit which, but for a mislaid teddy bear, could have been straight out of central casting for Evelyn Waugh's Brideshead.

Just as it all seemed to be calming down and life returning to sober normality, we came across some political demonstration by cyclists, every one of them wearing a mask of the prime minister David Cameron. We never did find out why. It was surreal. Like being trapped in a David Lynch movie. On that bizarre, unreal afternoon, I could almost swear that a British tennis player had won Wimbledon for the first time in 70-odd years...

After we'd parted from our friends we dropped into a cafe/ bar on the Cowley Road to give me a chance of preparing myself for what promised to be a long limp back to the boat. I needed an analgesic and fortuitously I found one packaged attractively in a bottle labelled Chilean Merlot. Opposite, a couple of young women who looked as if they'd never travelled further than Ibiza gave an impromptu, and perilous, performance of Indian dance on the narrow parapet of a facing building. I used the restaurant Wi-Fi to check emails on my phone. I hadn't looked at them for a day or two. It was a good job I did.

'It seems as if the surgery at home has managed to get me an appointment with the specialist,' I said. 'Tomorrow. 2.15 p.m. I'll have to go back to London.'

Em looked at me, uncertain whether this was good news or bad. 'How do you feel about that?' she asked.

'How am I supposed to feel? They might be able to do something to help, they might not. I'd be a fool not to find out though, wouldn't I?'

I suppose at that stage I had some notion that I'd twisted a ligament and that if I got any treatment at all I was likely to be offered a course of physiotherapy along the lines I'd had when I'd first damaged the knee ten years before. Regular sessions would be impossibly inconvenient now I was living on a boat. It would mean having to go to hospital from wherever we happened to be moored. Worse, though, would be that having to return to London regularly would effectively end our itinerant lifestyle almost before it had begun. It would mean we could never properly leave London.

I needn't have worried, however. The next day after I limped into London, the specialist had an entirely different idea about how to deal with the problem. At the hospital I had the knee X-rayed, and once in his office he called up the image on a monitor on his desk.

'Look,' he said, swinging it around so that I could see it. He positioned a cursor between the obvious outline of two joints and a number appeared on the screen. I can't remember what the number was now except that it was a very small one. 'That's the thickness of your cartilage,' he explained. 'No wonder you've been getting pain. We'll have to replace it...'

For a moment or two I thought I'd misheard, and then when I realised I hadn't, I thought I'd misunderstood him – though which part of the word 'replace' I could have misconstrued was difficult to say. Especially since, like a mosquito trapped inside my head, I could hear his voice droning on, clarifying what he'd said. I heard the word 'operation' mentioned. I heard the words 'recovery time'. I found myself holding some shining stainless-steel contraption in my hand. It looked for all the world like something you might see on display at Tate Modern. As his lips moved I could just about grasp what he was saying. He seemed to be trying to explain to me how he would fit this monstrous construction into my leg. Into my leg! My leg! I couldn't take him seriously. It seemed he was intending to hack out my old joint and insert this in its place. It was state of the art, he kept saying; it was the cutting edge of medical technology.

Cutting edge, maybe. But it involved cutting me and that was a cut too far. Old-fashioned though I am, I had become rather attached to my old knee over the years. It and I had shared some good times together; we had had some good craic. It seemed, well, a bit disloyal to dispense with it so dispassionately.

'I'm sorry,' I said. 'What was that?'

'I asked whether you had any questions,' said the specialist, bringing me back down to earth with a bump.

'So, what did you say to him?' asked Em that night when I was back on the boat on Osney Island.

'I told him there was no way I was going to agree to any operation without having more time to think about it.'

'And how did he respond to that?'

'He wasn't very encouraging. He told me to come back and see him again when I was screaming in agony. But apparently there are things I can do in terms of exercise and diet. I've been looking it up on the net on the train back. Fish oil can be very helpful, by all accounts. I think I'll give it a try.'

Em looked at me uncertainly. 'Are you sure this is the right thing to do?'

I shrugged. 'How can I be sure? It's a shot in the dark. All I know is that if I go ahead with an operation that would be the end of this journey. We couldn't go on with me an invalid. We'd have to moor up somewhere. There'd be time in hospital and then recuperation time afterwards and physiotherapy after that. And these things don't always work out as planned, you know. Sometimes people are left in pain even after a new knee...'

'But you're in pain now.'

'Yes, but I'm used to it,' I said with a blasé indifference I wasn't at that moment actually feeling. 'I've had problems with my back for years. I can handle pain...'

And I got up from the chair where I'd been sitting to signal the end of this conversation which, suddenly, had begun to bore me. It had been a long day and I was tired. I was sick of my knee, sick of all this talk of infirmity and pain. Ironically, though, as I rose I unthinkingly put my weight in the wrong place, twisting it in just about the worst way possible. An agonising jolt shot up my leg from my foot to my hip.

But I didn't react. I didn't curse or kick the cat. I didn't even wince.

The fact was, if I was going to play the hero then I was going to have to do the job properly.

CHAPTER FOUR
Narrowboat Nomads

It took a month or so for us to get used to the fact we were living on a boat. Until then it was a bit like being on holiday. Well, actually, until then it was exactly like being on holiday. We'd get up, cruise for a few miles, moor, do a bit of exploring, have something to eat, a glass or two of wine, and then go to bed. The difference was that normally after a holiday we'd pack up our toothbrushes, cram Kit into her basket and go home. This time we hadn't got a home to go home to. I think that's when it finally dawned on us what we'd done. For better or worse we'd got no fixed abode. From now on we weren't taking time out from life by being on the waterways: this *was* our life.

And it was a very different life to being on holiday. The main thing was that there were no constraints. We didn't have to be back at work, we didn't have to take the boat back anywhere. We had no schedule, unlike being on holiday when you'll have one even if you don't think you do. Everyone on holiday has a schedule. Even if it's not written down anywhere. Even if it's one you're not strictly tied to. It'll be there anyhow, like an alarm clock in the back of your head ticking louder and louder as it gets closer to ringing.

Having a holiday schedule has an effect on the way you travel, it's bound to. You might see a spot where you'd love to moor, but it'll be too early in the day to take a break so, reluctantly, you'll press on. There might be a nearby town or village you'd like to visit, but you realise that would take too much time, and so you'll keep travelling – often hammering on late into the day, long after you'd prefer to have stopped. But you can't stop: you're locked into your schedule. The schedule is there like a worm in your brain. It's not your fault. It's what life does to you all the time. It sets you targets. Or you set them for yourself.

Even living on the boat we would discover that we weren't entirely immune from constraints. There would be times we had to shop for provisions, times when we were running low on water, or when our cassette lavatory was getting dangerously close to full. And sometimes we'd have to move from a mooring where we'd have preferred to stay longer, because there are restrictions on the time you can stay in certain places on the cut: you can't just arrive somewhere and set up permanent camp as some newcomers seem to think. All the same, in the months to come we'd have a good deal more choice over how we travelled than we'd ever had before. Now if we spotted that attractive mooring we could stop for a couple of weeks if we wanted; and if we fancied visiting that little village, or exploring that town, then we had all the time in the world to do it.

This go-as-you-please style of cruising gave us a different view of travelling; it made us more spontaneous, more patient, less agitated, and that was something that in the end altered not just our relationship to the waterways, but our relationship to the world and ultimately to each other.

It was just tiresome that friends and family couldn't always see it our way. They wanted to know where we were going to be, and when we were likely to arrive there and how long we were staying. They wanted to keep in touch, you could understand that. Except that wasn't the whole story because they could keep in touch easily enough by phone or email. Even letters would reach us in time, forwarded from London to my brother's address. No, it was something more than that. It was almost as if they wanted to define us by those things that limited them. Almost as if the way we were spending our lives was an affront to theirs. And it got irksome. How could we explain to them that we were living in a different sort of way now? That we weren't actually doing anything or going anywhere? It was that old Buddhist thing: the journey really *was* more important than the arrival, because for us the journey was the whole point now.

It may sound an ideal existence, but there were some early readjustments we had to make to life aboard that weren't easy for us. Living in such cramped conditions was the greatest of them. We'd moved from a large three-storey Victorian house into a boat smaller than our back room. Of course, space was going to be a problem. How could it not be? Em's new-found talent for fitting quarts into pint pots had at least ensured that we could cram our stuff into the available drawers and cupboards, but even her magic couldn't work for us as people. Not when we were the ones taking up the space. Even she couldn't make one of us disappear when we were getting on each other's nerves. And we did get on each other's nerves. Of course we did. Tell me a couple who don't get on each other's nerves from time to time, even in a house.

We'd spent enough time on boats in the past to have a good idea of what it was going to be like, but I don't think either of us really grasped how exasperating it would be living on top of each other day in and day out. I don't think anything can prepare you for it except, perhaps, a spell inside with a difficult cellmate. Narrowboats are... well, narrow – just a little over 6 feet wide. And while it's true that they're long – as long as 72 feet sometimes – if you're going to live on one with another person you need to know that all privacy will go out of the window. You have to get used to living in each other's pockets.

This struggle for space was to be a recurrent theme to our lives.

Kit was another problem we hadn't properly thought through. Everyone warned us she'd be running away every five minutes, and that we'd spend half our lives waiting for her to come back. But we were confident she was too old for that. That was the sort of thing she did when she was a kitten straight out of cat rescue and as unfamiliar with the countryside as she was with boats. In those days I used to travel with her alone and I swear she used to tease me with her antics for no better reason than to wind me up. She was older now, though, more savvy to the ways of the cut. And besides, as cats do, she worked out pretty quickly what was in her best interests. Her conclusion was that, although the woods and fields could be exciting places to roam, filled with all manner of creatures she could hunt, torture and kill, the boat was where it was warmest and safest, with soft chairs and luxuriant rugs and enslaved humanoids at her beck and call to top up the biscuit bowl.

No, the problem we hadn't anticipated with Kit came about because she's a long-haired cat. She's just a mog, nothing special; but years ago, through some friends who know about these things, we discovered that there was a good deal of American Maine Coon in her genealogy. Quite apart from her extravagantly bushy tail – a characteristic of the breed – she has a fluffy ruff around her neck and a thick black-and-white coat, so abundant that in the right light it's as if she's floating in a miasma of fur.

That's because she's always moulting. You can deal with cats moulting in a house. For short periods you can deal with them moulting on a boat. But it becomes insufferable when they're moulting on a boat for any significant length of time. They can groom themselves as much as they like but it doesn't help. It doesn't help much either if you groom them as well. There'll still be cat hair in everything you eat. There'll still be great wads of it gliding across around the boat like tumbleweed in cowboy films.

By Oxford we had decided we'd had enough of it and we determined to get to grips with the problem once and for all. The truth is, it was beginning to get us down. For heaven's sake! We hadn't been living on the boat that long. Another few months of it and we'd be suffocating in cat hair, buried under the weight of it like polar explorers trapped by blizzards.

So while Em cleaned out the inside of the boat, vacuuming and scrupulously wiping down every surface to which a malign cat hair might possibly cling, I took Kit on to the bank for a good brushing. This is a procedure she generally enjoys – not just because she takes pleasure in the brushing itself, but because it allows us a little intimate time together, owner and pet united in trust and confidence. Except when she thinks I've taken too many liberties with her tummy. Then she attacks me. Which she probably enjoys just as much as the brushing, being the sadistic creature she is.

I use an ordinary pet brush to groom her – one of those contraptions that looks like a silver-spined hedgehog on a skateboard. It collects cat fur like it's harvesting it. The problem, though, when you're grooming a long-haired cat is that two or three strokes is enough to clog it up. You have to constantly clean the thing by pulling the fur off the bristles. I took a couple of dozen brushfuls off Kit, but it seemed to make no difference to her so I took a couple of dozen more and a couple of dozen after that, until eventually I'd collected enough to fill a bag to busting. It was a big bag too. Enormous.

I'd hardly started, however. True, her fur looked glossier. Yet there didn't actually seem to be much less of it than before and what there was still seemed to be blowing about all over the place in such profusion that people on the towpath were coughing and spluttering as they passed. I stripped her of another couple of bagfuls, and a couple more after that. Who would have thought a cat had so much fur on it? I'd collected so much of the stuff now that I could probably have made a sweater. I'd been at the job nearly an hour. The supply seemed inexhaustible.

What wasn't inexhaustible, however, was Kit's patience. She had tired of this game and was becoming bored. When I'd started grooming her she'd been purring contentedly. Now she was growling deep in her throat in a way that brooked no misunderstanding. She was conveying the clear message that if I didn't back off she would soon be producing sharp claws from the ends of her fluffy little toes, the purpose of which I would rapidly discover.

Luckily it didn't come to that. I must have loosened my grip on her and, taking advantage of it, she wriggled free and dashed back to the boat where Em was just putting the finishing touches to her sanitary blitzkrieg on the cabin. Without pause Kit leapt inside, leaving in her wake a vapour-trail of billowing fur, like a jet airliner in a summer's sky. It filled the cabin like a cloud and within moments settled over the floor in a dusty patina.

It was the last time we tried this.

From now on we realised that if we were going to live on a boat with a cat we were just going to have to live with cat hair too.

***

It was another beautiful morning when we untied our mooring lines the next day, the sun blazing relentlessly in an unblemished sky. We slipped through Osney Lock to Folly Bridge near the reputed site of the Saxon cattle crossing, or ox ford, which gave the city its name. How anyone can be sure of this I don't know, but there's a lot of dodgy conjecture like this which has become embedded in the story of Oxford – much of it, you sometimes think, created for the delectation of gullible tourists who are always wandering around the town in flash mobs pointing and shouting at each other.

There's a better example of this sort of thing on the island at Folly Bridge, where there's an unusual red-brick, castellated building hung with iron balconies and decorated with statues tucked away in alcoves, like saints on Italian cathedrals. Except these aren't saints. These are supposed to be the women who worked here when the place was a brothel.

Now really, I ask you, what sort of a credible story is that? What self-respecting prostitute would want herself advertised so blatantly? What madam worth her salt would pay to have it done? The story sounds to me more like the sort of thing an upper-crust Edwardian undergraduate might have let slip to his visiting mother to shock her. The sort of thing he might have muttered sotto voce to his pater in order to let the old man know that as well as being tutored in Greats he was learning a thing or two about the ways of the world too.

I'd love to have the chutzpah to concoct this sort of stuff myself. There are innumerable places on the waterways begging for it. Bridges with odd names just crying out for someone to fabricate myths about them. Old warehouses ripe for someone to create them a fallacious history. Creepy canalside houses desperate for their own ghosts. *Ah, yes, the Old Junction Toll House. That's where Bill Drummond murdered his young bride on their wedding night in 1782 over an argument about the recipe for suet pudding. On windy nights in winter they say you can still hear her anguished cries: 'Two ounces, Bill, just two ounces. Any more and it sticks to your teeth.'*

Not that there aren't genuinely creepy places on the waterways. A few miles downstream is Sandford, which has a lock nearly 9 feet deep, the deepest on the non-tidal section of the river; and as a result the infamous weir pool here – the Sandford Lasher as it's known – has particularly powerful undercurrents which have claimed more than their fair share of young lives over the years. At least half a dozen schoolboys and students had already drowned there in swimming or boating accidents prior to 1843 when Thomas Gaisford, an Oxford undergraduate, got into trouble and his friend Richard Phillimore dived in to save him. Both drowned, swelling the casualty list, their deaths commemorated (along with other drowned undergraduates) on an obelisk mentioned by the humorist Jerome K. Jerome in his famous book *Three Men in a Boat*. He makes a strained stab at a joke, observing that the steps of the memorial were used by swimmers wanting to see if the place really *was* dangerous.

Even so, he didn't underestimate the danger of the pool. 'The Sandford Lasher,' he wrote, 'is a very good place to drown yourself in.' Jerome was a close friend of the writer J. M. Barrie of *Peter Pan* fame, and he may have later regretted making the comment for in May 1921 one of Barrie's adopted sons, Michael Llewelyn Davies, became a victim of the pool himself, drowning in it with his friend Rupert Buxton. They were both students at Christ Church and described as 'inseparable'. Llewelyn Davies was not yet 21, and he and his brothers were already celebrated as the models for the Darling brothers in *Peter Pan*. This alone would have ensured that the drowning was newsworthy but the circumstances of it ensured even more publicity; for though the coroner concluded the two men had died accidentally, the truth almost certainly was that they were lovers and their deaths a suicide pact.

One witness reported seeing them together in the water – holding on to each other but not struggling. They were found the next day 'clasped in each other's arms', and there was talk they had even tied their hands together. Despite the official verdict, Barrie himself was in no doubt it was suicide. He described the death as 'in a way the end of me', a grief no doubt exacerbated by the earlier death of Michael's brother George, who'd died in the First World War, shot in the head at Flanders.

Another brother, Peter – the one who has the greatest claim to have actually inspired if not the character of Peter Pan then at least his name – died under tragic circumstances too. Plagued for years by being associated with what he called 'that terrible masterpiece', Peter became an alcoholic and committed suicide like his brother Michael. He'd been editing family papers, assembling them into a collection he sardonically called *The Morgue;* and had got to documents relating to Michael's drowning at Sandford weir pool when he walked out from the bar of the Royal Court Hotel in Sloane Square in London, went down into the Tube and stepped under a train. His own son Peter committed suicide too, ensuring that the tragedy associated with that archetypal story of innocent childhood has rippled through the generations to the present day; the chilling paradox is that, like Peter Pan, the boy who never wanted to grow up, so many of those associated with the story seemed never to want to either.

***

We weren't unhappy to leave the distressing history of Sandford Lock behind us and to get back to enjoying the warmer pleasures of a classic English summer's day. It was blazing hot, the river slow and sluggish. We passed the public school Radley College, where the comedian Peter Cook was educated; and soon afterward Nuneham House, where the gardens designed by Capability Brown stretch down to the water's edge. Rousseau stayed here in 1767, and George III described it as 'the most enjoyable place I know' – an accolade which can't have been much consolation to villagers of the former Nuneham Courtenay, which was demolished wholesale when the house was built because it got in the way of the view.

We moored that night by the flat grassy field opposite Abingdon. By now the glorious afternoon had turned into an evening as soft as meadow moss, the sky slashed by the scarlet of a sinking sun which coloured the glassy and unrippled river as if someone had washed out a paint brush in it.

We sat on the deck and surveyed the town over the rims of a couple of glasses of beer which had come straight from the fridge and were so cold we could barely hold them. Abingdon's a difficult place to get a fix on as a casual visitor. In many ways it's a typical Thames town: affluent, elegant and rich in history. But there's an underbelly of gentle privation to it as well – something difficult to identify and which you couldn't for one moment describe as poverty but which nevertheless seems to hint at it. There's a tacky precinct which you wouldn't associate with a town like this, too many charity shops, and too many people wandering the streets looking as if the economic recovery hadn't quite got as far as them yet.

The next day we wandered around trying to figure it out. On the one hand Abingdon seems to have everything going for it: stylish and graceful churches, and an extraordinary old gaol, now converted to flats, which looks as if it was built to withstand a siege. There's a ruined ancient abbey, which once used to be among the richest in the country, and a fine arcaded civic hall, built by a pupil of Christopher Wren and described by the famous architectural commentator Pevsner as the most beautiful municipal hall in England. It towers over Abingdon's small market square, a constant reminder of the proud years when it used to be the county town of Berkshire.

Look on Mumsnet and it will tell you Abingdon's an ideal place to live, full of preschools, toddler groups and family-friendly cafes. But scratch a little harder, or chat to any of the young kids kicking around the streets, and they'll tell you different stories about the 'chav estates' (their words) between the river and the 'lobotomised ley line' (their words again) which is the A34. Stories about the night the Weights Crew from Boulter Drive lost it after they nicked a case of vodka and went steaming through the town, so pumped up the police 'daren't come near us'. Accounts of pitched battles between the 'Sakkies' from Saxton Road, and the 'Peachies' from the private 1970s Peachcroft Estate who, from what I can gather, tend to be younger and physically smaller, and whose strategy seems to be to get lagered up on a Friday night and hunt in feral packs using McDonalds as their HQ. There's always a lot of booze or cheap drugs in these tales, a lot of stolen and unlicensed vehicles, and always a lot of blood after the inevitable punch-up.

And they say the art of storytelling is dead.

I got talking to a bunch of kids on the street one night, and to listen to them, or to read the stuff they write on the net, you'd think Abingdon had been on a downward trajectory since some band called the Lemon Creams played the Horse & Jockey three or four years ago before it closed down. If they showed the remotest interest I could tell them that it started a lot earlier than this – in Victorian times actually, when Abingdon missed out on getting a railway station, and when it lost its status as county town to Reading. Afterwards – and don't ask, please, you don't want to know – it got banished from Berkshire completely and somehow finished up in Oxfordshire.

More significant than this was that in 1980 the famous MG motor plant – which had been located in the town since it had moved from Cowley in 1929, and had been its biggest employer – closed down after the collapse of British Leyland.

This was a car crash to surpass all car crashes, although why it happened, why MG was a part of British Leyland at all and why this once world-famous British marque ended up in the hands of the Chinese, is beyond the scope of a book like this to explore. But brought up as I was in the Midlands, where as a child I watched hosiery factories close by the week, the deterioration and decline of our traditional industrial base makes me angry. And what makes me angrier still is that it continues to happen, our politicians pinning their hopes for the future of our country on rising house prices and a busted banking system that's already proved itself corrupt.

But what do I know about the world? All I've done is live in it a long time.

Mind you, the MG factory at Abingdon has left us an enduring reminder of its presence which we can enjoy at our leisure, for in 1979 the local brewery Morland was asked by the company to produce a commemorative beer to mark the company's 50 years in the town. It was named after an old car which was brought to the factory when it moved to Abingdon and got used as a runabout on the shop floor. The vehicle was originally painted black, although over its time regularly visiting the paint shop it developed a more flamboyant Jackson Pollock-like livery. After a while the shop floor workers nicknamed the car, somewhat disrespectfully, the 'Owld Speckled 'Un'.

Like Abingdon, and the MG plant itself, the brewery never made it to the twenty-first century and was closed down soon afterwards. But Old Speckled Hen, as the beer became known, is still brewed in Suffolk by its new owners Greene King. And a fine drink it is too (complimentary crates gratefully received c/o my publishers).

CHAPTER FIVE
Guns and Roses

The weeping willows were in seed. Wherever you looked, lines of delicate white down had washed up along the bank like drifts of snow. More hung in the air above the river: wads of gossamer floating aimlessly in the still atmosphere, light and insubstantial. Sometimes the seed descended from trailing branches in a gentle fall; at other times, with a breeze behind it, it fell like a blizzard, so thick you could scarcely see across to the other bank through the stuff.

On occasions when there was no wind, it draped itself across the river motionless, and then it didn't seem like snow at all but more like clouds, like diminutive versions of the cotton wool cumuli that had been the backdrop to our cruising since we'd been on the Thames. It was pretty, but it got everywhere. Wherever we moored it would settle and we'd be covered with it the next day, layers of the stuff spread across the deck and on the roof, and around the doors and in the porthole recesses where it clung to old spiders' webs, making them look like lace curtains. It got inside the boat as well, and into our clothes and on to our skin, where it stuck to us as if it had been glued there.

Worse was that we breathed it in: it got up our noses and into our sinuses and on into our chests where we couldn't get rid of it however much we coughed.

Even Kit began to suffer from the effects. It disturbed her as she was napping, playing about her nose until eventually she'd spring awake with a frustrated squeal and set about a clump of it as if it was some new breed of vermin waiting to be exterminated. Not that we were sympathetic. We'd had to live for long enough with her hair all over the place. As far as we were concerned she was getting a taste of her own medicine. There was a sort of natural justice to it. Justice on *Justice*, you might say.

One morning I was attempting to clear a load of willow seed from the roof when the occupant of a neighbouring boat wandered over for a chat. His boat was unusual, difficult to ignore. I'd noticed it when we'd arrived. It was a sort of beat-up sailing barge except that what lines it once possessed had been ruined by the addition of a series of home-built shacks across the top. These were stacked with logs and bits of old bikes and broken engines. Its masts were hung with tattered Tibetan prayer flags and drying washing which didn't look as if it had been washed. Up in the riggings the skull and crossbones of the Jolly Roger hung limply in the sunshine.

When Em and I first got interested in canals in the early 1970s there weren't anything like the number of boats afloat as there are today, but the diversity of craft was much wider. In those days any old thing sufficed as long as it floated. It might have been a decommissioned lifeboat, or a plastic cruiser, or a punt with an outboard motor, or a cut-down wooden working boat. It didn't matter. You name it, someone somewhere would be happily pottering up and down the water on it whistling a merry tune as they went.

Boaters were as varied as their craft then, a miscellaneous mix of the weird and wonderful. There were young hippies looking for a quiet place to skin up, middle-aged would-be sea captains, and ageing professionals playing at explorers as they drifted into their twilight years. All that united them was their love of the waterways and their determination to travel as many of them as they could – not always easy in those days with the canals in the state they were, shallow and undredged, the towpaths crumbling and some of the locks, especially in towns, pretty well on their last legs.

Today, craft on the waterways have become more homogeneous, and it's unusual to find old-style eccentrics on unconventional boats. This guy was one of them, so rare and distinctive he really ought to have been in a museum. He was an American from the mountains who claimed to have travelled the full length of the Mississippi three times as well as sailing around Manhattan and the Statue of Liberty. He must have been in his late sixties, perhaps even older, and he regaled me with a succession of stories about his adventures. One was an account of the time he'd been attacked in the bayou by alligators; in another he'd been pursued by backwoodsmen in Minnesota. Another I vaguely remember finished up with him being arrested for something or another in some godforsaken town in Arkansas. All of this I took with a large pinch of salt – but, hey, he was a good raconteur with a great fund of stories which I could have listened to all day. Or at least I could have listened to them all day until I noticed that every one of them featured guns tucked away in the narrative somewhere. As he went on, the stories themselves seemed to shrink as the importance of the firearms amplified.

As an advertisement for the superior quality of North American dentistry, this guy wasn't exactly an exemplar. He had a mouthful of tobacco-stained teeth which I might not have noticed as much except that the middle four on the top row were completely missing, making him look like the skittles in a 10-pin bowling alley after a bad first ball. He had a habit at key moments when he was talking of sucking his gums in the gap as if to give you time to react to what he was saying.

'So, without messing, this guy comes straight at me,' he said at one point. He had a particular nasal drawl. It was great for comic effect. It made him seem laid-back even when things were getting dramatic. 'So he came at me,' he said again, 'and there in his right hand…' – he pointed to his right hand as if I couldn't have worked out myself which one it was – '… I could see a 50-calibre Action Express supercharged Cody "Killer" cocked and ready to start blazing.'

He sucked his top gum while I expressed suitable shock and awe.

Or again – in that same nasal tone of voice – he concluded a story about drug smugglers he'd somehow got involved with. Mexican drug smugglers. Cartel members like in *Breaking Bad*. So like *Breaking Bad* I couldn't help but feel he'd based this tale on the TV series. 'So they opened up the bag,' he said, staring into my eyes, his own so wide open you could see the whites around them, 'and there in the bottom was an M240, 7.6-mm, open-bolt, gas-operated machine gun with a disintegrating M13 linked belt…' More tooth sucking. More time for a pause as I expressed further shock and awe.

Eventually this all became too much for me. I suspected that if it went on much longer the stories would be totally subsumed by gun talk. Then – who knows? – the conversation might get political. I might get pressed on my views on UK gun control. Or the government's policy on an unarmed police force. And he might have guns of his own to reinforce his opinions.

I made my excuses and went back to cleaning the willow seed.

* * *

Canals in the early 1970s were the last vestige of an England before bankers and bean-counters finally did for it, before it started sinking under the weight of accountants and estate agents. They were a refuge for the disenfranchised, the disengaged, the disinterested; a bolt-hole for antisocial anarchists, social revolutionaries and the plain bloody-minded who'd had quite enough of the present, thank you very much, and preferred to spend their weekends living in the past, exploring the oily backwaters of Birmingham, or sitting on wooden settles discussing old engines in pubs which hadn't changed for decades. They were a breed apart, incomprehensible to anyone else. Except steam railway enthusiasts. Often they were steam railway enthusiasts too.

Difficult as it is to believe today, what with all the edicts emerging from the Canal & River Trust, which runs the system nowadays, there was a period when the inland waterways were a bureaucracy-free zone, a sanctuary of the libertarian and a bastion of free-thinkers. Over the years, however, as the idyll of canals became a marketing opportunity, things changed. Overnight, as more people got drawn to them, they began to attract regulation – a change I can date almost precisely to one spring Saturday in 1980 when the postman arrived just as we were preparing to go out for the weekly shop. He handed me a flat package, the dimensions about those of a large letter box. I ripped it open, intrigued.

'Oh, you must come down and see this,' I shouted to Em who was upstairs prettying herself in the bathroom. 'You just won't believe it…'

The package was a set of cheap aluminium number plates. Number plates, can you believe it? Number plates like the ones on cars, like the ones the police use to trace you when you've gone through a red light or driven too fast in a 30-mph zone. It was a preposterous idea for the waterways, absurd. Oh, how we laughed…

Nowadays most of the laughing about boat number plates comes from newbies to the waterways, who don't believe there was ever a time when boats didn't have them. They think I'm winding them up when I try to tell them how things used to be. They simply can't conceive of a world in which you could travel the waterways of Britain without let or hindrance and without anyone knowing who you were or where you came from.

But number plates were just the beginning of it. Soon there were rules for where you could stay, rules for how long you could moor, rules about insurance and rules about safety. These got encapsulated in a draconian set of regulations for a four-yearly test – a boat MoT – which had the effect of taking most of the cheap boats off the water at one fell swoop. OK, it stopped us blowing each other up with faulty gas installations, or suffocating ourselves with our coal-burning fires. But do you know what? There was never a lot of that happening on the waterways. There was never a moment in waterways history when you picked up your paper to be regaled by accounts of boat explosions sweeping the country or thousands of boaters asphyxiating themselves from faulty fires. Some of us thought the rules were just a ruse to clear the canals of its eccentrics. Some of us thought they were part of a policy to sanitise the waterways for mass consumption.

It's probably why I have a soft spot for American oddballs with a proclivity towards lethal weaponry.

* * *

Em and I decided to go to church. It's not that we're particularly religious but for years we've used a set of waterways guidebooks that were written by a bloke with a profound ecclesiastical bent. They're filled with descriptions of churches, scattered about all over the text like confetti. Whenever we're cruising, in whatever part of the country, there are always descriptions of churches coming at us from all sides like traffic at a busy road junction. Bam! Bam! Bam! Every town seems to have its 'Romanesque church with its sixteenth-century stone-vaulted fan roof'. Every village has an 'ornate rood screen'. Every tiny hamlet has its church spire 'of handsome proportions', or its 'notable box pews' or its 'unusually broad nave'. God knows where this bloke finds all these churches. Maybe God tells him about them. One way or another he digs them out everywhere. Sometimes he even finds them in the middle of fields with nothing around them for miles on either side. Rest assured, though, they will have a 'Palladian-style' exterior, or inside – if you can get inside, since most of them are locked nowadays – will be an 'intricately decorated transept' or a 'remarkable chancel arch' or a 'series of ornately carved corbels'.

Nine times out of ten you don't have the first idea of what he's on about. All this technical terminology he tosses about is worse than Alan Hansen used to spout on *Match of the Day*. It's a specialist vocabulary he uses to make him seem like an expert and it's nothing to do with communicating with ordinary punters like us. It makes me feel like screaming. 'It's a church, mate, a bloody church. Just how many technical words do you need to describe a church?' You can't help wondering what the bloke's like in the rest of his life. He probably never gets toothache. He'll get a nervous impatience in a maxillary molar. And his car will never get a flat battery either. He will just find himself with an exhausted electrochemical power storage unit.

Em and I cast off from Abingdon and after a short journey we moored just beyond the bridge below the lock at Culham, from where we walked back to Culham village. It's an unsettling place is Culham village, one of England's 'lost' villages, wiped out by the plague or bad harvests or heaven knows what else, because no historian seems to know – or at least not with any level of conviction. Judging by the street patterns leading down to the river it was once a good deal larger than it is now, yet what little remains has an atmosphere of its own, so locked into the past that you could shoot a costume drama here without any need to dress the set.

Just a couple of narrow unmetalled roads bordered by grass verges link the few dwellings that now comprise the place: old manor houses for the most part hidden behind walls and topiary. It claims to have a population of 400 but for the life of me I can't see where they all live.

It was another still, scorching day and opening the groaning door of the church of St Paul, which we'd come to see, was like walking from the dry goods to the freezer aisle of a supermarket. Inside it was predictably gloomy, although parts of the church were bathed in an extraordinarily vivid light from shafts of late-afternoon sun which shone through the stained-glass windows like spotlights, the radiance from outside set against dim pools of darkness.

We walked around, soaking up the centuries of history which seemed to leach from the fabric of the place. Every detail of its design spoke of bygone ages, of times past: history deposited on history down to the present day, the layers making up the whole.

Roses left in a vase under the pulpit had been reduced to dried husks in the heat, dead petals scattered across the red and black tiling of the floor. The place smelt the way old country churches always smell: it's the odour of floor polish, a thousand spent candles, incense, damp rugs and fusty copies of *Hymns Ancient and Modern*. As we walked around, marvelling at the wooden roof beams which had sheltered generations before us, our feet threw up clouds of soft dust which had accumulated since the last cleaning but which seemed to us to represent much more: a poignant reminder of those from long ago who'd worshipped here and become dust themselves...

Except that St Paul's isn't that old. And it's not really that authentic either. Well, actually, it's not authentic at all. True, there's been a place of worship on the site from as early as the ninth century. And true, too, a parish church named St Paul was built here 300 years later. But the whole of that church with the exception of the tower (which was anyhow a later addition) was knocked down in 1852. This church – the actual building we were admiring for its antiquity – is a Victorian confection, built by the Gothic Revivalist architect Joseph Clarke, whose name might as well have been Walt Disney for all that's genuinely thirteenth century in this thirteenth-century-style building. The whole thing was like a carefully constructed stage set. And we laugh at the Americans for the faux castles and Renaissance-style gambling palaces of Las Vegas.

Em and I left the church and walked back towards the river. From the bowed wooden footbridge across Culham Cut we could see the tops of the cooling towers at Didcot Power Station. Skirting round a couple of fields we were soon under a canopy of trees, threading our way through the confusion of tributaries and backwaters which lead to the pretty village of Sutton Courtenay and its parish church of All Saints. This was to be our second dose of religion that day.

All Saints' is an altogether different kettle of fish to St Paul's at Culham. Whereas St Paul's is a reproduction, All Saints' is a genuine village church which has been kicking around for centuries and in turn has been kicked around a bit itself. Which is to say that architecturally it's something of a mishmash: a patchwork of alterations and additions which date back to medieval times. Even so, oddly enough, it seems very modern. That's because it's very bright inside. It has a lot of windows, including a row of them just underneath the roof. I was certain these windows would have a technical name but when I went back to my guidebook, the writer – garrulous on so many other ecclesiastical terms – was silent on this one. So it was left to my friend Mr Google to tell me they were called clerestory windows.

All Saints' is a working church, as much a social centre for the village as a place of worship – which is the way of these things nowadays. Just what this involves in terms of effort I had discovered some years ago on a previous visit – not long before Christmas, as it happened. I had fallen into conversation with the newly appointed vicar and made the mistake of implying that the job of running a church in an attractive village like Sutton Courtenay must make for a comfortable living.

Now while it's true that I didn't actually use the phrase 'cushy number' during our chat, I can see with the benefit of hindsight how what I said was unlikely to win me prizes for tact. Especially at Christmas, when the workload of any church increases exponentially. Take it from me, what I said didn't go down well. The vicar rounded on me – or she rounded on me as much as any polite, well-brought-up officeholder of the Church of England can round on any casual visitor to her church who has just put his foot well and truly in his mouth. Mainly this entailed her listing all the services she had to take, and the visits she had to make, and the sermons she had to write, and the parish societies she had to address. Eventually she ground to a halt and went harrumphing off to the vestry or wherever clergy do harrumph off to. Served me right.

A board on one wall lists all the previous incumbents stretching back in an unbroken line to 1091. One of the most colourful was Thomas Fitch, a Parliamentarian during the Civil War. In 1643 when the Royalists were holed up in Oxford, Fitch decided to take direct action to further the cause he supported, and he allowed the church to be used to store gunpowder and munitions.

Unfortunately – well, accidents happen, don't they? You can't think of *everything*, can you? – the church blew up. Fitch was later sacked from his job under provisions in ecclesiastical law for the 'Ejection of Scandalous Ministers'.

No one comes to visit All Saints' for the church itself, however – its big attraction is its churchyard, in which are buried one former prime minister, one media mogul and one of the best writers this country's ever produced. The prime minister is Herbert Asquith, buried in an imposing tomb in a prominent spot. Asquith, who was in Downing Street for eight years until halfway through the First World War, had a house in Sutton Courtenay which he used as his country retreat. It's marked today by a blue plaque and it's said that the decision to declare war on Germany on Tuesday 4 August 1914 was actually taken while he was there.

His great-granddaughter still has a house down the road – though she's less famous for her connection to him than she is in her own right. She's the actress Helena Bonham Carter, whose partner, until they separated recently, was the eccentric Hollywood film director and producer Tim Burton, who made the classic *Edward Scissorhands*.

The media mogul buried in a slightly less prominent position in the churchyard is the newspaperman David Astor, who owned and edited *The Observer* during its heyday of the 1950s. At that time it was the only British newspaper to have the bottle to finger the prime minister, Anthony Eden, for lying over the Suez Canal fiasco when he attempted to cover up a conspiracy he'd cobbled together with France and Israel to invade Egypt. This embarrassing episode in our contemporary history was supposed to allow us to seize the canal from those who actually owned it, thus ensuring the continuity of the British Empire for a thousand glorious years. Or something like that.

'Anthony, have you gone out of your mind?' the American president Dwight D. Eisenhower said to him after it became apparent what he'd done. To which, sadly, the only conclusion history can reasonably arrive at is that he had.

Astor was an old-style, hands-on newspaperman with a strong sense of decency which informed his life. He was one of the earliest opponents of the white apartheid government in South Africa, and one of the earliest sponsors of the human rights group Amnesty International, which came about as a direct result of an article he published about political prisoners by the group's founder Peter Benenson. Astor was also a great friend of the journalist and writer Eric Blair, better known as George Orwell. Both shared a suspicion of state control and big government, so that when Blair died, and there was difficulty in finding a place in consecrated ground to bury such an overt atheist, Astor arranged for him to be interred at All Saints', where I guess he was able to call in a favour from the local vicar.

It's a plain grave, simple and unassuming. Just a small stone with the simple legend 'Here lies Eric Arthur Blair' and his dates. It's tucked away in the churchyard, difficult to find: the sort of grave you'd easily miss if you weren't looking for it. But it seems fitting that it's so modest. Orwell's real legacy is his work: his essays and books like *Animal Farm* and *1984*. It's in the concepts he left us like 'doublethink' and 'newspeak', and the language he bequeathed us in phrases like 'Room 101' and 'Big Brother'. Most of all it's in the political philosophy he left us, the most persistent message of which is that personal freedom is not something you can always take for granted: it's something you have to constantly fight to preserve.

He chose the name Orwell as his pen name after the River Orwell in Ipswich. It seemed somehow appropriate to be visiting his grave from another river.

CHAPTER SIX
Another Lovely Day in Paradise

The early mornings were the loveliest. When there was still a whisper of the night in the air and when the new day felt so fresh that each breath was like sherbet exploding in your lungs. Some mornings – before the sun had time to burn it off – a gentle mist rose provocatively from the water, spilling over the banks on to the fields where it hung in pools over the countryside so that houses and trees appeared to float magically in the miasma, like a scene from some barely remembered dream.

Day after day, we'd wake to sunshine glistening on the water and streaming through our portholes. By mid morning it was hot, too hot to touch a steel boat comfortably and far too hot to do anything energetic. We'd sit on the deck reading, shading ourselves under umbrellas and floppy hats; or we'd take a gentle stroll up the riverbank or around whatever town or village we happened to be moored in. By afternoon, though, as the heat increased, movement itself became too much and lassitude set in. The air became heavier and breathing wearisome. We sought the shade of the boat, opening every porthole and hatch with the determination of hunters laying traps to catch passing breezes. We measured out our days in ice creams and cold drinks, rarely eating until the evening when the temperatures began to fall; and then we'd sit on the deck until midnight and beyond, gulping down the cooling air along with glasses of Sauvignon served straight from the fridge.

Sooner or later we'd judge that it was bearable enough to sleep and so we'd open our bedroom roof hatch to the baking night, and despite the dragonflies the light attracted, stumbling up the walls suicidally like demented extras from a zombie movie, we'd cautiously risk ourselves to bed. If we were lucky we'd fall straight off into a sort of heat-induced coma; but more often than not it was too oppressive even to snooze and we'd toss and turn fitfully throughout the night, until eventually wedges of the morning forcing their way through the cabin curtains announced that another new day had begun.

Everyone was infected by the weather. 'Good morning!' people would shout joyously from other boats as they passed. 'Good morning,' they'd say brightly as they went by on the towpath, winking at us as if we were involved in some conspiracy against the rest of the world.

'Another lovely day in paradise!' someone said to us one morning, paraphrasing the title of the song by Phil Collins. At first it disturbed me. Hang on, I thought, that song's about homelessness, isn't it? It's about people not having anywhere to live. No one on a boat is homeless. Far from it. Most of us have got the boat and a house too. Probably more than one house judging by some of the boats in these parts.

Yet the words fitted the moment so perfectly they became a part of it. Soon everyone was using them. 'Another lovely day in paradise, isn't it?' people would bellow at us from their moorings on the bank. 'Another lovely day in paradise, eh?' they'd shout to us smiling, when we passed them on the water. After a while any impact Phil Collins intended the words to have faded and we started using them between us as a catchphrase. Soon we were using it to other people as much as they used it to us. 'Another lovely day in paradise,' Em would say to people when she passed their boats on the way to the shops. 'Another lovely day in paradise,' I'd say when other boaters stopped to pass the time of day while I was tinkering about on the towpath. And we'd chuckle together conspiratorially like primary school kids in the playground. It was – let's be honest – a bit of a smug thing to do. It was a bit up ourselves, you might almost say. But it was how everyone on the river felt. We were just acknowledging to ourselves how privileged we were to be free to experience such an exquisite summer while so many others were having to trudge off to work to spend hours in stuffy offices and factories.

* * *

It was a Sunday when we cast off from our moorings, cruising downstream. After an hour or so we passed under the magnificent red-brick bridge at Clifton Hampden designed by George Gilbert Scott, who was also responsible not just for the Albert Memorial and the hotel that fronts St Pancras Station but (since Phil Collins' song was on my mind) about 40 workhouses too. A couple of miles on we arrived at Day's Lock, which lies in the crook of the dog-leg bend that takes the river around the old Roman town of Dorchester-on-Thames, and which is the main gauging station for measuring the flow of the river. It can't have been registering much that day for you could see the current was barely moving at all now, the mighty Thames reduced after a month or so without rain to an inert lake.

The local kids at Wallingford where we moored that afternoon were taking advantage of the conditions and it didn't matter to them that the open-air swimming pool in the park on the banks of the river was chock-a-block and turning away customers. They'd all congregated on the shallow beach at Riverside Meadows, downstream of the venerable old town bridge. There, 20 to 30 of them of all ages were having a whale of a time bombing off the parapet and playing about in rubber dinghies in the shallows. The place was like Blackpool on a bank holiday Monday.

I loved it. I loved their unadulterated happiness, their vitality. I loved their noisy exuberance and their unselfconscious *joie de vivre*.

There's a distinctive sound of summer we all recognise, and kids squealing in delight around water is as much a part of it as the chimes of ice-cream vans playing *Greensleeves,* or the noisy squabbling of ducks in park ponds competing for scraps of bread. It doesn't matter whether it's adolescents messing about on the river, or toddlers splashing about in inflatable paddling pools in suburban back gardens: wherever you go in Britain when the sun shines there'll be kids and water, that top-of-the-bill double act of the season.

We went into town for provisions, heading for a Waitrose which I knew from a previous visit was nearby. Towns are usually defined by their architecture, mostly buildings from the past which people think say something about them. Wallingford certainly has enough of these. It has a colonnaded corn exchange and a ruined castle on the hill and a church on the river with a spire that looks as if it's dropped off a wedding cake. But these don't really say anything about Wallingford – or at least not contemporary Wallingford. What *does* say something about it is its Waitrose, which stands guarding the approach to the High Street like a fortress.

Of course, any Waitrose says something about the town it's in. Usually it says it's affluent and full of itself. The Waitrose in Wallingford is no different – it's just that it says it really loudly. That's because it's huge. Colossal. So big they should name the town after it – Waitford or Roseford, something like that. It's a corner building on a junction, with a rounded facade dominating the street. At the top is a narrow row of windows like wraparound virtual-reality glasses. Below is what appears to be the entrance, like a mouth ready to gorge on you – which, considering Waitrose's prices, would be about right. Except what appears to be the entrance isn't the entrance. The entrance is somewhere up the back tucked away inconveniently to one side so that if you go round the other side by mistake you have to walk around the whole damned block before you can get in.

Really, how did such a brutal, user-unfriendly monstrosity come to be built in such a small riverside market town as this? Did the architect knock it off one morning with a hangover? When plans for it were first released in the architectural press the place was described as 'a cross between a private US prison and a bunker from the coast of World War II Normandy'. And that, in my opinion, was a kind judgement. It's so out of scale with the rest of the town, so totally at odds with it, that when I went searching for the place on my first visit I stood on the pavement next to it and didn't know it was there because it towered so high above me. Eventually I had to ask someone.

'Isn't there a Waitrose around here?' I said, accosting an elderly woman pushing a shopping trolley. She gawped at me gone out, did a backwards shuffle and pointed upwards with her index finger, where 20 or 30 feet above me was the store name in letters a yard high. 'Ah, yes, sorry… It just looks like a wine warehouse,' I blurted out as some sort of excuse – though she didn't hear it. She'd gone scurrying up the street first chance she got, the better to put distance between us.

Well, it *does* look like a wine warehouse. That's because the front bit is a wine warehouse. How's anyone to know there's a complete supermarket hidden behind it?

Not that Em and I were going to get into a debate about the declining standards of supermarket architecture. Well, not on a Sunday, and not on a day as hot as that. The truth was we were happy to find any supermarket open because nowhere else in Wallingford was. We got quite excited about the prospect and started planning a meal. We were going to spoil ourselves with a smoked salmon salad, and maybe some strawberries and ice cream to follow, and perhaps a bottle of chilled Prosecco to wash it all down…

It would have been a lovely meal, if we'd ever got it. Unfortunately we never did. There'd been a power cut and there wasn't a fridge in the place working. Indeed, there were hardly any lights working either – though this did at least have the advantage of hiding the embarrassed faces of the staff as they had to explain to customers that the electrical cabling in this state-of-the-art building hadn't been able to take the strain of the hot weather.

We stayed in Wallingford three or four days. Badly designed supermarkets notwithstanding, there's a comforting, old-fashioned feel about the place to which you can't help but be drawn. As well as beautiful buildings it's got lovely parks, which we never tired of visiting, wandering about in them aimlessly for hours on end. And that was an odd thing because normally Em and I aren't the sort to spend a lot of time wandering around aimlessly anywhere. But it seemed a natural thing to do as part of this new life we were beginning to settle into: a life in which we could do things like that, things that in the past we'd watched other people do but dismissed as a waste of time. Now we could happily waste time ourselves looking at roses, or trees or bedding plants. Or the boats going by on the river. Or the people passing in the street as we sat drinking a coffee at a pavement cafe. We could waste time because we had time to waste and because, for the first time in our lives, there wasn't the constant pressure on us to do things all the time.

I guess we'd moved from an active to a passive stage of our lives, and it suited us both down to the ground.

'Another lovely day...' Em began one afternoon as we walked back to the boat after a purposeless stroll around town. And before she could complete the phrase I'd interrupted: '...in paradise.' We both fell about laughing in the street. People must have thought we were mad.

Wallingford is so quintessentially English, it's no surprise to learn that it's a centre for the 'cosy crime' whodunnits that we as a nation seem to delight in producing. For more than two decades it's been the model for Causton in TV's *Midsomer Murders,* and this has brought it international fame. Nearby too is Winterbrook House, where 'Queen of Crime' Agatha Christie lived for more than 40 years until her death in 1976 and which she used as the model for the home of her famous detective Miss Marple.

To read the Miss Marple mysteries or to watch *Midsomer Murders* you'd think it was impossible to venture out of doors in these parts without stumbling across a dead body or, worse, ending up as one yourself. Some social scientist once did an analysis of the murder rate in Midsomer and concluded that it was almost exactly three times higher than the real-life murder rate in England and Wales. Some may ask how TV scriptwriters get away with it. Me, I wonder at the researchers who dig up these sorts of statistics: how do *they* get away with it?

I mean, what do you expect researching the amount of murders in a TV murder programme? That you won't find any? That you'll discover all the characters having afternoon tea and going to garden fetes? It's a murder programme, for God's sake. They kill each other. You can't have a whodunnit without someone who does it in the first place. And what about that team of otherwise erudite scholars who wrote a paper for the *British Medical Journal* analysing the mortality rate in *Coronation Street* and *EastEnders*? They concluded that it was higher than average. Well of course it was higher than average. What did the muppets expect? *Corrie* and *EastEnders* are television dramas. The clue's in the word drama. In drama people die: they kill each other and catch deadly diseases and get knocked over by cars. What did the researchers expect the characters in soaps to do? Sit around embroidering?

It's the same as that professor who wrote an essay in which he counted the atrocities in Shakespeare's tragedy *Titus Andronicus,* generally acknowledged as Shakespeare's most violent play. He discovered there were 14 killings, six occurrences of severed male organs, one live burial, one case of cannibalism and three or four rapes, depending on how you defined them. It worked out at an average of 5.2 atrocities per act, or one every 97 lines.

Now what possible interest could there be in research like... though, hold on! – actually, thinking about it, it *is* quite interesting when you see it all listed like that. Well, I find it interesting, at least. It makes me wonder how the levels of Shakespearean violence might compare with those of our modern-day dramatists or filmmakers. With Quentin Tarantino's, for instance. His *Pulp Fiction* and his two *Kill Bills* must have a greater incidence of violence than that.

Maybe somebody should research it.

***

It's our final night in Wallingford and we are sitting on deck in silence over the debris of dinner watching darkness fall on the river. It is that stage in the evening which the Scots, using an Old English word, call the gloaming – that brief period of twilight when day turns to night. Scientifically it's the point at which we begin to rely less on the light-sensitive cones in our retina which respond to photopic, or daytime, light levels, and more on the colour-insensitive rods that allow us to see better in the dark. This technical explanation says it all, but at the same time it says nothing. Because nightfall's so much more than this: it's a phenomenon which defies analysis – more mood than reason. It's the unsettling intersection of two worlds, the threshold of the barely known: a mystical time when the depth and dimension of the universe seem to shift about us and when our perceptions become heightened but strangely distorted too. It's something you're so much more aware of from the deck of a boat than from on land.

There is a lazy crescent moon lounging in an indigo sky so dark it seems to glisten with stars, as if the cosmos had been scattered with sugar. We watch as the last of the swallows skim the surface of the river before flying off to roost. A single coot with its white beak luminous in the shadow dives for a late supper, and from time to time a boat passes, its headlight cutting through the blackness as it hugs the bank searching for moorings.

The streetlights have come on across Wallingford Bridge and the older kids are still messing about on the nearby beach, as they have been the whole time we've been here. Some of them are still wet from swimming. The girls in thin summer dresses and long, straggling hair clutch themselves and stamp their feet for warmth while the boys – most of them bare-chested – strut around like peacocks. They are loud-mouthed, brash and profane; struggling with the perennial problem of puberty, which is how to impress girls while at the same time ignoring them. Their antics make no impact. The girls huddle together giggling. There are odd bouts of laughter from them, outbursts of inexplicable tears. Occasionally a boy makes a move and sidles up to the group only to retreat crestfallen, his mates jeering and taunting him for his failure. At one point another drives straight into the group on his bike and the girls scatter in all directions like tenpins, shrieking and angry at the assault but elated at the attention it signifies.

It is a masque which is being played out, I understand that, a ritual as old as humankind itself. And watching it I can't help but be thrown back to my own adolescence, me and my mates sporting ourselves with the girls around the unlit bus shelter which was the nearest we got to a youth club in the small Leicestershire village where I grew up. We'd let them sit on our laps while we teased them with forbidden cigarettes or squares of chocolate. Or we'd steal their hairbrushes and dare them to chase after us. We'd steal kisses too and odd, furtive moments of intimacy, groping underneath their dresses and cardigans until the bus arrived and cast a guilty spotlight on us all. Then we'd know it was time to go home. Home to our mums who'd tell us off for getting in late. Home to our dads who'd barely look up from the telly when we did.

Gazing at the kids at Wallingford that stifling summer's evening I feel old, so very old. In their bravado they are like a different species. Or maybe it is me that is the different species, not human at all but something tired and wasted, like some husk of a butterfly that had once shadowed the sun flamboyantly. I watch them until they leave and feel distraught when they are gone, a straggling line of them disappearing into the night. Despite the chasm between us I feel for them with such intensity it hurts. There is a bliss in adolescence that comes from living life as if it were never-ending; but there's a delicious anguish associated with it too, as you come to learn that it's not.

Watching those kids that night I felt envious of their youth. The truth is I wanted to be them.

***

Beyond the extraordinary Moulsford railway bridge (which is actually two parallel bridges built more than 50 years apart) the river enters one of its most attractive reaches as the Berkshire Downs meet the Chilterns. Meandering gently through the heavily wooded section of the Goring Gap, it arrives at Goring itself, where a precarious-looking bridge separates it from the village of Streatley on the other bank.

We were parched and stopped to top up our fluid levels. We'd have stopped longer except the beer was so pricy it made us weep – which rather defeated the object of the exercise. So we continued on to Pangbourne to moor on the meadows below the town, where three or four more hot, sunny days slipped by so languidly we barely noticed the time passing.

Pangbourne's that sort of place. The sort of place where days slip by without your being even aware of it until the moorings warden politely reminds you it might be time to think about moving on. It's very comfortable is Pangbourne, very at ease with itself. Laid back, you might say, except that no one in Pangbourne would think of using that sort of vernacular. It's got airs and graces, that's what I'm trying to say. But it's also got a high-class cheese shop, its own bakery, an award-winning butcher and an organic wholefood store selling wet fish. Take it from me, you won't go hungry for posh nosh in Pangbourne.

But that isn't all of Pangbourne – oh no, that isn't the half of it. Pangbourne has a Bentley dealership too. And not only a Bentley dealership but a Lamborghini dealership as well. Getting some idea of the place now, eh? Getting some sense of what the houses might cost? It's a pretty cultural place too, Pangbourne; bang on the rural zeitgeist. It has a performing arts group and a painting club, a choral society and even a silver band – though I'm not sure if that's posher than a brass band or not.

On our first morning there we were waylaid passing a bus stop. 'Are you intending to catch the bus,' a woman enquired, 'or are you going to the theatre?' Why she thought we were queuing at a bus stop at all, let alone for the theatre, intrigued me too much to let it pass. She explained that it was because the Pangbourne Theatre Club, or whatever they call themselves, organised regular coach outings to London to see shows, and that the pick-up point was the bus stop. Apparently the play they were going to see that day was *Merrily We Roll Along* at the Harold Pinter Theatre, a fact worth noting because the words 'merrily' and 'Harold Pinter' are not ones you often see together in the same sentence.

Pangbourne's most famous resident was Kenneth Grahame, author of *The Wind in the Willows*. He was brought up downstream at Cookham and moved to Pangbourne after his retirement from the Bank of England, where he had worked for 30 years. He retired early on grounds we'd recognise today as stress, something almost certainly related to an ongoing dispute he'd had with one of the directors. However, an odd incident a few years before couldn't have helped his state of mind. A visitor had blagged his way into the bank demanding to see the governor and when Grahame was sent to deal with him the caller suddenly produced a gun and started firing it off all over the place. Grahame was unharmed and managed to lock his would-be killer into a waiting room until the latter was overpowered by bank security staff using a fire hose. The man was declared insane and sectioned soon afterwards.

Imagine that happening nowadays. The poor devil wouldn't get within a mile of the front door before the Anti Terrorist Squad had him spreadeagled on the pavement with a gun to his head and probably a couple of bullets inside it too.

Grahame lived in Church Cottage which, as its name suggests, is tucked away in a narrow lane behind the village church of St James the Less. It was here the famous illustrator Ernest (E. H.) Shepard came in the early 1930s after he'd been commissioned to provide drawings for an edition of Toad, Ratty and Mole's adventures. Shepard had made his name creating the celebrated drawings for the Winnie the Pooh stories and he took the reach of the river between Cookham and Pangbourne as the inspiration for this new commission. A number of local houses claim to be the model for his drawings. Some of them claim to be the model for the same drawing.

It was one of these houses – Mapledurham House, which might or might not have been Toad Hall – that had brought Em and me to Pangbourne in the first place. Now this may seem curious since Mapledurham House lies downstream of Pangbourne on the way to Reading, and you'd be right in thinking that it would have been easier for us to visit the house as we passed on the boat. We'd certainly have done it that way if it had been possible, but we were prevented from doing so because the place is kept inaccessible from the towpath – fortressed from it, you might almost say – by a wide weir and the stream to a restored watermill. There are organised boat trips from Reading, and on occasions the family owning the house do allow private boats to moor, but otherwise the only way of getting to it is by doing what we planned to do on our second or third day in Pangbourne, which was to cross the river at Whitchurch Bridge below the town and walk the back way to it by lanes and footpaths on the opposite bank.

It was a lovely ramble on a hot summer's day when the verges were thick with teasels and cow parsley, and the hedgerows heavy with the scent of wild honeysuckle and hypnotic with the droning of bees. Whitchurch Bridge is – extraordinarily – one of two river crossings on the Thames still in private hands. It's been owned since 1792 by The Company of Proprietors of Whitchurch Bridge (I wonder how you buy shares in that?), and tolls are still levied from motor vehicles, although sadly no longer from the porch of the pretty white-stuccoed cottage from which business used to be done. Today the money's taken by an attendant in a utilitarian red-brick kiosk in the middle of the road. From here he heroically battles to service oncoming drivers from both directions, who inevitably become impatient at the hold-up. When we were there, however, changes were promised. This version of the bridge, constructed in 1902, was on its last legs and scheduled to be rebuilt in the autumn for the third time. I was only pleased I didn't live in the area when it happened. With the nearest bridge capable of taking the displaced traffic 6 miles or so downstream at Reading, you just knew that complete chaos would soon reign in this otherwise serene fragment of old Albion.

We walked past an alpaca farm. A herd of them, looking more like a flock of toffee-nosed sheep, were grazing peacefully in the shade of a hedge. Soon afterwards we skirted the stud at Hardwick Farm, old Comet looking at us disapprovingly from his stall as we disturbed his afternoon. The place used to be the stables for nearby Hardwick House, a Tudor manor bought by the MP and racehorse breeder Charles Day Rose in 1909, just before he became a baronet. It's another house that might have provided the inspiration for Toad Hall, a fact that for some reason gets given greater prominence today than the fact that Day Rose is also said to be the model for the overbearing, arrogant and filthy-rich Mr Toad.

It's currently occupied by Sir Julian Rose, the fifth baronet, who succeeded to the estate in 1966. Being made of more ideological stuff than his ancestor he set about making it an ecological exemplar, converting the land to organic farming and managing the surrounding woodlands sustainably. Sir Julian was an early voice against global farming methods and an opponent of genetically modified food; and as you walk through the estate – almost past his front door – you're regaled by signs announcing that it's a 'GM Free Zone'.

The accessibility of the Hardwick estate is in complete contrast to the restrictions we found at Mapledurham House. After the inconvenience of getting there in the first place, you can then only see the back of the house through a set of forbidding wrought-iron gates, which separates it from the churchyard. And from that angle it's not a very prepossessing place, take it from me. In fact it's more like a prison block than a house. Frankly, even on a searing summer's afternoon, it looks forbidding, the sort of place where you really wouldn't want to have to spend a night alone. Mapledurham village was the setting of Michael Caine's 1976 film *The Eagle Has Landed* about a German plot to kidnap Churchill in the Second World War. In my opinion Mapledurham House would make a better set for a Dracula movie.

Completed in 1588 during the reign of Queen Elizabeth and sycophantically designed around the shape of the letter E to honour her, it's one of those unusual piles which has been in the same family since it was built. The Blounts were, and still are, a Catholic family, which explains a unique feature of the Anglican church of St Margaret's next door, which is that it has a Catholic aisle in it. Under the same roof but entirely separate from it. This is because for 500 years the Bardolf Aisle, as it's known, has been the personal property of the owners of Mapledurham House. And though in the interim there's been a Reformation and a Civil War and centuries of religious upheaval during which Protestants and Catholics have been at each other like cats and dogs, putting each other to death and torturing each other for their beliefs, throughout it all the Catholic aisle in the Anglican church of St Margaret's at Mapledurham survived untouched and unharmed.

It says something reassuringly comforting about us English that this could happen because, when you look at it, the religious confusion of those years was all too theological for us. It was about ideas, many of which, even at the time, were too arcane and complicated for most of us to understand. For we English, unlike our Gallic neighbours, are never comfortable around ideas. We become fidgety when things get too intellectual. On other matters though, concrete topics like who owns what – tangible, substantial questions of rights, tenures and titles – well, that's a different thing altogether. Here we're in our element and much more sure of ourselves.

The fact is, the Blounts own the aisle in the church and that's an end of it. Religion has got nothing to do with it.

CHAPTER SEVEN
O, 'Tis Reading

To be fair to the Blounts at Mapledurham, I can understand why they want to keep their bit of Olde England sacrosanct by ensuring it remains cut off from the rest of the world. Frankly, if I was in their position I'd want to do the same thing. Cruising down the river the following morning it became clear just how dangerously Reading is beginning to encroach on the village. When you visit by foot, it seems miles away from anywhere, locked into a past of its own; but by boat it becomes clear that Mapledurham's virtually part of Reading now. It's probably closer to the town centre than many of the city's outlying suburbs.

We were barely a mile beyond Mapledurham Lock – which is just opposite the house, remember – when, on the dock of the bay between a building site and an ad for some *Fawlty Towers*-type hotel, we spotted a tatty sign announcing 'Welcome to Reading'. At this point a railway line and a savage-looking row of palings, like spears stored in an armoury, separate the river from a suburb called Tilehurst. This is no bad thing as far as I'm concerned. I'm all for putting as much distance as possible between me and Tilehurst. I once spent months there investigating a murder for a television programme and I formed no good opinion of the place. My colleague formed an even worse opinion. He was approached out of the blue by a man on the street, who advised him to get out of Tilehurst straightaway and not to come back. Only he didn't put it quite that politely.

He actually told him to f*ck off. 'And if you come back,' he added, 'I'm going to rip your head off and shit down your throat.'

The three-times world champion racing driver Ayrton Senna lived in Tilehurst for a couple of years in the early 1980s before he moved to Monaco, which takes a bit of believing, doesn't it? But it was convenient for work, close to Woking where McLaren was based and Didcot where Williams had its HQ. He might have been a legend on the track, but the neighbours remember him as a dreadful gardener who was forever planting roses around the house with no idea of how to look after them. The brother of one of them ran into the side of Senna's Alfa Romeo reversing out of a drive one day. Such was Senna's combative character that if anything like this had happened in a race it would have signalled an immediate and lifelong blood feud. But apparently off track the Brazilian was charm itself. He told the man not to worry about it.

The delights of Tilehurst soon give way to those of Caversham, where solid, Edwardian houses with gables and turrets and expansive manicured lawns start to appear. Boathouses, old and new, are much in evidence in these parts. One of them, noticeably older than the rest, had a thatched roof and was probably a residential house itself once. Caversham may not be the best address on the Thames, but it's still on the Thames;

and these rambling eight-, nine- or ten-bedroomed properties – many of them mock-Tudor and painted in such vivid black and white they're as fresh as the remastered prints of old movies – would cost a lottery win to buy.

Reading is at its best from the river and as you get closer to the centre and Caversham Bridge there's a sense of spaciousness about the town, with parks and playgrounds lining the bank on one side and elegant blocks of mansion flats bordering the other in a way vaguely reminiscent of Torquay.

We pulled into a boatyard. We'd been having trouble with our electrics, our fridge labouring in the heat, and I wanted to buy new batteries. I was steering and as I came into moor I saw another boat against the landing stage, an ex-hire boat built like a military Bailey bridge. Standing by it was a couple, the man slight and nervous, the woman – who I took to be his wife – ample, loud and demanding. She immediately took command of proceedings and instructed me to come alongside. If she'd been in a car you'd have called it back-seat driving.

'Pull left a bit to starboard – harder, harder. Straighten out. More throttle now, more throttle...'

It turned out they were selling their boat and a potential buyer was coming to see it that morning. It was too heavy for them, they couldn't handle it any longer, they explained to me. Besides, they'd had enough of boating, they were fed up with it, the Thames particularly. 'Marlow is dreadful and Henley isn't worth visiting,' the woman complained. '£9 a night we had to pay, £9 to moor in a field...'

Trying to be helpful, I said that it might have been cheaper for them to have stayed on the town moorings. This obviously touched the wrong chord. It seemed to irritate them.

'You don't want to stay in towns,' she said, 'not when you're on a boat. That's the last thing you want to do.'

Her husband nodded vigorously. 'When you're on a boat you want to get away from towns,' he added for good measure, as if this was a completely original idea that hadn't been introduced into conversation just moments before.

'Yes, yes, of course.' I faltered. 'Pangbourne's a nice mooring, though. We've just come from Pangbourne. It's beautiful there, very rural. And it's free.'

This appeared to aggravate them even more. 'There's no shade at Pangbourne,' the woman snapped.

'No, no shade at all,' her husband concurred. 'It's far too hot in this weather; you could easily get sunburned if you stayed too long on the moorings in Pangbourne...'

'What about Goring then? Goring's nice. There's free mooring there,' I suggested.

'Goring's far too noisy,' she replied.

Again her husband nodded. 'It's like mooring on a motorway,' he proclaimed. 'Or spending a night in a car park.'

And so it went on.

'I don't think there was a single place I could have suggested that would have suited them,' I said to Em later in the day. 'There was something wrong with everywhere I mentioned. Either it was too close or too far away, or too busy or too quiet, or too many trees or not enough. Honestly, I don't think it's the waterways they're tired of, I think it's life itself.'

'You can understand it, though, I suppose,' said Em, with great empathy. She is a great empathiser when she wants to be. Given enough information on his early years and childhood she could probably empathise with Vlad the Impaler. 'They're an old couple and they've probably been boating all their lives. They've seen it all and feel it's time to move on...'

'They're younger than us,' I protested. 'And they've been boating less than a year. They only bought their boat last August. I was talking to the old bat while I was in the chandlery paying for the batteries. She told me that they're going to buy a motorhome now.'

'A motorhome?' Em went silent for a moment. 'What did you say to that, then?'

'I wished them the best of luck for the future. What else could I have said?'

'Good riddance, maybe?' she suggested wickedly. And not at all empathetically.

***

As the Thames leaves Reading it passes the entrance to the 87-mile-long Kennet and Avon Canal, which leads to Bristol. There's a Tesco on the bend here. The big supermarkets sited along the waterways are clued up nowadays about boats, and in the same way they provide car parking it's not unusual for them to make provision for their waterborne customers by providing short-term moorings too. You're lucky if you can get a space at the ones at Reading though. The moorings tend to act as a magnet for the sort of liveaboards who've generated considerable ill feeling on the waterways over recent years.

Officially termed 'non-compliant continuous cruisers', they're boaters who haven't got an official mooring and actually don't cruise at all, let alone continuously as they're required to do by the terms of their licence. Instead, in order to avoid the regulations, they potter between local bridges, moving but not moving – or at least not moving in any sort of meaningful way which could be construed as making a journey.

There've always been people living this way on the waterways. We have friends who brought up a family like this. But as house prices have risen and the property market has exploded, the waterways have attracted unsustainable numbers of people looking for a cheaper way to live. Unfortunately their arrival has coincided with a massive increase in leisure boat owning, so that now more than 35,000 craft of all sorts are licensed on the inland waterways. This – astonishingly – is more than there ever were at the height of the Industrial Revolution when canals were the backbone of our transport system.

Today what was once the obsession of a few enthusiasts has become the lifestyle of the many. And it's caused conflict, genuine canal rage. Leisure boaters – the weekenders and the holiday cruising types – dismiss the others as 'bridgehoppers'. They accuse them of hogging resources, stealing the best mooring spaces and staying on them for weeks on end; and their antagonism has spilled over to people who are living on the waterways perfectly legally, as we had begun to, observing mooring restrictions when there are restrictions and moving on at least every two weeks when there aren't.

A lot of it is jealousy. You get the impression from some of the more disagreeable weekenders that because they're not lucky enough to be able to spend as much time on their boats as they'd like, they're resentful about anyone who does. But they do have a point. If you've spent a fortune buying a boat and another fortune licensing it, maintaining it, and paying for overpriced marina moorings, then it must be galling to find that when you come to take your precious two-week annual holiday you can't even stop where you want.

The friction between the groups is worsened by cultural difference. Many of the bridgehoppers, especially in towns, are young. They play loud music and have tattoos and long hair or no hair at all. They're also, on the whole, not as well off as the leisure boaters. Their craft tend to be scruffy, unpainted and piled high with bags of coal and logs and old engine parts.

I have mixed feelings about them. I know that if I was young again and starting out a career in a big city, a boat moored in a community of other young boaters would offer a much more affordable and enticing option as a home than a bedsit up a back alley costing God-knows how many hundreds of pounds a week. The government recognises this too and has encouraged local councils to promote mooring in cities, which many of them, especially in London, already do. Indeed, if it wasn't for the fact that many National Health Service staff, social workers and teachers already live on canals, public services in many London boroughs would be a good deal worse than they are.

Also, as anyone who's had a boat on the cut for more than ten minutes can't help but notice, boats in built-up areas enhance the urban landscape. For years the public perception of a city canal was straight out of Ewan MacColl's song 'Dirty Old Town'. It was the place down by the gasworks where you kissed your girl by the factory wall: a place where you dreamed your dreams – most of which were about getting away from the environs of the canal as quickly as you could. Boats brighten up city canals, though, even scruffy boats. They may not seem much of an attraction in themselves but on a messy section of urban canal even a tatty boat is better than no boat. Canals draw people to them: they provide mental breathing space in the midst of the city scrum. Boats can help regenerate parts of cities which have become derelict, no-go areas. They can make cities safer by populating the towpath rather than abandoning it to the yobs and muggers.

That's why if I hear anyone on a boat complaining about not being able to moor overnight in Victoria Park in Hackney in London because of the liveaboards clogging up the towpath, I know one thing. I know they haven't been boating long. If they had been they'd know that in the past, without the liveaboards being around to provide security, you'd never have moored there overnight even if your life depended on it.

You wouldn't have had a boat the next morning if you had.

You should never judge by appearances, but even so I confess that it was hard to imagine how the liveaboards around the moorings at Reading's Tesco that morning could do much for any urban environment. They eyed Em and me suspiciously as we brought our boat into the bank and, after we'd tied up, their dogs gathered in a pack and started edging towards us, snarling viciously. I couldn't understand it. Until we arrived they'd all been quietly gnawing bones. Probably the bones of boaters. That's probably why our arrival had disturbed them. It was the scent of fresh meat.

Mind you, to be fair to them, the liveaboards and the dogs were very much in keeping with the general tenor of the surroundings. The weather had drawn people outside from the supermarket to the river and there seemed to be a convocation of the fat and their offspring taking place. Young and old alike were all resolutely stuffing crisps and chocolate into their mouths as if it were an Olympic sport, the purpose of which was to distribute discarded wrappers on the grass over as wide an area as possible. Further along were a crowd of drinkers knocking back Special Brew and Buckfast. Shaded from the sun by the black clouds of the cigarettes they were incinerating on an industrial scale, they were entering into the spirit of things by tossing their empty bottles, fag ends and cans into the water.

A biker in leathers and dripping with chains sat surveying the scene on his machine. It was polished to a lustrous shine, its coachwork gleaming in the sun, the shimmering chrome of its headlight and exhaust pipe blindingly bright. There wasn't a spot of dirt on it, not a fleck of misplaced mud, not a speck of disoriented dust.

Only it wasn't a motorbike: it was a mobility scooter. The motorbike accessories were just faux decoration. Pretty cool faux decoration, I grant you, but as artificial as plastic grass.

I assumed that since he'd got no kids with him to stuff with sugars and trans fats, before long he'd be swelling the ranks of the drinkers. I couldn't have been more wrong. We had to pass him on the way into the supermarket and he made his views clear to us in no uncertain terms. Pointing at the river and the various tribes of people enjoying the morning in their inimitable fashions, he said: 'Bloody disgrace, the lot of them. You'd think they could at least keep the place decent.'

Appearance may count for a lot on the beautiful waterways; but as I say, you should never judge character by it.

***

We moored at Sonning, pronounced 'Sunning'. This seemed a particularly apt place to stop considering the gorgeous weather we continued to have, the long heatwave making headlines overseas as well as here. The place is only 2 or 3 miles by water from Tesco's at Reading but it's an entirely different world.

Hollywood actor George Clooney and his new wife, human rights lawyer Amal Alamuddin, have just moved there into a £10 million house. That's how different. That evening we walked through the churchyard to the Bull Inn where we sat in the courtyard under a trellis of wisteria still heavy with fragrant flowers, talking about our progress so far. Or rather our lack of progress. Weeks had passed by since we left Banbury, more than a month. Yet it felt as if we'd only just left a couple of days ago. We weren't cruising at anything like the rate we had done in the past; now we had the time we were tending to stay in places much longer. But this was part of the way we'd chosen to do things. This was the difference between living on a boat and taking a holiday on one. We weren't cruising to any set pattern, we weren't trying to get anywhere. Neither had we got any plans or schedule we were keeping to. People didn't understand this. They were so caught up in their own frenetic lives that they kept demanding answers from us: the same old questions over and over again. Where are you going? What plans have you got?

I wanted to scream. Haven't you got this yet? Can't you get this into your head? That's all the old stuff. We don't do that any more. Now we're living on a boat. We don't have plans now. We're not going anywhere. We're just being.

Later we walked back to *Justice* in the balmy darkness, past the lock where crowds were spilling out across the lawns after a performance by the Yorkshire-based Mikron Theatre Company, which for decades has travelled the length and breadth of the waterways performing musical shows on waterways themes.

You could sense the people before you saw them, from the odour of bruised grass beneath their feet. It's an aroma which for me is so redolent of childhood summers that it transports me instantly back to my youth. One hint of it and I'm a teenager on a tennis court with the light fading and the match to win; or I'm dragging my feet across fields after a long walk somewhere; or at some county show with my dad and my uncles, in a tent where even the heavy odours of the exhibition flowers on display can't mask the sweetness of it in my nose.

When we got back we discovered an enormous Dutch barge had moored adjacent to us. It was a hotel boat, plying its trade carrying guests on short cruises; and at twice our length, more than double our width and three or four times our height it dwarfed us completely. As we sat on deck enjoying the last of the evening air we felt out of our league with this huge, looming presence in front of us. It was as if we were suddenly next door to a pub, except a pub without closing times so that as we prepared for bed we could still hear customers around the bar ordering drinks and laughing at each other's jokes.

It wasn't the best place on the river to moor that night, and it certainly wouldn't have been a good place for the moaning couple we'd come across in the boatyard in Reading while we were buying new batteries. It would have given them something worth complaining about for a change.

The hotel barge moved off the following morning before we'd even woken and we stayed on in Sonning a few days longer, enjoying the peaceful ambience of what is actually the place Jerome K. Jerome describes in *Three Men in a Boat* as 'the most fairy-like little nook on the whole river'. It's a small place, no more than a couple of thousand inhabitants, and though it has its share of grand houses, at its core is the old village of twisting lanes and picturesque cottages hung with wisteria and Virginia creeper. It was hard to drag ourselves away, and when we eventually made our break through the lock which had become our barrier to further progress, it was as if we'd escaped from one of those American retirement communities where you can never be sure whether the guards on the gates are there to keep intruders out or the residents in. Almost immediately afterwards we passed under the elegant Sonning Bridge, built in 1775. This was once the ancient border of Wessex and Mercia; today it's the county boundary separating Berkshire and Oxfordshire. A stone on the bridge carved with the inscription BIO marks where the change takes place, the centre stroke showing the exact boundary line.

Glancing backwards, we caught sight of a postbox set into one of the central bridge arches – and did a double take. Surely it was too far out in the river for anyone to use? What on earth was it there for? We joked about eccentric locals of the parish who for reasons best known to themselves wouldn't post a letter from anywhere else. And about the trials and tribulations of the local postie who had to use a rowing boat to make his collections. We'd never seen anything like it before and we could hardly keep *Justice* under control taking pictures of it.

Afterwards we conjectured more seriously about why it was there. I, ever the analyst, became convinced that when it had originally been mounted it must have been accessible from the bank which had since been washed away. Em wasn't having any of that. She thought the whole thing had to be a joke – and in a way she was right. We learned later that the postbox had appeared one morning without warning, puzzling local residents including Uri Geller, who, as a psychic, should know about mysterious things. It turned out to be an installation by an artist who calls himself Impro.

Impro's been responsible for a few outbreaks of guerrilla art in this neck of the woods. He once put an enormous Google map pin on a local roundabout, and we boaters have been the recipients of his humour before when he erected traffic bollards in the river with a skid warning sign. He says he does it to make life 'a little more magical', which touched a chord with me that summer when so many things on the river seemed that way. But the Royal Mail didn't like it. They said it was 'not an operational posting facility'. And the local council took it down soon after, I heard, boring old farts.

***

Our original plan that day – if you can call it a plan – had been to head for Henley and stop for a few days at the town moorings I'd recommended to the couple in Reading. We never got that far. It was oppressively hot and in that sort of weather it can be uncomfortable to be on the river on a narrowboat. Not only do you get the full force of the sun shining on you directly, but you get the secondary glare off the water which is just as capable of burning you to a cinder regardless of how much suncream you've applied.

Rounding the bend just after Shiplake Lock, about an hour out of Sonning and a couple of miles short of Henley, we were already exhausted with the heat when we spotted an isolated mooring at Wargrave Marsh tucked between willow trees and hardly visible from the water. On a whim we pulled in. It turned out to be a delightful spot, cool and shaded and private too: on this reach of the river there's no continuous towpath, so the only people who pass – and then only rarely – are locals out for a stroll or walking their dogs. It was ideal for Kit and she was soon cavorting on her back, wriggling around in the grass, the way she does when she's at ease with the world.

We set off for a walk. We decided that if we weren't going to Henley by water we'd go by foot. We planned to climb out of the river valley and drop down into the town using public footpaths as far as we could and cutting across fields when we couldn't. This, however, turned out to be more difficult than it first appeared. In fact it proved impossible.

For a start, getting away from the mooring wasn't easy. We were cut off from anywhere by Hennerton Backwater, which was behind us like the string on the bow of the river. It's a narrow water channel, but it's wide enough, so that to cross it we had to walk back on ourselves, away from Henley, to a bridge in the Wargrave direction. After that we had to double back along the busy A321 until we found a footpath that took us away from the traffic. It led us up the hill, through fields of waving barley, until eventually from the summit we could see the escarpment over the other side of the river valley. On it was the green outline of what we took to be Lambridge Wood.

So far, so good. However, the footpath soon petered out and we were in trouble. We tried to take a short cut to avoid walking around the lanes but we found our way constantly blocked by the increasingly fortified walls, fencing and banking of what was obviously an estate of some kind. When we eventually found a break in the defences it was only to be confronted by a grey steel gate topped by a row of discouraging spikes. A mile or so further on we came across a similar opening, this one with a security hut behind it complete with arc-lights like something out of a prison camp. Indeed, as we walked around the boundaries of the estate, it was difficult to get this image of a prison camp out of our minds. Except that this wasn't a prison camp built to keep people in, it was one constructed to keep people out. Who would do that to themselves? Who would be so frightened of the outside world that they'd incarcerate themselves like this?

A clue came halfway down White Hill, the steep and busy A4130 that drops down to Henley Bridge. There we passed the estate's main gates, through which you can just about make out the house. I was taking pictures of it when a disembodied voice asked me what I was doing. I nearly jumped out of my skin. The voice, I couldn't help but notice, had a creepy Russian accent, like the villains in old Bond movies. When I recovered myself sufficiently I realised that it was coming from a steel stanchion set into the ground just in front of the gates. There must have been a camera around somewhere since it was evident that every move I made was being monitored.

'I'm taking pictures,' I said.

'You cannot do zat,' the voice replied.

'Why not?' I asked, affronted by his impertinence.

'Zis is private land,' the voice responded.

'This is a public road I'm standing on,' I said. Before long we were having a row about rights and freedoms in the United Kingdom. It stopped when I realised the absurdity of having an argument with a steel stanchion halfway down a hill into Henley.

Later, sitting over a drink at The Angel, the celebrated riverside pub just over the bridge, we fell into conversation with a bloke who explained it all. 'It's called Park Place,' he told us. 'It belongs to Andrey Borodin, the former head of the Moscow Bank. After he was granted political asylum here in 2011 he bought the place for £140 million. It's the most expensive house in the country.'

I discovered afterwards that this wasn't the half of it. Borodin – who's made the Forbes rich list and is said to be worth £640 billion – is wanted by the Russian authorities on fraud and corruption charges. They say he embezzled money; he claims he got on the wrong side of President Putin and that the allegations are politically motivated. One way or another, it seems the Russians are out to get him and in 2013 he became the target of a potential assassination after what were described as 'Chechen political figures' put a $1 million contract on his head.

'And you had an argument with his security man?' the bloke in The Angel laughed. 'You should make sure you keep your door locked tonight.'

I didn't know whether he was joking or not.

CHAPTER EIGHT
Rowing Rows

It is a truth universally acknowledged that once a boat has moored for the night it will be surrounded by waterfowl of every description scavenging for food. Geese, ducks, swans, coots, moorhens, you name a breed: none is so proud that it won't sell its soul for a slice of bread. They all do it, though they do it in different ways. Mallards are probably the least embarrassed at the practice and no sooner are you tied up than a rabble of them surrounds your boat, fighting and squabbling like a ruck of medieval peasants gathering under the castle walls in the hope someone will toss them a few groats from the parapet.

Canada geese only seem slightly more guilty about abandoning their dignity for a handful of carbohydrate. When they become aware from the behaviour of the ducks that there's food on offer they affect not to be interested. They start circling the feeding area indifferently in an attempt to preserve their distance and their self-respect for as long as they can. That's not usually long. Temptation invariably gets the better of them. Soon they're muscling in mob-handed like a street

118

gang, hoovering up what they can and stealing what they can't. An emboldened Canada goose will snatch bread out of your hand before you get the chance to feed it. And it won't mind if it takes one or two of your fingers with it.

Swans, as befits their reputation as the royalty of the waterways, tend to do the whole thing with more dignity. They do it unwillingly, as it were. As if they're under duress. Well, they really shouldn't be taking food like this, should they? Not from those human thingies. Really, it's beneath them. Just too demeaning. But. On the other hand. Conversely. If the thingies will insist on forcing their tasty fare on to one... well, one would be foolish to refuse, wouldn't one?

We'd no sooner moored up in Henley, adjacent to the park, when half the wildfowl population of south-east England descended on us. Being a bit soft this way, Em unwisely tossed them a few slices of stale sliced white which had been in the bread bin for a month. (Well, sliced white's got so many chemicals in it, it *has* to be in the bread bin a month before it goes stale.) Immediately, the other half of the south-east's anatine population descended on us as well and all hell broke loose. There were so many birds in the water you could have walked across the river on their backs. They were going at each other like football hooligans, kicking up such a froth of water between them it was as if some transcendent barista was vainly trying to whip up the Thames into a cappuccino.

Then – as soon as the bread had gone – it all calmed down and they disappeared, vanishing as quickly as they'd assembled. We left the boat to go into town. Further down the towpath we came across them again, regrouping on the bank. They were eyeing up a young family who were laying out a picnic blanket, and it was clear a new riot was about to kick off.

Wildlife, don't you love it? Livelier than you think, wilder than you'd imagine.

***

Henley's a resort town, especially in the summer and especially for the month or two either side of its world-famous annual regatta, which is held in the first week of July. Even outside the rowing season the river dominates the town, drawing visitors to the water for ice creams and boat trips in much the same way the sea does in coastal towns. During the regatta season, the river becomes an even more dominant part of the landscape with its temporary township of stands, marquees and stages springing up along the course between Henley Bridge, where the races end, and Temple Island, where they begin – a stretch of the Thames which is the longest naturally straight section of river in Britain.

Dickens described Henley as 'the Mecca of the rowing man', but he might as well have described it as the Mecca of boating and left it at that; for there are craft of every type littering its banks, from faux Mississippi river steamers to Dutch barges, from immaculately varnished slipper launches to plastic gin palaces three stories high. But it's rowing boats which dominate the river hereabouts – and by rowing boats I don't, of course, mean those heavy clinker-built vessels with rattling rowlocks and oars the size of pine trees which you can rent for a few quid an hour for a picnic trip. No, when you talk rowing boats at Henley you're talking about those racing constructions, as thin as matches and as flimsy as matchwood, in which you win Olympic medals. Almost all the year round there are swarms of them from local rowing clubs – sculls, pairs, fours and eights

– zipping up and down the river like gnats, trying not only to avoid hitting narrowboats, but to avoid even looking at them.

This is because, at Henley, narrowboats are a big builder's bum. They are, after all, vestiges of our industrial past. They don't fit in well with a place which is – let's call a spade a spade here – a bit stuck up. Well, very stuck up, actually. It's the only place in the country, London notwithstanding, where the waiters in restaurants make me feel inadequate. The only place where I'm never sure of the reception I'll get walking into a shop to spend my money. For heaven's sake, it's so up itself that its rowing course isn't even a round mile. Or even a round mile and a quarter. It's a mile and 550 yards. Blimey! What sort of conceit is that? What sort of arrogance?

Of course, it's nowhere near as bad now as it used to be, but the Henley Royal Regatta – to give it its formal title – is still part of the London 'season' along with Wimbledon and Royal Ascot; and it's still rooted in the type of attitudes which, in 1879, when it framed its first definition of an 'amateur', precluded anyone taking part in the races 'who is, or has been, by trade or employment for wages, a mechanic, artisan or labourer'. Even that was felt too loose a definition to keep out the oiks and so a rider was added in 1886 barring anyone 'engaged in any menial activity' – which pretty much allowed the stewards a free hand in deciding who was going to compete and who wasn't.

It was an outrageously snobbish policy even for its time, yet it survived until 1920 when the organisers went too far and banned six-times US National Champion Jack Kelly, America's most accomplished oarsman of the era. He went on to win three Olympic gold medals but Henley vetoed him because he'd once done an apprenticeship in bricklaying. Hearteningly, this display of class prejudice backfired badly since Kelly's daughter was the actress Grace Kelly, who later married Prince Rainier III and became Princess Grace of Monaco. In time this made Jack the grandfather of Prince Albert II of Monaco and, as far as I can discover, the only member of a royal house ever to be banned from Royal Henley.

We had a good stay in Henley, though. We explored St Mary's Church, which dominates the town; we drank at the iconic Angel on the Bridge and marvelled at the beautiful bridge itself, carved with the faces of Isis and Old Father Thames. And we explored further afield, walking up to Friar Park, the 120-room mansion where Beatle George Harrison lived until his death in 2001. All in all we felt very well inclined towards Henley as we pulled away from the bank. Then a man on a bike shouted to us. I took him to be a coach. The loudhailer he was carrying was the giveaway clue.

'You'll find a lot of rowers around here,' he said after one had nearly run into us.

Yes, I should imagine so, I thought. This is Henley, isn't it, synonymous with rowing the world over?

'You should realise they can't always see you,' he went on, treating us like a couple of toddlers whose nappies he'd be changing before the day was out.

I gave the patronising pillock the benefit of a plastic smile. I've been boating around rowers for decades; I used to row myself at school. Of course I know they can't see me. Especially when they don't even bother looking because they're depending on you, their coach, to give them some small indication of the state of river traffic...

'You should give them a wide berth,' he told me. 'You should use your horn...'

Now, generally I don't like using my horn in the vicinity of rowers – especially on still summer mornings when the sound of it shatters the tranquillity for miles around. It works from compressed air, you see. It makes a monstrous sound like an industrial foghorn and it can give other river users a nasty turn. It can make them feel they've got their bearings wrong and finished up in the Channel with an oil tanker heading straight for them.

That morning, after the run-in with the man on the bike, I was cross. Very cross indeed. And a couple of minutes later when a sculler who should have known better pulled out into my water, rather than simply adjust my course to take account of him which I'd have normally done, I let fly with the horn. It was on a level with his ear when I fired it off. A yard or two away.

The sculler rose vertically from his seat, pulling on his oars at the same time. But his oars weren't in the water any more and he went flying backwards into his boat, which began wobbling so much it was only divine intervention that prevented it from overturning completely and depositing him in the water. When he'd scrabbled back into his seat and recovered himself he gave me a look which would have curdled milk.

'Sorry,' I shouted as I cruised away. 'Your coach told me to use it. Blame him.'

* * *

There's been a common law right of navigation along the Thames since time immemorial, and so to ensure the river's kept open with all the rowing taking place in Henley it's been divided down the middle by a series of white posts set in the riverbed. During the regatta these separate the races from the rest of the river traffic; but during the remainder of the year they become like white lines in the middle of a road, dividing boats travelling in different directions. This means that leaving Henley to go downstream, as we were, you cruise along the whole length of the rowing course from finish to start. With its stands and viewing tents lining the route, as they are for a large part of the summer, it's a remarkable experience for a narrowboat, like cruising along the front of the Stretford End at Old Trafford.

Temple Island, the start of the course, is one of the most photographed locations on the entire river. It's named after a building on it, which, I suppose, in the right light, if you squint your eyes hard enough, does look a bit temple-like. It's a small, bow-fronted folly topped with a colonnaded dome, built in 1771 as a sort of summer house for nearby Fawley Court, which you can see set back a little from the river on the Henley side.

To have a summer house that grand should give you some idea of what Fawley Court's like. Suffice to say that to call the place Fawley Court does it a grave injustice. Fawley Court should really be called Fawley Palace. And if that doesn't help you picture it, get your head around the fact that a few years back a couple of property developers were squabbling over it in court, hoping to make a profit of £32 million on it. That's the profit they were hoping to make, not the price they were going to pay for it.

Just round the bend from Temple Island you pass Hambleden Lock, which ought to be called Temple Lock except, confusingly, that's 4 miles further on and named after a mill once owned by the Knights Templars, having nothing to do with Temple

Island at all. Soon afterwards is Bisham Abbey, reputed to be one of the most haunted houses in Britain. One of the ghosts frequenting it is Elizabeth Hoby, who is said to have locked up her son in one of the towers and starved him to death for some minor misdemeanour like not tying up his shoelaces. She's often reported wandering the corridors screaming in agony. The place is currently the National Sports Centre and until recently it was used by the Football Association for preparing the English team for international matches. This probably explains Elizabeth Hoby's screaming. She'd probably watched them play.

***

OK, so I wasn't planning to take up ice skating or competitive downhill skiing, but since seeing the specialist about my knee I had at least got to the stage where I could potter gently along the riverbank without wincing in agony all the time. This was a significant step for me. Well, a lot of significant steps, actually. It was also a great comfort to others using the river. Believe me, when I winced it was not a pretty sight. And it wasn't improved by me trying to smile stoically through the pain. In fact, smiling stoically through the pain made matters worse. When I smiled stoically through pain, and winced at the same time, I could set babies crying in their buggies and cause elderly ladies to choke on their tea. Even so, I knew that sooner or later the knee would give out and I'd be left begging a local doctor for painkillers. It wasn't anything I could plan for, just something I'd have to deal with when the time came.

In the event, however, it was Em who needed a doctor first. She'd picked up some infection along the way and approaching

Marlow she realised she needed antibiotics. Our priority now was finding a practice willing to treat her.

We weren't optimistic. In London our experience was that doctors were reluctant enough to treat you even when you were registered with them, let alone when you drifted in off the streets anonymously, pleading to be healed. They set you obstacles which you had to overcome to convince them you were sick. You had to navigate their telephone answering services. You had to understand their appointments systems. You had to deal with their receptionists. Then, unless you were incontestably dead – in which case you'd go to the back of the queue – you might get an appointment a week or so later. It was usually a waste of time. More often than not you'd have recovered in the interim.

In London going to a doctor's surgery is enough to make you ill if you aren't ill already. Before you finally get into that holy-of-holies which is the consulting room, you have to battle your way through hordes of screaming kids, and multitudes of the bleeding, the infected and the clinically depressed. Even then you won't see the doctor at the time scheduled. If you're lucky you might see him an hour later or maybe even two, depending on whether he's having a bad day, a really bad day or a truly atrocious one, thank you very much for asking but I'd rather not talk about it now…

In London, the idea that you'd be able to walk off the street and get an immediate appointment would be so outlandish as to be laughable. You might as well expect a seat on a rush-hour tube. Or people to be polite to you in shops.

However, in Marlow it was all so different we might have been on another planet. At the top end of town a chemist suggested a nearby practice that turned out to be just a step or two away. It was newly built, clean and accommodating. A cheerful receptionist with a smile on her face greeted Em. Soon Em had a smile on her face. Within an hour she'd seen a doctor and had a prescription. Inside a couple of days she was well.

It was reassuring for us both to know that it was possible to get this level of medical care under the NHS. Living on a boat, especially as you get older, it's unfeasible to think you won't need a doctor at some stage. Indeed, the potential problems of getting medical treatment while we were on the move was one we'd discussed in the early stages of planning our trip. And it's something anyone thinking of living on a boat should reflect on. We had a permanent address, which made things easier for us: it meant we were registered with a practice and could slot into the NHS system. A permanent address made it easier for a hundred other things as well, from taking out a mobile phone contract to reserving items for sale in a shop. I dread to think what we'd have done without one. Without an address in this country you are seriously disadvantaged. The gypsy life is a romantic notion, redolent of the open road, and brightly coloured vardoes, and wild-eyed girls dancing around an open fire. But *being* a gypsy doesn't quite cut it, does it? Not these days. It makes you unusual and that makes others suspicious of you, which brings out their worst prejudices.

It was ever thus. In the past – even at the height of the Industrial Revolution when they played a key role in Britain's manufacturing success – the original boat people who crewed the actual commercial boats that did the canal carrying were reviled by those who 'lived on the land', treated as outsiders and less than human. The result was to make them inward-looking and suspicious of people who lived in houses. Eventually the boat people became a closed community with their own habits and customs, as resistant to outsiders as outsiders were to them.

Living on a boat, I began to understand this in a way I never had before because for the first time I began to feel a little of it myself. It wasn't just that friends and associates couldn't understand the lifestyle Em and I had chosen, what attracted us to it and what we saw in it. It was just that after a while we both lost the will to explain it to them. Eventually it became easier talking to other people on the cut, even people you'd think we'd have little in common with. That didn't matter. We had the cut in common. It meant we shared various attitudes; there was no need to talk about them. We all understood the attractions of the travelling life, for instance. We all appreciated the freedom it afforded us. We shared the feeling of living close to the natural world too, the satisfaction of being self-reliant. And we knew, without the need for it ever to be mentioned, that by living this way we were all to some extent rejecting the values of the contemporary world.

***

Like Henley, Marlow's another elegant and well-tended riverside town with a similar vista of church spire and venerable old bridge. Indeed, the two towns are alike in so many respects that visitors from the river often get them mixed up and spend hours in one place looking for a shop that's in the other. Well, some visitors do. By which I mean that I did once. It was embarrassing, I don't want to talk about it.

Marlow, like Henley, is also a rowing town, so there's a good deal of rivalry between the two. Henley may have the reputation and the regatta and the oldest and most successful rowing club in the world; but all this pales into nothing against Marlow, which has Sir Steve Redgrave, not just the greatest rower of all time, but arguably Britain's greatest Olympian, winner of five gold medals at five consecutive Olympic games, not to mention so many world championships and Commonwealth Games medals that he probably lost count of them years ago.

A statue of him stands outside the leisure centre in Higginson Park, which borders the river where we moored for two or three days. It's a fine park, so clean and well kept that I can almost forgive the council charging a higher rate to moor there than at Henley. The statue is a little larger than life, as statues are, and as Sir Steve himself is too. Though in my opinion this statue does no favours to his stomach, which in the flesh may be rock-solid muscle but which on the plinth looks unflatteringly like he ate all the pies.

The next day I began washing down the boat and doing some light brass cleaning while Em, who was already feeling better, set off into town to find a laundrette. Laundrettes had become an important part of our lives since we'd been living on a boat. We'd made a decision not to have a washing machine, not because we couldn't afford one, or hadn't got the space for one or a dependable electricity supply to power one, but because Em had pointed out that without a drier – which we certainly hadn't got power for – we'd be either living with wet washing draped around the cabin all the time or dependent on the weather to put up a line.

We'd not used laundrettes much since we'd been at uni, and it was a surprise to find that so many of them still existed. More of a surprise was that on the whole they were much better than we remembered them: cleaner, better equipped and more efficiently run. Most of them did service washes as a matter of course, so we didn't have to go through that spiritually demeaning (not to say tediously hypnotic) process of looking at our clothes as they revolved incessantly in the drum. We discovered a booklet published by the Aylesbury Canal Society which listed laundrettes nationally, but even without it Google maps was invaluable in telling us where they were located and how we could get to them. It also showed reviews from people who had used them, so we could avoid the worst.

Even so, some horrors got under the wire. There would be one in Rugby that was so grimy it could have benefited from being put in a washing machine itself. Another was so appalling that we've expunged it from memory and couldn't tell you where it was to save our lives. Em recollects that none of the machines there worked because they were gunged up with grease. I just remember that the old crone who ran the place cackled like the witch in Hansel and Gretel. I felt relieved we got away from the place without being incarcerated and fattened up for the table.

Em wasn't away from the boat long in Marlow. She came tripping back with a step so lively that I knew she'd had a good outing before she told me.

'So where we taking it today?' I asked her.

'We're taking it nowhere, my love,' she replied brightly, kissing me lightly on the cheek.

And sure enough a few minutes later a woman appeared and loaded our dirty washing into a small van. The next day she brought it back, not only washed and clean, but starched and ironed too, my shirts retextured and feeling like new. Of course, it cost an arm and a leg. So much, in truth, that we could have bought a washing machine for the same outlay.

That's when we began to realise that, in this part of the world at least, the social conventions governing the use of laundrettes had shifted completely. When we'd used them in the past they'd been for those who were less well off. The rich had their own washing machines and wouldn't have been seen dead in a laundrette. However, in Marlow today, the position's reversed and washing machines are for the poor. The rich, like the grandees of former times, don't want anything to do with cleaning their own clothes. And they can afford not to.

But then we were getting closer to London, weren't we? Where people can afford these services. Where the economy depends on them, in fact. Every mile we travelled now took us nearer to the bloated city-state that was once our home. We realised just how close we were getting that night when we sat on deck relaxing with a glass of something or other after dinner. It had been another lovely day in paradise and the evening, warm though it was, was still a respite from the heat of the day. The sky was velvet and, although we seemed a million miles from the city, we sat and watched the jets flying in and out of Heathrow by the light of a full moon, the planes passing across its luminous face like ET on his bicycle.

CHAPTER NINE
Paints and Sinners

*L*isten, I know you don't like art; I can understand that, who would? Especially Art with a capital A. Even so, if you happen to be on the river near Cookham with an hour to spare, then do search out the Stanley Spencer Gallery. Of course you don't understand modern painting – who does? I'm with you on that one. Some of this abstract stuff is rubbish, it looks like nothing on earth. But go and have a look at Stanley Spencer's paintings in Cookham. Cookham is where Spencer was born and spent much of his life. You won't be walked off your feet for hours on end: it's only a small place, an old Wesleyan chapel, in fact, no bigger than a two-up/two-down terraced house. It won't cost you much more than you'd pay for a pint in these parts and, believe me, you'll kick yourself if you don't.

That's a bust of Stanley near the front doors there. See? Just an ordinary bloke, nothing about him to frighten the horses, is there? No horns coming out of his head, no long hair or arty-farty beard. Just nerdy glasses, that's the worst you can say about him. And his eyes; can you make out his eyes? You can

132

see them better in his self-portraits. They're penetrating eyes, artist's eyes. And his paintings – see them over there? Nothing to make you run screaming for the door, eh? Some of them are quite comical, can you see that? A bit like Beryl Cook. You know Beryl from all her fat lady prints, the ones you can buy as birthday cards. She was a great admirer of Stanley Spencer. You can see it, can't you, in the way she inflates her figures like he did? He makes them almost caricatures, and yet they never are caricatures because they never lose their humanity. He's not doing it that way because he can't paint any differently. Oh no, don't go running away with that idea. Look at his portraits if you don't believe me. They're like people you'd see in the street. And they seem to live, don't they? Or maybe they've got a life of their own, which isn't quite the same thing.

No, the style was just Stanley's way. He used to wander around the village pushing that pram – yes, that one over there on display in the corner. He used to load it up with his paints and canvasses so that he could get out and about to do his painting. He wanted to make his work accessible to everyday people and so he got among them and painted them. A lot of the figures he depicted were just friends and neighbours from Cookham, which is the place where he found his inspiration, a place he called 'a village in Heaven'. That was the sort of man he was. He was exceptionally talented but at heart he was just an ordinary bloke from the village who just wanted to paint things that ordinary people would recognise and relate to. He did that even when he was painting mystical subjects, which he did a lot because in his idiosyncratic way he was deeply religious. He called these paintings his 'queer ones' and you can see why. That's one of them over there – that large unfinished canvas on the wall. It's called *Christ Preaching at*

Cookham Regatta and it's always on display here. Strange title, don't you think? Why would Christ preach at Cookham Regatta? But why wouldn't he, I suppose? Cookham could be anywhere or it could be everywhere. Maybe that's what Stanley was getting at.

Can you see the Christ figure in the wicker chair there? He's on the deck of what was the old horse ferry barge which used to be moored by the Ferry Inn next to the bridge – though you'd barely recognise the place today now they've knocked it about and made into one of those awful 'child-friendly' eateries. I think he looks a bit fearsome, sermonizing like some mad evangelical preacher – though he doesn't seem to be making much of an impression on that bloke there in the white flannels standing on the riverside with his hands in his pockets. Or on those women in the punts, for that matter. They all seem to be half-asleep, their drowsy English day bathed in sunshine, just like today, and untouched by his rantings. What's all that about then? What do *you* make of it?

***

Even without the Stanley Spencer connection, Cookham would be a lovely place to moor. It's a large, rambling village, with a common near to the station, and a Norman church, and some lovely pubs and gorgeous houses scattered like gemstones around the lanes. You wonder if there's not a workshop somewhere making these pretty Thameside hamlets. Some offshoot of John Lewis maybe. A factory unit somewhere churning them out in a way that manages to get the balance between the attractive and the twee exactly right: a place that understands the importance of detail so that the trailing roses hang in precisely the way they should, and the streets meet at exactly the right angle, and the houses blend together so flawlessly that people think it's all come together naturally and not been conceived in the design shop at the back.

We spent a few days on Cookham Meadow where the bend of the river has cut into the field, creating a mud cliff so that on a narrowboat you can only get to the bank by climbing on to the roof and stepping across from there. The first night we had a barbecue on the grass with chicken I'd marinated in a spicy Moroccan sauce. A group of youngsters camping in tents nearby were our only company since the adjoining moorings were empty – remarkably so. But then the whole river was surprisingly empty and had been the entire time we'd been cruising on it. We couldn't understand it. The weather had been unchangeably hot for weeks now and the forecast was that it would continue for weeks yet.

Why on earth weren't people using their boats? Or hiring them if they didn't own one? Why weren't people at least visiting the river in their cars in droves? Every weekend we were expecting to be overrun by hordes coming at us from all sides, on water and on land; but, astonishingly, it never happened. Summer is an ephemeral season in England: one minute it's here, the next it's been ruined by raucous crowds wearing shorts and back-to-front baseball caps. Yet in this most perfect of summers, the best by far for a decade, we felt we had the river to ourselves, and we could only conclude that some benign nymph or river sprite was keeping it like this for us.

The river was so quiet that the following day, splayed on the bank sunbathing, we watched for an afternoon as a middle-aged man in a pair of loud check shorts attempted to teach himself paddleboarding. He was a lost cause; any fool could have seen that. This was partly because he didn't seem to have a great deal of balance – which is something of a disadvantage in a sport where the prerequisite is to stay upright. But it was also partly because he was overweight too, with a belly bigger than mine. Indeed, on the belly front, he was as badly out of proportion as Sir Steve Redgrave's statue in Marlow.

He'd clamber up on to his board with all the grace of an elephant preparing to tap dance. Then he'd stand there teetering uncertainly, wobbling like a jelly on a Slendertone. Then he'd fall off. This went on for hours. Honestly – I'm not exaggerating this. Hours. He'd get on, fall off; get on again, fall off; get on once more, fall off yet again... The only variation in his routine was *how* he fell off. Most times he'd conspire to do it with such inelegance it was wondrous to behold how much public indignity a man could endure in the name of leisure. Sometimes he'd tumble into the water like an acrobat falling off a high wire, legs akimbo and arms flailing wildly. Other times he'd do it as if he was walking in the street and he'd tripped, so that he went tumbling in head over heels, no idea of which bit of him was up and which down. On odd occasions, however, he managed to fall with genuine poise, slipping into the water like a diver chasing a 5.5 from the judges to be in with the chance of a medal.

Once, just once, he managed to stay on the board for long enough to use the paddle to propel himself forwards a few feet. We felt like applauding. He probably felt like he'd won the lottery.

Then he fell off and had to start all over again.

***

There are a few things they don't mind you knowing about Cliveden, the stately old Italianate pile which lies above the wooded chalk cliff between Bourne End and Maidenhead. And there are a few things they'd rather you didn't.

What they don't mind you knowing – what they positively delight in telling you, in fact – is that the place is associated with sexual scandal. Indeed, the most notorious sex scandal of modern times happened at Cliveden when in the early 1960s Spring Cottage, which lies in an idyllic riverside setting in the grounds of the house, was rented out to society osteopath Dr Stephen Ward. I'm old enough to remember the details of it perfectly. As a young man in my early teens, the name Stephen Ward was burnt into my consciousness along with others like John F. Kennedy, John Lennon and Jimmy Greaves.

Day after day, the papers were full of how Ward had 'pimped' for his rich and famous friends, introducing them to 'showgirls' like Christine Keeler and Mandy Rice-Davies – more names imprinted on my smutty adolescent mind. For a time my mum and dad tried to discourage my curiosity in this first bit of news, outside of the football results, in which I'd ever taken genuine interest. They'd hide the papers when they'd finished reading them, and switch off the telly when it came on the news.

It was a hopeless task, like expecting me to get my head round quadratic equations. As kids, the goings-on at Cliveden were the only thing we talked about at school – though in truth the subtleties of events there were a bit baffling to us. We knew all about prostitutes and pimps and that sort of stuff; everyone knew about *that*. What we didn't know – and what no one seemed inclined to explain to us – was what on earth an osteopath was. We didn't have osteopaths where we lived.

For some reason not unconnected with the playground gossip I was hearing, I imagined they dressed in leather and carried whips. My mate Tony said that was bollocks. He thought they were doctors who put things up your bum. And he wasn't having any of it when I tried to put him right and told him that what he was talking about were called enemies.

'What? Enemies? Like the Germans? That's bullshit, that is. And you, Haywood, you're a twat, you are,' he said, using another word the full import of which we didn't quite grasp.

They prosecuted Stephen Ward for living off the immoral earnings of Keeler and Rice-Davies, and to ensure a conviction they enlisted corrupt Scotland Yard officer Inspector Samuel Herbert to arrest Rice-Davies for the non-existent theft of a TV. In Holloway Prison she was softened up until, reluctantly, she agreed to testify for the prosecution. Ward himself, depressed by the deceitfulness of the whole charade, killed himself before his trial ended.

There was never evidence that Ward was living off the earnings of prostitutes because there was never evidence that Keeler or Rice-Davies were prostitutes rather than just sleeping with men for the hell of it. But sadly for them, the men they consorted with were rich and powerful operators, one of whom was a Russian naval attaché and the other John Profumo, the Secretary of State for War – a man so stupid he lied to Parliament when his enemies began to suggest there were security implications to what he was doing.

As kids yakking in the playground at breaktime, we treated the whole unfolding story of sexual conniving and nude poolside parties like a bawdy soap opera – not unlike that *Coronation Street* programme which had started on the telly not long before, with Elsie Tanner putting it about all over the place. Actually what we were witnessing were the first shiftings of the tectonic plates that would eventually redefine the values of our society. In truth, the stuff they did at Cliveden in the 1960s wasn't much different from what they did there in the 1660s when George Villiers, later the Duke of Buckingham, used it to entertain his (many) mistresses until the husband of one of them challenged him to a duel and got run through with a rapier for his trouble.

The Profumo affair is often referred to as the beginning of the Swinging Sixties – which gives it a warm and cosy feel, as if the whole thing had been set up so that afterwards we could have Carnaby Street and the Beatles and win the World Cup. The truth, I fear, is that it was the beginning of contemporary cynicism, a way of thinking that's corrupted our age. After Profumo the British public lost confidence in the moral probity of its leadership, and I don't think it's found it again since. Indeed, after Profumo it began to associate leadership with hypocrisy.

It still does.

***

We tucked behind one of the small islands lining the riverside of the Cliveden estate, and moored *Justice* in a secluded, woodland cove where we stayed for two or three days, barely aware of whether there were other boats nearby or not. Cliveden's owned by the National Trust now, and although Cliveden House – and indeed, Spring Cottage – is leased out to a luxury hotel chain, Trust moorings are available for a modest fee and the grounds are open to members to wander around at liberty. Once we got our bearings we discovered we were only a step or two away from Spring Cottage anyhow, so we got the same view as the guests inside did, at a fraction of the £1,800 a night they were paying.

That evening – and, indeed, every evening of our stay – we ate on deck, cooled by the overhanging trees. In the mornings we developed something of a routine, climbing the steep paths to the main house where, in the burning sunshine, volunteers were valiantly replanting flower beds on the lawn. Nearby, of course – it being a National Trust property – was the inevitable NT cafe, this one located in the beautiful orangery. We took to having lunch there, and afterwards, with temperatures gradually becoming cooler throughout the afternoon, we'd wander around the dappled beech woodlands taking in the panoramic views of this luxuriantly verdant reach of the river which is often described as the most magnificent on the Thames.

When it finally came time to leave, it proved a wrench – as it so often does on a boat after you've stayed in a place and made it yours. Providence itself seemed sad to see us go too, for no sooner had we untied our ropes than a couple of clouds in the sky darkened for a few moments as if showing their displeasure, and it looked like we might have a drop or two of rain. The threat only lasted an instant, but it was a close shave, close enough to remind us that this was England in the summer and that the weather we were experiencing was unusual and not to be taken for granted.

We pulled up that night in the backwater below Boulter's Lock in Maidenhead, overlooked by a boisterous crowd strung across the terrace bar of the Riverside Brasserie. The next morning we went out on a search for supplies, which had been running dangerously low since emerging from the Waitrose belt in Marlow. Neither of us particularly liked Maidenhead, and that doyen of waterways writers Jerome K. Jerome, who'd been inevitably accompanying us on our trip since Oxford, didn't like it either. In one of the bitterest diatribes of *Three Men in a Boat* he had a go at it for being 'snobby' and 'showy', 'the haunt of the river swell and his overdressed female companion'. We didn't like it because it was noisy, dirty and hectic; and because it took an age to get to the shops from the lock, and because there was nowhere to cross the busy roads to reach them once you did.

More problematic is why Jerome took such a dislike to the place since there's not a word in the book to explain his prejudice. You can't help wondering if at some stage in his life he'd had a bad weekend there. Or a dirty one, at least. It's the sort of place he might have done. In fact, in the past Maidenhead had the sort of reputation for illicit liaisons that Brighton later inherited – something you can hardly credit when the present-day Maidenhead oozes such suburban respectability. 'Are you married,' it used to be said in late-Victorian times, 'or are you from Maidenhead?'

Perhaps poor old Jerome, who was working as a bank clerk then, had tried his hand with one of the secretaries. Perhaps he'd attempted to take her for a 'spot of supper' at one of those 'capital', out-of-the-way restaurants he knew and been snubbed on the door for some antiquated breach of the dress code. Perhaps – and who knows the levels of bad behaviour a man in a cheeky, striped blazer might sink to? – he'd been rebuffed booking them into the now-demolished Skindles Hotel, where the Prince of Wales, the future Edward VII, used to take the actress Lillie Langtry, setting the trend for his age.

It's ironic that Jerome had such a downer on the town because ultimately he did so much for it. After *Three Men in a Boat* was published, there was an exponential growth in pleasure boating on the river, and Maidenhead was in pole position to benefit from it. It was an hour from London by train, with the river easily accessible from a bridge over the lock, where you could stand and watch the world go by and maybe, if you were lucky, even see a music hall star or a member of royalty. What could be a better place to go to enjoy this new fad than Boulter's Lock? Edward Gregory's famous painting of the place on a Sunday afternoon in 1895 captures the giddy freedom the river offered in that era, and the absolute chaos that resulted from people taking advantage of it, with canoes, rowing boats and steamers jostling for space. In fact, the painting depicts a relatively quiet day. One Sunday in 1888, 72 steamers and 800 unpowered boats of various sorts passed through the lock; and it got even busier in Edwardian times when some of the photographs taken show the lock jammed to bursting with not so much as an inch of water to be seen between the boats squeezed in there.

Nearly 20 years ago we left *Justice* at Boulter's for a couple of weeks. A strict condition of the mooring was that we had to undertake to move away by a stipulated date and time, and not a moment longer. Unfortunately we cut our deadline perilously close. We arrived back from London flustered after a delayed train journey and a sphincter-tightening taxi trip from the station with a driver whose innate trade tendency towards the kamikaze wasn't improved by us offering him the promise of a fat tip to put his foot down. The reason for the strict deadline became apparent when we finally arrived to find ourselves in the middle of a flotilla of extraordinary Victorian and Edwardian boats, every one of them looking as if it had just emerged from a museum.

There were gleaming slipper boats, lustrous with varnish, their low, sweeping sterns barely above the waterline; and impeccably presented steam launches with highly polished copper and brass engines. Of row boats and camping boats there were so many you could barely count them, but each came with its full complement of crew: the men all in blazers and flannels and straw boaters threaded with colourful neckerchiefs; the women in long, sweeping skirts and tight lace blouses, carrying frilly parasols draped with tassels. Many of them had tiny dogs, bedecked with ribbons, on their laps.

What they were doing, we soon discovered, was attempting to reproduce Gregory's painting in real life – an idea, like many ideas before it, that probably sounded a good deal more attractive at the planning stage than it turned out in practice. It rained, you see. Heavily. Bucketed down, the way it only can in England on a normal summer's day, especially when some special event is on the cards and God fancies a laugh at our expense.

Sadly, the whole event was washed out.

***

That evening I was out on deck enjoying the last of the day's sunshine when I suddenly became aware of a heady and yet slightly repugnant smell in the air. I couldn't place it. It was too sweet to be natural, a fusion of flowers and fruit but with an overtone of some pungent – and not particularly pleasant – spice. At first I put it down to the brasserie. It wasn't a food smell, but I wondered if was a floral air freshener, or perhaps some deodorant from the urinal which had somehow seeped into the river. I went to investigate but found that the closer I got to the restaurant the more the smell faded; so I retraced my steps and started to investigate in the other direction. This time there was no mistaking that I was getting closer to the source of the stink. With every step the odour got more powerful until at last it became so sickeningly intense I could hardly bear it.

I found myself standing on the rim of the lock, where a bed of broadleaf bushes 10 to 12 feet high were growing above the path, each of them hanging with clutches of long trumpet-shaped flowers of red or yellow. Something drew me to the plant. But something about it repulsed me too. It was too assertive and dominant, too blowsy and in-your-face. It seems a strange thing to say of a plant, but I felt instinctively there was something dangerous about it.

And my instincts weren't wrong. The next day I discovered everything there was to know about the plant from the lock-keeper, who'd developed an obsession with the things after someone had given him a cutting a few years before. Its formal name turned out to be *Brugmansia*, though the plants are better known as angel's trumpets after the shape of their flowers. It's a native of South America and prefers a warm climate, although tucked against the south-facing wall of the lock at Boulter's these were doing very well in our temperate surroundings, thank you very much. In fact, so well did they appear to be prospering that if I'd been on Maidenhead Council I'd have been anxious about them taking over the town, like the triffids in John Wyndham's novel. This wouldn't be advisable. Angel's trumpets may not be man-eating but every part of the plant is poisonous, with its seeds and leaves particularly toxic. However, this hasn't prevented it getting a reputation as a hippie hallucinogenic – though I'm uncertain what sort of high it would be to kill yourself. One expert described the plant inducing a powerful trance with violent and unpleasant after-effects and, at times, temporary insanity. Mind you, that doesn't sound too bad to me. But then I worked in the TV industry for most of my life.

An odd coincidence occurred involving these flowers months later on an overcast October day when the memory of this glorious summer was gently fading to brown, like the leaves on the trees. I was walking along the towpath in Braunston in Northamptonshire when I ran across a bloke called Ivan, the son-in-law of Joe Gilbert, who for many years ran the dockyard in Bedworth near Coventry where Em and I moored a boat for almost a decade. We paused for a while to chat as people do on the cut, and after a while we fell into conversation about a couple of mutual friends who used to work at the dock: Arthur, a mechanic, and Ted, his sidekick, who was always talking about the fights he'd been in, but who was actually rather a sweet-natured man who used to light our fire for us when we were coming up from London for the weekend.

Suddenly a smell in the air stopped me dead. It didn't take me long to work out what it was. There, on the front deck of Ivan's boat, was a towering angel's trumpet, still just about in flower despite the season. Its odour was unmistakeably imprinted on my memory.

'Where on earth did you get that monstrosity?' I asked.

'Oh, I was passing through Boulter's Lock on the Thames a year or two back,' he explained. 'The lock-keeper gave me a cutting...'

CHAPTER TEN
Of Queens and Castles

*E*very day now was bringing us closer to London, which may seem odd, given that we'd come on to the boat partly to get away from London. But there was business with the house we'd left undone, and friends we hadn't managed to say goodbye to properly before we left. The main reason for going back, however, was our enthusiasm to cruise the Thames, for part of the package of the river is that if you want to experience all it has to offer, you have to recognise it will lead you inexorably into the capital since the city has been intrinsically connected to the river since it was first settled.

We arrived in Windsor. Even without *that* castle Windsor would be a pleasant enough riverside town, unusual only for being constructed on one of the very few rock outcrops which stand above the Thames. With the castle, however, it's something special and an unforgettable place to visit by boat. Approaching it from upriver as we did, we'd already passed some sufficiently impressive places along the way, but in this neck of the woods everything's impressive for one reason or another. The railway bridge just below Bray Lock, for instance.

That isn't just any old railway bridge. It was constructed by Isambard Kingdom Brunel for his Great Western Railway and it's the flattest, widest brick arch in the world.

And overlooking Monkey Island, just after we cruised under the M4, is the attractive but unexceptional house where in 1910 the composer Edward Elgar worked on his famous *Violin Concerto*. The house once went by the humble name of The Hut – although when it was last on sale it would have cost you a cool £2.5 million for the pleasure of storing your garden tools in it.

Even the shabby grey edifice with dustbins out the back, which you go past on Dorney Reach, is renowned. This is Bray Studios, which for nearly 20 years was the HQ of Hammer Films, purveyors of low-budget horror movies to the world. Every potential location worth screen time around here was used at one time or another for a film, the Gothic-style Oakley Court next door featuring regularly – presumably because directors could shoot a scene or two there and still get the cast back to the canteen for lunch. In its time it's been everything from Dracula's castle to Tommy Steele's house in *Half a Sixpence;* and it's still used for film and TV production today.

All this is interesting enough if you go everywhere with a guidebook in your back pocket and treat travel as if it's a challenge to collect places by ticking them off a list. Some people seem to believe that if you do that you somehow own them. You know the sort of thing I mean. They're doing it in every newspaper and magazine you pick up these days. *The Hundred Things You Should See Before You're Fifty. The Thousand Places You Should Go Before You Die.* But there's more to journeying than just this, surely? And more to the Thames than just making it into an I-spy game?

What you can experience, travelling along it, if you're willing to make yourself accessible to what it has to offer, is the harmony that the river affords. Every now and again you'll turn a bend or come out of a lock and there'll be an extraordinary vista stretching out in front of you: the river and the surrounding countryside and the carefully positioned houses along the bank all, suddenly, coming together in exquisite concord. Seeing this can't be described as sightseeing. Or at least it can't if you're seeing in the right way, opening yourself to the emotional experience that places can offer. Then boating on the river can be an experience verging on the spiritual. I felt it the morning we cruised Port Meadow, in Oxford; and the afternoon we passed under the bridge at Clifton Hampden; and the day we cruised below the wooded heights of Cliveden Deep. You might find it in a dozen different places, though it's not something you'll ever possess. Rather it's something that, if you're lucky, will possess you.

Windsor Castle does something like this to me. I find it a remarkable spectacle, and like the Taj Mahal or the Grand Canyon, it's one of those sights that can take your breath away – as impressive in real life as you've been led to believe it would be. Approaching on a boat, it's at its best in the early morning when the mists are beginning to rise from the water; or on a warm summer's evening when the temperature is falling and they're starting to descend again. This is how it was when we arrived. The river was swathed in vapour, undulating like a coverlet of fine muslin in a breeze. The castle, emerging out of the haze, seemed ethereal and dreamlike, as unreal as those castles we waterways enthusiasts are so familiar with from traditional narrowboat painting.

The castle sits on a hill, high above the town, a fortress of a place surrounded by a high wall and punctuated with bastions and turrets that dominate Windsor. We've all seen so many photographs and paintings of the place it's impressed itself on our minds as the archetype of what a castle should be. It sits as a stern sentinel surveying the river, so that wherever you are you can't avoid seeing it. It's everywhere you turn, so much a part of the panorama of the Windsor skyline that Windsor wouldn't be Windsor without it.

There's always been a castle here – at least there has since William the Conqueror built a fort on the site in 1070. It was gradually improved and developed so that by the time of Henry III in the thirteenth century it was not just a military garrison but the royal palace it remains today, the oldest occupied palace in the world. The castle will be forever associated with royal history, but since 1917 it's become increasingly linked with the current royal house following George V's decision to choose Windsor as the family's new dynastic name. This was towards the back end of the First World War when it finally dawned on the only person on the royal staff with more than two brain cells that carrying the name Saxe-Coburg-Gotha while millions were getting slaughtered in a war with the Germans wasn't exactly doing a lot for royal PR. Not to mention being a bit of a mouthful after a glass or two of wine. (And, to our contemporary ears, sounding like a couple of Bundesliga football teams.)

In recent years Windsor's become intrinsically associated with our present Queen, especially after the castle caught fire in 1992, capping what she called her *annus horribilis* – a year in which her son separated from his wife, her daughter divorced, and her daughter-in-law was caught topless by the tabloids having her toes sucked by her 'financial advisor'. If it wasn't one thing, it was another. But it could have been worse, I suppose. At least her husband didn't leave her for a soap star.

I was delighted on this trip to be able to visit the place the Queen lived because when I last met her she'd been visiting the place I lived.

Of course, I use the word 'met' in this context in its loosest possible sense. Ours was an unusual encounter, bizarre you might even say. It happened some miles downriver in Thamesmead, on the outer fringes of south-east London where I was living at the time. It was 1980 and Her Majesty had been on an official visit, allowing the royal presence to be used to bolster the morale of this modernistic new town, which had once been used to film Stanley Kubrick's *Clockwork Orange* and had never got over it. I was working for the London listings magazine *Time Out* which at that period in its life – before its owner Tony Elliott made the *Sunday Times* rich list – prided itself on its anti-establishment radicalism. One of us in the newsroom – probably me, I'm mortified to admit – suggested that it would be a bit of a wheeze to cover a royal visit in a facetious way from the point of view of a resident.

Actually, it's hard to be facetious about a royal visit because the Queen hardly does anything worth being facetious about. She goes to a school and shakes a few hands and talks to a few kids and teachers, and then she goes to a church and shakes a few more hands and talks to a few priests and curates, then she goes to a... well, you get the picture. It's fair to say that three or four hours later, the royal hand still pumping like a steam piston and the royal smile set in rictus, even a hard-bitten journo like me on a mission to file 500 snotty words had to confess to a certain admiration for the old girl. The level of her commitment to the job was staggering to behold, the stamina she brought to bear on it made all the more impressive by the relentless, mind-numbing tedium of her task.

I'd had enough by then, though. I looked at her schedule and decided I'd go along to one more of her appearances before calling it a day and heading for the pub. Next on her list to visit was a health centre, and being acquainted with Thamesmead I took a short cut through an underground car park and up a narrow spiral staircase. Unfortunately I was late arriving and Her Majesty was early leaving. For it was there, ascending the spiral staircase, that I happened with some horror upon the royal legs descending towards me.

It's easy to say that with all the security surrounding the royal family as a result of today's unstable political situation, this sort of casual encounter just couldn't happen now. But actually, it shouldn't have happened then. This was 1980, remember, not long after a kidnap attempt on Princess Anne. It was the height of 'The Troubles' in Ireland, just a matter of months after the Queen's cousin Louis Mountbatten was blown up by the IRA on holiday in Donegal Bay. Bombs were going off almost daily in Belfast and London. An encounter of this sort must have startled the Queen much more than it did me.

I backed off, alarmed more on her account than my own; and at the bottom of the staircase I stepped back a pace or two, bowing my head more to indicate that I represented no danger than as any mark of respect. Her face was ashen and – something I shall remember to my dying day – there was fear on her face, a look of unmistakeable apprehension. This was not something she expected, I could see that. I wasn't a man in a uniform or a familiar face from her security detail. I was a young radical with long hair wearing jeans. And I could have been carrying a revolver. Or worse.

And she knew it. I could see it in her eyes.

* * *

Thankfully, the memory of this didn't impair my enjoyment of Windsor and we decided on the spur of the moment to stay a few days, one of the advantages of living on a boat when you can live more spontaneously. In summer, especially when the sun's shining, the town feels like it's by the seaside and you'd have to be a hard-hearted cynic not to get caught up in the spirit of it. Every day is like a bank holiday weekend: the flags are flying and the bunting is out, and there are kiosks selling ice cream, and boats touting trips, and families picnicking on the beautifully mown lawns of the adjoining park.

And there is a constant stream of tourists from all parts of the world looking at the boats. We soon realised that in our small way our brightly coloured narrowboat was a tourist attraction in itself. In fact, having visited Windsor by river a couple of times before, I'd anticipated as much and waxed our paintwork and polished our brasses for the occasion. It was just as well. We were photographed constantly, a source of wonder not just to the Japanese (who – take it from me – are not ones for confronting the national stereotype, and genuinely *do* take photographs of everything, from every conceivable angle, at every opportunity) but also to tourists from Britain who really ought to know a tad more about their heritage and geography than they seem to.

'You mean, you're going all the way to London? In this boat? You can do that, can you?' one man asked me as he took a snapshot. And he wasn't winding me up, that much was sadly obvious. 'Yes, of course I can, you lobotomised halfwit,' I felt like saying. 'What river do you think this is? What do you think the river which goes through London is called? Has it ever occurred to you that they might possibly be connected? Or do you think there are two SEPARATE rivers called the Thames in this neck of the woods?'

In keeping with the festive feel of the place, during our stay there was even a travelling fair on the meadow on the Eton side of the river opposite our mooring. At nights, sitting on deck after our evening meal (which we continued to eat outside because it was too warm to be in the boat), the flashing lights from the stalls and the Wurlitzers, and the dull, barely audible thud of bass from a dozen speakers, became the soundtrack on which we'd end our day.

One afternoon we walked over to Eton, strolling across Windsor Bridge and down the charming High Street lined with restaurants, antique shops and old-fashioned gentlemen's outfitters. These sell various items of Eton school uniform including the multitudinous designs of tasselled caps that as a pupil you're entitled to wear for anything, it seems, from winning the Nobel Prize to learning how to read. We were able to nose around the famous school more than normal because it was outside term time and the kids had gone abroad to St Moritz or Bermuda or wherever rich kids go for their hols. We were with some friends who'd come up for the day to see us. One was a cricket enthusiast and he was gobsmacked at the standard of the school's pitch, which, he said incredulously, could easily be used for county games. He was also a teacher and his response to the cricket pitch paled into insignificance compared with his response to the size of the school's careers room, which he discovered after he'd stood on tiptoe and pressed his nose randomly against some venerable old Gothic windowpane.

But that's privilege for you, and although we English rail against it constantly there must be something about it we find irresistible. How else can you explain the survival of royalty? How else can you understand our proclivity for voting for prime ministers educated at Eton – 19 of them at the last count and more expected soon?

Mind you, we had someone who went into politics at my school. Well, he won a seat on the local council, which he said was going into politics. But he was the school nerd so it was the sort of nonsense you'd have expected of him. He was a Liberal at a time when you could have fitted the whole party into the back of a taxi, so we weren't impressed. But then, neither was he in the long run – he resigned a couple of years later. He grumbled about the shrinking influence of local democracy and the onerous workload of a councillor, but we thought it hadn't been as useful to him in his career as he thought it would be.

You get a glimpse of real privilege from the river as you leave Windsor; for the Thames at this point in its passage to the sea is the boundary of Home Park, which is the private section of Windsor Great Park and essentially the Queen's back garden. Except it's a back garden on a scale of which most of us couldn't conceive. We might have a bit of a vegetable patch: she has a farm. We might have a lawn for the kids to kick around a ball: she has a golf course, a cricket pitch, a bowling green and more tennis courts than a lot of suburban clubs. She also has a large lake and her own private burial ground – though I don't suppose this cheers her up any as she's stomping around on her morning constitutional in her headscarf and green wellies.

You can't stop along the 2-mile section of Home Park and, in case you're tempted, there are ominous signs telling you that it's a criminal offence, the site apparently 'protected under Section 128 of the Serious Organised Crime and Police Act 2005'. Every few minutes – or so it seems at the slow speed of a canal boat – you find out what 'protected' actually means when a black Land Rover with darkened windows speeds by on the river path. Presumably it's filled with police. And presumably, if called to action, they wouldn't be toting traditional bobby's truncheons. Or hanging around to ask too many questions of intruders either.

I couldn't help but wonder in today's world how long I'd last on that spiral staircase in Thamesmead.

Mind you, even privilege has its limits, and I have to be honest and say that for all its grandeur I wouldn't want to live in Windsor Castle. It's on the flight path to Heathrow and all the privilege in the world can't stop noisy planes passing over every couple of minutes. One tourist is supposed to have asked why they built the castle so close to the airport. It was a joke. Or at least I think it was. But judging by the one who asked me if it were possible to get to London from Windsor on a boat, I can't be absolutely certain...

***

Approaching Windsor we'd seen a cormorant perched on a high mooring post, posed like an heraldic griffin, its wings outstretched, bent downward at the joint, gently shimmering as it dried its feathers in the sunshine. It was, as Em observed, vaguely reminiscent of Antony Gormley's statue *Angel of the North,* though the cormorant was more menacing than Gormley's welcoming icon, and altogether more primitive with its green, intimidating eyes and its savage beak topped with a curved bill as sharp as a scimitar.

Cormorants can be big birds, with a wingspan of 3 or 4 feet across. But there was another, even bigger bird with which we'd become familiar during our trip down the river. This was the red kite, which has an even wider wingspan and which, like the cormorant, was hunted to virtual extinction in the past. Red kites were once a common sight across the country and their diet of carrion flesh made them valued in the early Middle Ages, when they were seen as a sort of avian street cleaner and protected by royal decree.

By Tudor times, though, their star was on the wane. They were considered pests and included in Henry VIII's vermin laws along with hedgehogs and – astonishingly – kingfishers. As numbers reduced they became rare and this increased the value of their eggs for collectors, which made them rarer still. Even those few that survived were hunted by farmers who erroneously believed they killed livestock. By the 1890s they were effectively extinct in Great Britain apart from a small colony in Wales, which survived only because of the support of local landowners and early conservationists.

It's estimated the total population at that point may have fallen as low as ten breeding pairs – although recent genetic research suggests the situation could have actually been much worse, and that there was only one female among these which was successfully reproducing.

However, one of the country's most successful conservation programmes began in 1989 when the first of 88 red kites from

Sweden, Germany and Spain were released into the Chilterns by English Nature and the Royal Society for the Protection of Birds. Twenty-five years on, there are an estimated one thousand breeding pairs in the UK, possibly more. Red kites are now the 53rd most common bird in British gardens according to the RSPB. They are a particularly familiar sight in Oxfordshire and Berkshire, especially along the Thames where you'd be unlucky indeed – even out for a gentle Sunday afternoon stroll – not to see the burnished underbelly and distinctive fantail of one gliding in the air.

On the boat we got blasé about seeing them, and not just seeing them but seeing them at close range as they circled over our heads when they were hunting, sometimes no more than 10 or 20 feet above us. Even so, coming out of Old Windsor Lock, I was treated to an unprecedented confrontation with one.

We were passing through the lock out of hours, when you operate them for yourself without the help of lock-keepers. Em had worked the paddles and had just opened the bottom gates to allow me to exit. Suddenly, like drawing back the curtains on a stage, I found myself not just witness to a life and death drama, but a central player in it. Before me was a distraught mallard, vainly flapping at a red kite which was hovering in the mouth of the lock, clearly intent of having one of the half a dozen or so chicks which were cowering behind their mother. It was a pathetic mismatch and without my chance intervention it could have only ended one way.

For a second or two the kite hung in the air as I approached, so close I could feel the draught from its wings in the restricted space. But then, torn between its prey and the monstrous 60-foot boat coming towards it, the bird decided that it was safer to back off. It flew upwards in the neck of the lock, angling its wings to avoid the boat and the lock wall, before rising steeply into the air, the feathers on its tail curiously twisted with the effort of the aerodynamics. I watched it disappear into the clouds, astonished that just moments before I could have almost touched it.

CHAPTER ELEVEN
Doing it Their Wey

*W*e decided to go up the River Wey. *When* we decided to go up the River Wey – the precise moment we made the decision – I can't tell you. Em has a friend who lives near it and I remember us talking vaguely about how nice it would be to visit her by boat. At that stage, though, I'm not sure that we actually knew where her friend lived in relation to the river. But then we weren't too sure of where the Wey was either. I had some notion it was near Godalming. I'd been to Godalming once and I was convinced Godalming was on the Wey. But then I began thinking about it and I became equally convinced that it wasn't. One way or another, I'd got some idea that the Wey was somehow connected to the recently restored Basingstoke Canal – though that didn't help much, because I couldn't have told you where Basingstoke was either.

But cruising along the Thames towards London, we kept getting asked if we were planning on going on to the Wey. It was almost as if the River Wey PR department had got its people out in force trying to tempt passing boaters – like those annoying waiters you sometimes get overseas trying to tempt you into their restaurant. 'It's a lovely river, the Wey,' people kept saying. 'It's worth making the effort.' Or, 'It's really pretty, unexpectedly picturesque. You should explore it.'

After a couple of weeks of this I felt like screaming. OK, I've got the message now, I wanted to say. The Wey is a cute river; it's very attractive and you get to it by turning off the Thames. But you have to pay to go on it, don't you? It's run by the National Trust. And you don't even get a bloody discount for being a member, do you?

Anyway, who'd want to cruise a waterway through the Surrey commuter belt? Through towns whose names alone were enough to chill your soul and strike despair into your very heart? Weybridge, for heaven's sake. Guildford. Who on earth wants to visit places like that? Em and I had it up to our back teeth with Commuterland when we were working. We didn't want reminding of it now we weren't. No, we were heading straight to London to see some friends we hadn't been able to meet up with before we'd left, and to clear up some details left on the rental of the house. After that… well, after that we would go where the wind took us.

But then we met a lovely couple in a boat called *Weyward Lass*, and after chatting to them we softened a bit. Their permanent mooring, as the name of their boat suggests, was on the River Wey and they did a bit of work for the NT too. They were as fulsome in its praise as everyone else had been, eulogizing its beauty and its rural charm. They even waxed lyrical about its towns – even Guildford, can you believe? Now, admittedly, I'd never been to Guildford, but I'd never been to Tallinn either and frankly, though both of them might be among the most beautiful places in the world, life's too short to do all the exploring yourself. Sometimes it's just easier to go along with your prejudices. As far as I was concerned Guildford wasn't a place I was going to like and that was an end of it.

Even so, all this soft-sell about the river must have worked on us at some level because over the next few days we gradually changed our plans – probably no bad thing, because on the waterways plans are only made for changing.

For the moment, though, we were still on the Thames. We cruised next day past Runnymede and Magna Carta Island, where in 1215 the barons forced King John to put his seal to a humiliating charter requiring him to remove his fish weirs from rivers so that they could put theirs in the same places instead. In the words of W. C. Sellar and R. J. Yeatman's *1066 and All That*, they also forced him to agree that 'no-one was put to death – except the Common People', that 'everyone should be free – except the Common People', and that 'everything should be of the same weight and measure throughout the Realm – except the Common People'. A few odd clauses of the charter are now seen as the cornerstone of English liberty and the basis of the freedom of the Common People. No, I don't know how it happened either.

On this section of the river around Staines the planes landing at Heathrow were so close they looked as if they were going to come down on our roof. I was steering and probably taking more notice of what was happening in the air than on the water because just after Shepperton Lock I went swanning by the signpost directing us right to the Wey, even though I'd been looking out for it and knew I was going to be passing it at any moment. By the time I'd realised what I'd done I could only rectify my error by swinging the boat back on itself at an angle so severe I almost knocked Em into the water with the tiller. It was a tricky manoeuvre, and like all tricky manoeuvres on a 60-foot narrowboat, it required some concentration. By the time we were back on course, the environment around us had changed completely. It was as if we'd gone through one of those *Star Trek*-type warps, just as we had leaving the canal for the river at Duke's Cut in Oxford. From being on a wide and spacious river we were now in a narrow channel so enclosed by bushes and overhanging trees that we could have been cruising through a wood. There was something surreal about the abrupt change, and this feeling persisted when a short distance further on we emerged from the foliage only to be confronted by the nearest thing I've seen to a waterways roundabout.

There were exits going off all over the place, up tributaries and streams and backwaters leading God-knows-where. None of them was marked on the map I was using. Mind you, given that the map I was using was a map of the River Thames, and we were no longer on the River Thames, this was understandable enough – though in my opinion unhelpfully literal. I was hopelessly confused and brought the boat to a standstill. It was only then that we were able to make out a sign to the Wey, hidden behind a veil of thick willows. But things still weren't as they should have been. We continued through a set of lock gates which a lock-keeper had obligingly opened for us; but instead of finding ourselves at another lock gate which would normally be the way of things, we found ourselves in the long banana-shaped cutting of a second lock where we had to wait for an hour or so while water levels equalised. It was what's called a staircase lock, where the front gate of one lock is the back gate of another.

However, I didn't understand why the water levels needed to be equalised at all – they looked equal to me already. And I didn't understand why the whole business took so long. Were they filling the lock from a tap? But hey, it was another hot and sunny day and there wasn't much else to do so we settled down on the grass to wait. On the River Wey they do things their way, by methods they've always used; and you're best advised not to be too inquisitive about why. After all, boats have been coming up here for a very long time – since the seventeenth century, in fact, when local landowner Sir Richard Weston, who'd travelled widely in the Low Countries, realised the commercial possibilities of a navigable waterway linking Guildford with the River Thames.

This surprises a lot of people who've been fed the primary school view that canals were more or less invented in England at the time of the Industrial Revolution. The truth is that man-made canals date back to the Roman period, and locks similar to those we're familiar with today were probably invented in Imperial China before the first millennium.

But that's history for you. It's like the Magna Carta myth. You look at the facts and decide how you can best use them in the interests of the national narrative. At the same time you ensure that you don't teach kids at school about the past in any dispassionate way, so they never catch you up to your tricks. This way, as Voltaire says, history becomes 'a series of accumulated imaginative inventions', and everyone from English Heritage to the Boy Scouts can spout as much nonsense as they like with no one being any the wiser.

It put me in mind of the ornate plaque on that house which stands sandwiched between the Globe and Tate Modern on the river in London. The one that announces: 'Here lived Sir Christopher Wren during the building of St Paul's Cathedral.' No, he didn't. The house wasn't built until

1710 – two years after the cathedral was completed. The plaque probably stood on another house, long demolished, further down the river; and it was almost certainly erected in its present location in 1945 by Malcolm Munthe, a man described as 'a fantasist' and 'a dreamer'. Even so, it's his version of history which has survived and all over the world there are people who will swear blind it's the house where Wren stayed because, look, they can show you a photograph of it.

We stayed in Weybridge, just the other side of the lock, for a few days. We moored opposite an old warehouse which had been converted to flats, a process which had involved erecting an ugly gantry up the side of it, cantilevered over the water. I assume the architect had thought it justified as a reference to the building's industrial past. Sometimes I wish I could have been an architect. I'd particularly like to have designed an office for other architects. I'd have put a large turd on the top. This would be a reference to the work done by those in the profession over the past 20 years.

Weybridge actually turned out to be a pleasant enough town, much nicer than either of us imagined. It had a few surprises up its sleeve too. Walking around one day we stumbled across the original monument that stood at the meeting point of the seven streets that converge on Seven Dials in Covent Garden on the edge of London's Theatreland. Seven Dials is a salubrious area nowadays, abounding with hotels and posh pubs, but in the 1690s it was the haunt of every ruffian and low-life in the city. The monument was removed by the authorities because, they said, it was attracting disreputable elements. However, because it was popular – considered one of London's 'great public ornaments' – they excused their behaviour by putting about the fantastic story that it had been demolished by the mob who believed there was treasure buried underneath.

Oh, these simpletons who lived in those days of yore; they'd have believed anything, they would. They'd have probably even believed there were weapons of mass destruction in Iraq.

Eventually, after sitting around for years at the house of the architect who'd bought it, the monument was sold to Weybridge Council. They used it to commemorate some minor royal with a local connection who obviously wasn't worth a monument of her own. Even so, when London began agitating to get it back some years ago, Weybridge wouldn't budge an inch and London had to make do with a replica.

Just across the road from this displaced bit of London was an incongruous-seeming plaque on a shabby semi-detached house. Expecting it to be one of those memorials put up to commemorate someone who we'd never even heard of, we went over to have a look, curious as to what nonentity it honoured. In fact, to our surprise, we discovered that it was the house where the writer E. M. Forster had lived for a large part of his life with his mother, and where he had written all six of his major novels. It was a gloomy and cheerless place, obviously rented out to young people; and it looked as if it could do with a lick of paint and some TLC. Downstairs it was clear the tenants were as unimpressed with their celebrated previous occupant as they were with visitors like us peering through their windows; so they'd erected their own replica plaque by the front door announcing that 'Nothing Happened Here'.

We couldn't work out why more hadn't been made of the house. Forster is one of the greatest British twentieth-century novelists. He's so famous there's an International E. M. Forster Society in his honour. And wasn't he a fellow of King's College,

Cambridge too? Aren't the colleges supposed to look after their own? Surely you'd have thought someone might have bought the place, if for no other reason than to prevent it going to rack and ruin, which seems its likely fate. Surely, you'd have thought, Weybridge itself might have been interested in doing something with the house. After all, it fought hard enough to hang on to a carved column with barely any relevance to the town. Surely the house of a front-ranking writer who did his major work in Weybridge would be more important to them? Surely there'd be tourist potential in it? Or is Weybridge too genteel and suburban to want tourists?

***

The bridge across the Wey from which Weybridge gets its name is to the south-east of the town, a stylish three-arched structure topped by attractive filigree cast-iron railings. Cruising the Wey you don't pass under it though, for at this point the navigable route becomes canalised and you have to swing 90 degrees to a lock on the right, through a second bridge of much narrower and more industrial construction. As you approach, it seems to be just a hole in a brick wall, a steel joist above it marked 'Navigation' the only indication of where you're supposed to be going. Again I was on the tiller. I wasn't expecting this sort of complication that early in the morning and my approach was hopelessly misjudged, my angle completely wrong. I hit the bridge side on and jammed the bow of the boat which stopped dead, skewering the stern around and slamming it against one wall of the bridge before bouncing it on the rebound back against the other, like a snooker ball rattling around in the jaws of a pocket.

Em stood on the lockside watching all this in horror, wincing and shaking her head. I didn't need to see her scorecard to know I was getting *nul points* for that manoeuvre. But at least I was in the lock and the worst was over. Or that's what I thought. Both of us had been shaken by what had happened. The boat had been shaken even more. We'd have been better taking time out to compose ourselves before going on. Instead we began to go through the lock without thinking. It was as if we were consoling ourselves in routines we were familiar with and which we'd done a thousand times before.

The problem was we'd forgotten that they do things differently on the Wey.

It was entirely our fault. We'd been warned by the lock-keeper coming on to the river that the locks on the Wey could be particularly fierce and that going uphill we shouldn't depend on being able to control the boat with a single centre rope as we would in normal locks. We were told – no, 'instructed' would be a better word – to use both bow and stern ropes together. We'd even been given a Visitors' Guide which said the same thing, so we had it in writing as well.

But still stressed by the trauma of getting into the lock in the first place, all this went out of the window. I wound our single centre rope around a bollard as usual and Em opened the paddles. Moments later the force of the water hit us. The rope tightened and I attempted to restrain it but it was a waste of time. When water flows this furiously there's no holding any boat against it. Em tried to close the paddles but it was like trying to get an omelette back into eggs: the damage had been done and there was no retrieving it. The surge wrenched the rope out of my hands and all 20 tonnes of *Justice* shot forward with an irresistible inevitability, smashing against the top gate with an almighty crash of glassware and crockery from inside.

Afterwards we surveyed the damage. The breakages were no better or worse than we'd had in previous collisions, and it didn't matter anyhow. We only have cheap glasses and crockery on the boat, so everything could be replaced. Damage to the boat itself seemed marginal too. Luckily the full force of the collision had been absorbed by our bow fender – the tightly plaited cushion of rope that is there for just such an emergency.

The poor cat, though, had had the worst of it. Normally when we're on the move she settles under a coffee table, which offers her sanctuary and a place she can sleep undisturbed until the evening when the engine is finally switched off and she can come out to take the air. But that day, even after we'd tied up for the night, she refused to move. She was either sulking or traumatised. When she did finally emerge it was apparent from her demeanour that we could both drown in the cut for all she cared after putting her through the cruel ordeal we had.

She looked at us both accusingly, moving her eyes from one of us to the other, belligerent and resentful. People say cats are inscrutable and hard to know. Sometimes, though, it's all too clear what's going through their minds. She was thinking, 'Any more of those sorts of fun and games, you pair, and mark my words, I'll be looking for a new home…'

The collision lost us an hour, but it was no great problem. We had agreed to meet Em's friend Liz and her husband Brent that afternoon to go to a nearby country show and we were well ahead of schedule. We cruised past Coxes Lock and the imposing old watermill nearby, now converted to flats; and a few miles further on, beyond New Haw Lock, we finally located the Basingstoke Canal as it branched west off the Wey.

But when the canal got closer to the M25 at Dartnell Park near West Byfleet, we arrived at a section lined by gardens on one side and a small but dense spinney on the other. From a distance it seemed as if the trees were growing across the canal, blocking it. It was only as we got closer that we realised that this wasn't an illusion. Trees *were* actually blocking the canal. Well, one of them was, at least. It was a huge conifer that had fallen from one of the gardens, its trunk stretching from one bank to the other, completely preventing any boat getting past.

Even though it was morally and legally their responsibility, the owners of the garden seemed totally uninterested in the tree and the chaos it was causing. We drove *Justice* nearer to the foliage to take a closer look at the scale of the obstruction, and it was then we realised the reason for this: they were having a party. The bunting was up, the guests were arriving, the music was on. The last thing they wanted to be hassled with was a recalcitrant tree which had chosen that Saturday of all Saturdays to fall across the waterway, thoughtlessly interfering with their social life in the process. Eventually some bloke from the house did deign to wander across to stand for a while at the water's edge, glass in hand, assessing the situation while taking care not to look at me standing in the bow of the boat looking at him. Finally he wheeled round, ignoring both the tree and me. And that was the last we saw of him that day.

We tried to ring Liz and Brent to let them know what had happened but there was no phone reception and we couldn't even get a text through. We had no idea how long it might take before the canal would be clear.

Left to our own devices, Em and I decided to see whether we could make any headway getting past the obstruction without help. We carry an electric bullnose saw on board and we plugged it into the boat's 240-volt supply and began to lop off the most obvious branches until we'd assembled a sizeable pile of them on the towpath. Soon we were joined by the crew of another boat travelling in the opposite direction. With everyone mucking in the way boaters do, the tree – or at least that bit above the surface of the water – was reduced to a skeleton after a couple of hours. The trunk, however, was still below the waterline and despite our best efforts we weren't able to get to it, so for a while it looked as if our exertions might have been in vain.

However, after some deliberation between the boat crews, we decided to see whether one of us could somehow slither over it. As the heavier and more robust of the two boats, Em and I volunteered to give it a go in *Justice* and we tentatively edged towards the submerged obstruction with our engine in tick-over. Once we could feel the trunk underneath us, we engaged full power. Gradually we began to feel ourselves riding up over it.

Eventually, of course, we got stuck. But we'd anticipated that. By then we were far enough across the trunk for the boat on the other side to haul us the rest of the way across the canal. Our delight at having overcome the obstacle, however, had the edge taken off it by a neighbour of the man throwing the party. She had been standing at the waterside at the bottom of her own garden, arms folded like a bouncer outside a nightclub, watching the whole operation. Once the boat was over the tree she began glowering at Em, who was on the bow deck playing a key part in proceedings by helping to steer the boat back into deep water with the barge pole.

'Don't you touch my decking,' the woman said, jabbing her finger down to the timber edging which separated the canal from her lawn. 'Don't you dare touch my decking.'

I was on the stern of the boat and from there it looked as if Em hadn't heard properly, or hadn't quite believed what she had heard. She stopped what she was doing and walked over to the other side of the deck to get closer to the woman.

'Don't you touch my decking,' the woman exploded again, only this time more aggressively than before. 'Don't you dare...'

Now, had this been me rather than Em on the front of the boat, I might have been inclined to tell the woman where to put her blessed decking – especially since most of it seemed to be cantilevered over the river where by rights it shouldn't have been anyhow. If it had been me, I'd have told her that the best way of protecting her precious decking would be to have a word with her neighbour to ensure that no more of his trees fell across the canal blocking the navigation again. If it had been me, I would, at the last resort, being tired and fed up to the back teeth with hacking away at the tree for hours, have reversed the boat and accelerated it into her damned decking with the cheery exhortation to her to sue me for the damage if she wanted.

But thankfully it wasn't me and Em's response was pithier and altogether more controlled. 'Madam,' she said, 'I wouldn't dream of touching your decking – not even with my barge pole.'

Later in the day, we did get some redress for the indifference with which the guy with the fallen tree had treated us. We passed a workboat of National Trust volunteers who'd been alerted to the problem and were on their way to deal with it. A couple of hours afterwards, when we'd moored for the night, they passed us coming back.

It seems they'd shifted the remnants of the tree in no time at all, sawing the trunk up into pieces. Then they'd dumped it back in his garden along with all the branches we'd left on the towpath during the course of the afternoon.

'Well, it's his property,' one of them said. 'And it's his responsibility to dispose of it.'

'And of course we'll be billing him for our work,' another added with a twinkle in his eye.

CHAPTER TWELVE
Into the Stranglers' Lair

To be honest, we hadn't been that impressed with the River Wey up to now, despite its good billing. OK, Weybridge was worth a trip, and the old watermill at Coxes Lock was as impressive an example of industrial architecture as you'd find anywhere. But as for the rest... well, so far the natives hadn't exactly overwhelmed us with their friendliness; and the scenery was all a bit dreary, if truth be told. Indeed, the section up to the junction with the Basingstoke Canal was positively forbidding, even in the sunshine of a summer afternoon. With the M25 shaking the ground beneath us, and graffiti all over the place, it was like a transposed arm of inner-city Birmingham – which is all well and good if you're going through Birmingham, but doesn't really cut it on a waterway with a reputation for beauty and serenity.

The fact that we hadn't been able to get permission to go up the Basingstoke Canal hadn't made us feel any better either. Volunteers from the Basingstoke Canal Society have worked miracles over the years getting the waterway navigable. We thought everyone would want to show off the new baby;

we thought they'd welcome visitors. But when we rang the Basingstoke Canal Authority which administers the canal on behalf of Surrey and Hampshire Councils, its joint owners, we couldn't have had more obstacles thrown in our path if we'd been pirates wanting to bring a galleon to the top for the purposes of arson and plunder.

In other words, the authority sounded just like you'd expect a coalition of two bureaucratic county councils to sound. It was all red tape, rules and regulations. There were problems with water supply, there were difficulties with environmental issues, there were forms to be filled in, procedures to be observed. Frankly, what it seemed to come down to was that they thought it rather a nuisance that anyone should want to take a boat up the Basingstoke Canal; and really, they'd rather I hadn't asked. Even my announcement that I was writing a travel book about being on the waterways – not a card I like to play too often – had little effect. Someone would look into it. Someone would get back to me sometime.

In the garden of The Anchor at Pyrford near where we moored that night, we eventually linked up with Em's friend Liz and her husband Brent. They attempted to make us feel better about things. 'I wouldn't worry about the Basingstoke Canal, the Wey is much more beautiful,' Brent assured us. 'And I wouldn't trouble too much about the people near the tree either,' said Liz. 'They're all a bit snooty down that way, not at all like people in the rest of Byfleet.'

They were right on both counts. The following day we went to a Byfleet version of *Songs of Praise* organised by local churches on the village green and it was heartening to discover that people in that place didn't just want to ignore us or shout at us. They were all quite welcoming and cordial, in fact.

That afternoon we walked to the Royal Horticultural Society gardens at Wisley, where Liz worked. At 240 acres it's the largest of the four gardens run by the RHS, and it's impressive enough to warrant a detour up the Wey even if you were to turn around and go back to the Thames immediately afterwards. The long half-timbered house fronted with lily ponds, around which the gardens are built, has a red-tiled roof and high Tudor-like chimneys and looks for all the world like the seat of some old country estate dating back centuries. In fact it was only built in 1916 and today houses meeting rooms and laboratories which are still used for important botanic work. We're no gardeners, but even so we were so enthralled with the whole place and its spectacular complex of exotic greenhouses, lawns, flower gardens and woods that we returned a couple of days later with some friends who drove up from London on our recommendation. With all that sightseeing it was halfway through the week before we finally slipped our moorings and moved on.

Immediately we saw why everyone had been banging on about the beauty of the Wey, extolling it as they had. The river here meanders through serene water meadows scattered with summer flowers and punctuated every now and again by a copse or spinney. There is a haunting stillness about the quietly flowing water and with barely any boats on the move we felt we had it to ourselves. We set our engine to a gentle, almost silent tick-over and at that tempo we became aware of every small sound around us, whether cattle grazing in the adjacent fields or the banter of farm workers in the faraway distance. Above us in the trees a harmony of songbirds seemed to be serenading our passage; thrushes, finches and blackbirds in full-throated tune. Along the banks, thick with blue watermint and fiery orange balsam, chuckling warblers darted between the reeds; and occasionally, from behind some tuft of grass, came the chilling screech of a hidden moorhen alarmed by our wash. It was poignantly beautiful, the more so because the river is so close to the towns of commuter Surrey which it somehow manages to keep at arm's length.

This isn't a coincidence: in recent years the Wey has been carefully nurtured to protect it from encroaching suburbia and the increasingly rapacious demands of developers. Transfer to the National Trust in 1964 helped, but maintenance of a 20-mile navigation like this is an ongoing project and the Trust has been buying up odd pockets of land to protect it ever since. The RHS has helped too, and where the river borders its gardens at Wisley, it restored the original watercourse which had been bypassed by the construction of the canal, forming an oxbow lake and three islands in the process. This has created a series of distinctive wildlife habitats in which an extraordinary variety of birds, plants and invertebrates have been recorded, including 80 insects considered either nationally important, rare, or in some cases vulnerable to extinction.

A mile or two further on from Pyrford Lock, on the off-towpath side, is a small, square red-brick building which was once the summer house for the nearby old pile of Pyrford Place. It has latticed windows and an unusually shaped roof looking not unlike a pagoda with brewer's droop. Mounted on the outside is a blue plaque misleadingly proclaiming that the poet John Donne lived here for four years from 1600. He actually lived in Pyrford Place. Donne was what the experts call a 'metaphysical' poet but frankly, all the metaphysics in the world wouldn't have been any use squeezing him and his family into a building the size of that summer house.

He lived at Pyrford Place after he'd ruined a promising future as a diplomat by falling in love and eloping with Anne More, the 16-year-old niece of his boss who just happened to be the Lieutenant of the Tower. It was not a clever career move. Poor Donne lost his job, spent time in prison for his 'impudence and gross effrontery' and for the next ten years struggled with poverty – a situation he summed up in a pithy epithet: 'John Donne, Anne Donne, Undone'. Unfortunate though things were for him, they turned out more unfortunately for his wife. After his release she spent pretty much the rest of her married life pregnant, bearing him 11 children over 16 years until she died in childbirth with their twelfth.

I suppose the least you can say of this sorry story is that the ardour of their passion for each other never grew stale, though the cynic in me suspects that Anne often wished it had.

Matters of this nature – love, poetry, philosophy and death – are the sorts of things you find yourself pondering on during an afternoon in high summer cruising along the Wey. The river gets you like that. It's probably because there's a sense of timelessness to it; something which transcends the moment and speaks to another dimension of human experience. It appeals to that part of us which is quieter and more contemplative. Meandering gently through the countryside in the apparently aimless way it does, you'd be forgiven for thinking the Wey's an entirely natural river in an entirely natural landscape. But what landscape in England is natural in the sense of never having been carefully husbanded? The River Wey has been managed more than most waterways: channelled, dredged and straightened until you'd have thought it impossible that there could be anything left of its essential character.

And yet, paradoxically, its natural character has only been preserved by safeguarding it artificially.

If you want to know what happens when waterways are left to themselves without protection you need only look around you at the excess of appallingly designed residential estates that are springing up at the side of canals all over the country, as views over the water – any water, any views – have become the latest must-have design addition for those who have everything else. Shouldn't these waterways be protected from ugly encroachment too? It's true that waterways are better cared for than when we first began boating. In those days canals were still being abandoned and filled in, and even the ones which survived weren't being maintained and were silting up, their towpaths left to crumble. Nevertheless a residue of the old negligence is still apparent today. You saw it when the government released plans for HS2 – its proposed high-speed train route north from the capital – routing it close to the historic meeting place of the Trent and Mersey and Coventry Canals at Fradley Junction, even though it seems that all along there was a better and less disruptive course for the line.

The waterways community fought that one successfully, but we haven't been so lucky getting other parts of HS2 re-routed, such as the section which will gouge its way across the secluded summit of the Oxford Canal on the border with Warwickshire. This will destroy the isolation of a unique, 11-mile corridor of the canal that twists and turns with the contours of the land, through fields which we know haven't been ploughed for centuries because the outline of medieval strip-farming patterns are still embossed on them. And we haven't been successful either in stopping a thousand other lower-profile demolitions and developments and road widenings and bypasses and bridge strengthenings which, little by little, have eroded – and still are eroding – the character of the canals, destroying them bit by bit.

Oh, I know what people say. That canals were the HS2 of their time, and that you can't stop progress, and that we can't live in the past. And that's right, of course. But if the past is a different country, as they say it is, then surely we should value it differently too. Everyone recognises nowadays that we've a responsibility to preserve something of what we inherit for future generations: it's just that our waterways system presents a particular problem to modern conservationists. Because what makes it so special – unique, in fact – is that the whole is greater than its parts. There is the detail of the system, the fact that each individual canal is defined by the myriad features that compose it – the particular mechanisms of the locks, the unique lock cottages, the design of the bridges that cross it and the aqueducts which carry it across roads. But just as important is the scale of the system, whereby each individual river or canal is part of an intricate 3,000-mile network.

It's futile arguing that you can abandon the odd canal if it becomes too expensive to maintain, or discard an arm or two here and there if there's the chance of a killing to be made building an office block. The loss of even a part of the system would be a loss of the whole. You might as well argue that you could prise a few jewels from the coronation crown. After all, there's enough bling on it, isn't there? No one's going to notice that one or two gems have gone missing, are they?

Canals have benefited recently from a renaissance of interest. And not just in boating. More of us use towpaths for walking, running, cycling and fishing than ever before. Canals have become linear parks, opening up towns and cities. They've become long-distance footpaths too, linking cities with the countryside and with other cities beyond that. Yet the more people discover what a valuable resource canals are, the more environmental pressure they'll be under, for increasingly it's the people who use the waterways today who are the greatest threat to them. More and more people are walking or cycling the towpath, demanding improved facilities, so that towpaths are turning into narrow, metalled roads as a result. Ever more people are doing what Em and I are doing and continuously cruising. More yet are taking to the canal as a cheap housing option so that across parts of London boats are moored three abreast, the only chance some youngsters ever have of a home of their own.

Yet the centuries-old network becomes gradually more fragile, even a single boat cruising idyllically down the Wey in summer has an ecological footprint. Me writing books about the waterways doesn't help either. But what can I do? I'm stuck on the horns of a dilemma. I want to celebrate this living, breathing part of our heritage: I want everyone to know about it and celebrate it as I do. But I don't want people trashing it – though by 'people', of course, I mean 'other people'. That's what we always mean when we say 'people', isn't it? Because *we* wouldn't damage canals, would we? *We* just want to protect them.

Which – to be fair to it – is the dilemma the Basingstoke Canal Authority is wrestling with on its canal, much of which has been designated a Site of Special Scientific Interest, reflecting its rich ecostructure and biodiversity. Someone from the authority finally called with a date for our passage and I got very excited. But then he found something wrong with

Justice – I think it was too deep in the water or something – and we were back to square one...

***

We tied up that night at a pretty mooring near Worsfold Flood Gates close to Send, where the river re-joins Broadmead Cut after making one of its periodic diversions from the main navigation. Before long a couple of young blokes appeared in a small dinghy powered by an outboard engine and began messing around on the banks. It was a bright, balmy evening, the clouds idly drifting across the sky, and I sat on the deck with a glass of beer trying to work out what they were doing. Whatever it was, they were doing it systematically. They seemed to be following a set course between the river and the canal. They'd cruise for a few yards, stop and then begin fiddling with something or another in the water before moving to another spot.

Before long my curiosity got the better of me and I wandered up the towpath to talk to them. It turned out they were hunting for crayfish, emptying traps which they'd baited the previous day. They'd caught what seemed to me scores of them wriggling and squirming in a sack they showed me.

Crayfish look a lot like small lobsters and they've become a problem recently on the Wey, as they have across most of the country. In the past, if you were lucky enough to see a crayfish it would be one of our small native white-clawed variety, which you might glimpse hidden in a culvert or scampering over the wall of a weir. They were shy, reserved creatures that kept themselves to themselves, a small but treasured feature of the rich ecology of old Albion. But in the 1970s the world turned upside down for the native white-clawed when, in one of those brainless business initiatives which make you despair for the survival of the human race, thousands of larger North American signal crayfish were imported into the country to satisfy a commercial demand from the Scandinavians who apparently are partial to a crayfish tail or two on their smorgasbord.

Everything was hunky-dory for a few years until the bottom dropped out of the market. Maybe the Scandinavians just got bored with crayfish. Maybe they rediscovered herring. Either way, large numbers of signal crayfish were dumped in rivers and canals, where they prospered very well, thank you very much. The climate suited them down to the ground. Well, down to the riverbed at least. And food was plentiful too, their only competitor the puny white-clawed, half their size and not capable of putting up much of a fight if it came to a contest. Not that it did come to a contest, for the signals carry a waterborne fungus that is fatal to the native species. Before long they had wiped out the white-clawed in their thousands, without so much as a pincer being raised in anger.

Today the white-clawed is a protected species, with heavy fines for those who tamper with them. In contrast, signals have become such a pest that if you were inadvertently to catch one while you were dangling a piece of meat over your boat on a length of string (and signals are so stupid they'd bite at that), you wouldn't be allowed by law to return it to the water. You need a permit to fish them, and fishing is not discouraged – though whether it does much good as a control mechanism is problematic, because among their other captivating charms the signals are cannibalistic and some say that taking out the large ones merely relieves 'predation pressure' on the young.

Or putting it another way, if you get rid of the big bruisers who eat the little ones, then more of the little ones have the chance of becoming big bruisers themselves.

Signals do, however, taste very good. The guys in the boat were selling their catch locally, though sadly not to Pret a Manger where a crayfish and rocket on wholemeal – one of their signature sarnies – will cost you the better part of a fiver. Predictably the Pret crayfish comes from China, where else? Which, thinking about it, is probably what did for our domestic industry in the first place.

'Can you, like, erm, make any sort of a living from this,' I asked the guys in the boat. I was a bit wary, concerned that they might consider me an idiot for thinking that there was that much money in a hobby. On the other hand, if it was their livelihood, I was anxious that they didn't think I was mocking it by dismissing it as a pastime.

The two of them burst into laughter. 'Well, we *are* fishermen,' one of them said. 'But we fish out of Brixham for Dover sole,' said the other. 'We come up here most years in the summer for a week or two. It's just a holiday for us really, a change of scene. The crayfish pay for the beer.'

***

The next morning dawned, as they all seemed to do that implausible summer, with sunshine creeping into the cabin where we slept, prising open our eyes with the promise of the new day. On deck the glare from the water was unbearable, the reflection of the sun on the surface like a series of explosions of crystal shattering in the current. We'd talked the previous evening about putting our feet up for the day and doing nothing, but mornings like this challenge you to become a part of them and so we decided to join the world and cruise into Guildford. Maybe there we'd cast off our canal kit and treat ourselves to a night on the town. A film perhaps, a meal out.

Less than a mile from the floodgates at Worsfold is Triggs Lock, whose keeper in 1812 was William Stevens. His descendant Harry Stevens subsequently came to own the Wey, and it was he who eventually donated it to the National Trust. From this point onwards the river – or is it the canal now? I didn't know, I'd lost touch – begins to arc around the secluded country estate of Sutton Park by way of a couple of challenging 90-degree bends which have the effect of keeping the house out of sight, preserving its privacy. This was no doubt a plus point for Sutton Park's most famous recent occupant, the reclusive oil tycoon Paul Getty, who lived there for nearly 20 years until his death in 1976. For those of us on boats, however, it's got a much more celebrated past which stretches back much further, for it was originally the home of the Weston family. It was the agricultural pioneer Richard Weston three and a half centuries ago who started experimenting with a technique of water management that eventually led to the Wey becoming navigable.

Weston had travelled in the Low Countries and as a farmer he'd been intrigued by a cultivation system he'd seen there in which pastureland was flooded in the winter, insulating the ground below even when it was so cold it iced over. This way, when you came to drain it in the early spring you could graze the land at a time when animal foodstuff was scarce. More than this, once you let the grass grow again you could get an early cut, sometimes even two, significantly boosting hay yields.

In 1618 or 1619, between what are now the unprepossessing modern suburbs of Slyfield Green and Burpham on the approach to Guildford – a council rubbish tip on one side and the A3 thundering along on the other – Weston built Stoke Lock. It's one of the earliest locks in England except that it wasn't originally constructed for the passage of boats, but to control the flow of water so that he could flood his meadows below. However, it wasn't long before Weston and other landowners along the Wey saw the benefits of a fully navigable route to link with the Thames and the profitable markets of London.

After 1666, when London burned down in the Great Fire, there was a massive demand for materials for rebuilding. Much of it – like the Guildford Stone which Sir Christopher Wren used for St Paul's Cathedral – was transported directly down the Wey. The waterway was in the money – and so was Surrey.

It still is. It's the richest county in England.

* * *

And so we arrived in Guildford. Guildford, I have to say from the outset, was nothing like I expected it to be.

In fact Guildford – the real city, the one I found myself in – was so far removed from my perception of it that wandering around I frequently found myself baffled as to where exactly I was. Reminding myself I was in Guildford didn't help a lot either. I didn't actually believe myself. In my mind – and God knows where I'd picked up the idea – Guildford was a modern city of 1930s estates and ring roads and dual carriageways and out-of-town shopping precincts with cheap burger bars and fish and chip shops. That was my Guildford. I hated that Guildford.

This Guildford, however, seemed to be a splendid old city which could trace its history back to Saxon times. It had a gracious cobbled High Street rising from the river to the top of a hill from which it was possible to see the surrounding countryside. It had an ancient set of almshouses, old coaching inns, the remains of a Norman castle, a grammar school founded in 1509 and a Guildhall with an imposing projecting clock jutting lewdly from its frontage and an equally striking cupola crowning its top. That was this Guildford. I loved everything about this Guildford.

Well, almost everything. The Town Wharf overlooked by the dreadful 1960s Friary Court office block took a bit of stomaching. But then it was once voted the city's ugliest building, so I guess it's not been popular with people in Guildford either. Considering the wharf was once the source of the town's wealth, it's a great shame that it's been reduced to what seems like a derelict pub painted lime green and purple. I didn't much care for the red-brick cathedral either. But it'll mellow in time. Or I will.

Those exceptions aside though, Guildford was a lovely town. But mind you, it's posh. Really posh. In fact, I'll tell you how posh Guildford is: Guildford has a Heals. And if that name doesn't mean anything to you, you're in good company, for this exclusive emporium of contemporary design is so upmarket it's off the radar to most ordinary folk. It sells furniture and homeware and only has six stores in the whole country, three of them in London. We went to look around the one in Guildford more in the spirit we might visit a museum of modern art than a shop, and we found an office chair for sale costing £3,800. Yes: £3,800. Takes a lot of believing, doesn't it? A sales assistant let me sit in it, which must have been worth at least 20 quid. He told us it was an Eames chair, which may mean something to those who know about these things, but which meant so little to me that for months afterwards I was bragging to people that I'd sat in an Eels chair (provoking the predictable response from everyone that they'd always thought I was a slippery character).

We moored south of the town alongside the wonderful Shalford water meadows, where a gang of men was noisily pollarding the willows on the bank, hacking back their trailing branches and leaving them as tidier, but rather bulbous, stumps. Even so, it was as idyllic a mooring as you'd find in any city anywhere. The meadows are a Site of Special Scientific Interest now – grazed by organically reared cattle and closely protected. They used to be flooded in line with Weston's water-management techniques – though here the practice had a secondary function in protecting Guildford from real flooding. Actually, it had a third function too, for up until the early part of the twentieth century when winters became warmer, the water-covered meadows froze, providing Guildford with a huge public skating rink.

The city has always made a feature of its river, and the following day – a Saturday – the parks and gardens bordering the bank were bustling with mums with pushchairs and dog walkers and joggers. A little-known fact of Guildford is that the iconic punk band The Stranglers come from here. Indeed, they were originally called the Guildford Stranglers. But even knowing this, we still found it remarkable that a disproportionate number of young people coming our way that morning appeared to be Goths. Goths? You know, Goths: kids dressed in black, the girls with white make-up and purple lips, the boys all sub punk zombie: chains, leathers, that sort of stuff. Blimey, where've you been the last 30 years?

We were wandering and mindlessly enjoying the morning when we became aware of them. They were out in force and had all spent a lot of time and money on their appearance. A group of three or four passed us first, the girls pretty in a way that even their scowls and thick make-up couldn't hide, the boys trying to look like death but succeeding only in looking a bit poorly. A couple of more aggressive ones passed later, one of them staring at me as if he wanted to rip my throat out just as soon as he'd got rid of his milk teeth. Then an all-girl group sauntered by, maybe half a dozen of them, all dressed like Victorian widows in black satin dresses and a black lace headscarves. Soon afterwards an all-male group about the same size came along. They all had Dracula eyes darkened by mascara, their long straight hair looking as if it had been washed in coal dust.

'Hang on,' I said to Em. 'Something's happening here…' And with my curiosity excited I approached the next group who came along.

This crew did look a little less friendly than the rest, I concede. Maybe it was because they were older, and physically bigger; maybe it was because they looked more like Frankenstein's monster than Dracula, their faces apparently held together by studs of various sorts. They had studs in their cheeks and in their noses and along the edge of their ears. Some of the girls even had studs in the skin of their temples. Most of them, male and female, also seemed to have studs in their tongues which were impossible to miss since they were all chewing on gum with their mouths open, grinding it between their teeth in a manner designed to be provocatively insolent.

'Excuse me, I wonder if I could possibly ask a rude question?' I started. But then I had second thoughts. Maybe this wasn't such a bright idea after all. It might antagonise them. By now they'd all stopped and were looking at me expectantly.

I gulped. There didn't seem to be any going back now. 'It's just that there seem to be a rather large number of you guys around this morning,' I went on. 'I was, erm, curious what, you know, what was happening?'

Immediately one of the women stepped forward. In an instant she had whipped the gum from her mouth, and replaced the glowering grimace that had been weighing down the sides of her mouth with a wide and affable smile. 'Oh, we're all friends; we're just celebrating a birthday,' she said. 'It's a summer thing, you know, we just thought it would be a bit different to have a party in the park.' She spoke with such a perfectly enunciated Home Counties accent that she could have been a newsreader on the World Service. You could immediately sense too from her polite demeanour that she was a well-brought-up young woman from a good home.

But then they all were. And why wouldn't they be? They lived in Guildford where, because of their background, a degree of confrontation with establishment values might be expected and, I'd guess, probably encouraged. It would be seen by their parents as a natural phase in their lives before they all settled down to jobs in the Foreign Office, the City or the BBC. Em came over and we all began chatting. As soon as they discovered we were living on a boat they were bubbling with curiosity to know everything about us: where we'd come from, where we were going, how long we'd been doing it...

Eventually we had to break away. We'd have still been there now otherwise. However, it wasn't to be our final encounter with the youth of Guildford that day. Later that afternoon coming back from the shops we saw a drugs bust in the same river park – though to call it a drugs bust seems a bit of an overstatement. It wasn't exactly *The Wire,* I grant you. There wasn't much in the way of screeching tyres or shoot-outs. Some kids around 13 or 14 years old had been smoking dope – 'doing some blow', as they'd say – and they'd been raided by police who'd arrived in two or three squad cars, sirens blazing.

As we neared Millmead Lock close to Town Bridge one of them was being led away, so mortified by the episode that he was on the verge of tears. Which, thinking about it, was probably the police strategy in making such a big deal of the raid and marching him through a public area on such a busy afternoon.

Still, embarrassing though it must have been for the miserable wretch, I fear it was nothing compared to what he'd have to face when the police got him back to the station and rang his dad...

CHAPTER THIRTEEN
Carpe Diem

I'm not sure how long we stayed in Guildford. Long enough to have to buy another National Trust licence, I know that much. And long enough to feel sorry that we had to leave when the time came. But this happens on a boat. You turn up somewhere you've never been before and a couple of weeks later you feel like it's your home town and you're bereft that you have to leave. The go-as-you-please gypsy life has enormous attractions, and it's difficult to express the unalloyed sense of liberation, joy and delight which you experience being able to move your home on a whim, as and when you please. But people put down roots quicker than you'd think. And they aren't always aware it's happening.

We were beginners at this liveaboard life, yet I've heard the same said by old stagers who've lived on narrowboats for decades. They talk of favourite spots they keep going back to time and time again, locations they feel drawn to return to. There's a view they like, they'll explain, or a particular pub where they feel comfortable. Perhaps there's a village or small town they've grown fond of over the years. Maybe even a city they feel an affinity for, because people can be enticed by urban areas as much as the countryside.

Em and I had been careful about spending too long in any one place, though it was sometimes difficult to strike the right balance. During years of boating on weekends away and holidays we'd constantly been on the move, trying to get to somewhere or another. Living as we now did released us from the need to keep travelling and without this burden we were seeing the waterways as if in a different dimension, a dimension in which time became immaterial and distance only an intellectual idea. Yes, we wanted to visit new places, or experience old ones in a new way. But that was for the future and we were sick of the future. We'd been living in the future for years; our whole life had been focused on it. Now we wanted to live in the present and enjoy the moment. We wanted to relish the places we found ourselves in without this constantly gnawing pressure that there was somewhere better around the next bend if only we pressed on to find it.

In the event it was the simple recognition of how little distance we'd actually travelled that made us decide that we should get on with it and move more. It was months since we'd left Banbury, yet if we'd decided to return we could probably have been back there in a couple of weeks. This glorious summer couldn't last forever. We might not want to think about the looming winter yet, but it would be upon us faster than you could say falling temperatures and browning leaves. Insomuch as we'd talked about it at all, we'd agreed we didn't want to spend winter in the south, yet here we were getting on for September and almost back in London again. London! Where we'd started from. Where the whole adventure had begun. We needed to move faster, that's what it came down to.

So, fired with a new determination, we made up our minds to leave the next day. We decided that we'd go to the end of the canal so that at least we could say we'd been there; and after that we'd turn round and make a break for the Thames and London before doing some serious travelling north. The problem, however, was that even as we were formulating this plan we weren't entirely persuaded of it ourselves. It was too inflexible and prescriptive, like those initiatives managements are forever foisting on workforces to make them more efficient. They might be great in theory but they're often impossible to put into practice.

And so it was with the River Wey, which is so pretty there's no hurrying it. There's something bewitching about this waterway which compels you to take your time cruising along it. Its loveliness is like the song of the sirens, those mythical creatures of Greek mythology, daughters of the river god Achelous, who lured sailors to their death. It worms into your head, beauty like this; it tempts you to stay, if not forever then at least another week or so, or maybe just another few days, that wouldn't be too much to ask of anyone surely…?

Half a mile or so beyond the Guildford moorings, where we'd been tied up nearly a week, is St Catherine's Hill. Here, over the years, the river has worn away at an orange sandstone bank to form a shallow beach. For centuries this was a major crossing point on the Wey – the golden, or 'guilden', ford which gave Guildford its name. There was a ferry here for those who didn't want to get their feet wet, though today an attractive wooden footbridge spans the narrow channel. Nearby, at the bottom of a sunken lane leading down the hill, is a charming Victorian grotto built to make a feature of a spring which surfaces from the chalk hills before flowing under the towpath and into the river.

It's a delightful spot with a mysterious, spiritual feel to it; so it's no surprise to find stories about the place woven into local mythology. Legend has it that the spring, once guarded by a dragon, has wondrous medicinal properties especially for those with eye complaints. Beech and oak trees stretch down to the water's edge where you can sometimes see purple loosestrife, meadowsweet and hemp agrimony. But it gets prettier yet; and as the Wey morphs into the Godalming Navigation near the junction with the disused Wey and Arun Canal (which once took boats through Chichester to Portsmouth on the south coast) you cruise through a part of Surrey you'd hardly believe could still exist in the twenty-first century. The canal twists and turns, left and right, snaking between reed beds peppered with campion and yellow flags, and meadows filled with – get this! – haystacks. Real haystacks. Haystacks constructed from good, old-fashioned, square-shaped bales of hay and not these rolls covered with bin liners the size of buses, which are such a blot on the landscape nowadays. Nearly 200 years after he wrote about the journey between Guildford and Godalming in his *Rural Rides*, you have to agree with William Cobbett that 'there is hardly another such pretty four miles in all England'.

We cruised as far as we could up the river and tied up in Godalming at the intriguingly named Lammas Lands just down from the wharf. This was once a busy transhipment point for timber, stone and agricultural produce, but that day, with just one other boat moored around the bend from us, only the sound of the horse-drawn trip boat *Iona* passing its tow rope across our roof disturbed the stillness of the afternoon. We'd only intended staying there overnight. We finished up staying for three or four days. We could feel Godalming growing on us. Or maybe it was growing into us. Either way it wasn't healthy for a couple of people pretending to be travellers.

We got talking to Graham and Pat in the boat around the corner. 'It's very genteel, Godalming,' Graham said. 'But have you noticed how many charity shops and hairdressers it has?'

Well actually, we hadn't, though when we looked more closely he was right. It didn't seem to matter, however. Godalming may have seen more prosperous days, but where in the country except London hasn't? It had a certain charm which was compelling. We both felt we could have stayed there longer.

'But we can't stay here any longer,' Em protested one evening, emboldened by a surfeit of wine to confront the river sprites that seemed to have us in their grasp. 'We're just going to have to break away from this damned waterway. It seems to have put a spell on us...'

So we went the next morning, leaving before the sun had risen. It was chilly with the cold of the night still in the air; and as we started our engine, mists played on the surface of the water, swirling around our hull like ethereal fingers trying to prevent us escaping their clutches. In a copse nearby some unidentifiable bird screeched with a cry like cackling laughter. At the same time a breeze caught the back of my neck and I felt a sudden unaccountable chill down my spine.

We hacked down the Wey as fast as we could, as if we were being pursued; and before the week was out we were turning back on to the Thames again at Weybridge, skirting Rivermead Island at Sunbury where Pink Floyd's David Gilmour lives, and Hampton where he has a recording studio in a houseboat once owned by the theatre impresario Fred Karno. We both felt a sense of profound relief to be on the move again.

Mind you, that didn't last long. We hadn't gone more than a mile before we'd moored up again at Hampton Court for another longish stop. This wasn't part of the plan and I'm not certain even now why it happened. I mean, it's not as if we hadn't visited Hampton Court before by boat. But Hampton Court's at its best from the water and it's a very difficult place to ignore. Indeed, you're probably in breach of some ancient Thames by-law if you do. The moorings are along the riverbank directly outside and they're spectacular, especially in the twilight of a balmy evening, which it was as we were passing, on our way to Teddington, where we planned to catch the morning tide the following day. Along the darkening riverbank lights were blinking into life and in the enchanting half-light the palace was beguiling, its profusion of turrets and chimneys like a floodlit forest in the sky.

We both saw a mooring spot at the same time.

'Just one night then. Agreed?' I said to Em. She nodded. 'Just one or two beers at the King's Arms and off first thing in the morning?' She nodded again. 'No excuses?'

'Absolutely none,' she agreed. And she brought the boat around in a wide arc across the river, slotting into the space perfectly with our bow upstream.

It was then we got a call from my friend Dave who'd been following our progress since we'd been on the Thames. He was calling from London for a chat but once he realised where we were he lost no time in wheedling a visit. He'd never been to Hampton Court. It would be a shame not to see it and take advantage of seeing us at the same time, he said.

So instead of catching the tide as we'd planned, the next morning we found ourselves with him, mixing it with the usual mobs of tourists visiting this, the largest royal residence in the country – though no reigning monarch's lived there since the eighteenth century when George III developed an aversion to the place. There's certainly a lot to see and you can understand why the place attracts crowds from all over the world. The Great Hall, the state apartments, the chapel, the royal tennis courts – you could spend an hour in each of them and still see nothing. My top tip is not to even think about leaving the ticket office without one of the maps they offer you. If you do, steal someone else's the first opportunity you get. You'll thank me for this advice, believe me. Forget about the famous maze in the grounds: that's easy-peasy compared with the palace itself, which is so huge you can easily get lost trying to find a lavatory.

That's what I was attempting to do when I stumbled into the kitchens, which someone had told me was the way to the gents. It felt more like the way to Hades. It was like a furnace. I took a couple of steps inside and almost passed out with the heat. The reason for this, I discovered, was that they'd lit fires in the huge hearths where the Tudors roasted their barons of beef. They were vast conflagrations, bonfires piled high with logs and raging so apparently uncontrollably they looked as if they might burn the place down.

Eat your heart out, Gordon Ramsay. This was the real Hell's Kitchen. No one – but no one – was going to get out of the place that day without realising exactly what an ordeal cooking must have been in Henry VIII's time.

The fires would have made the kitchen impossibly hot even on a freezing day in December. On an uncharacteristically warm late-summer afternoon it was unbearable. The tourists from overseas just didn't know how to handle it. Lectured before leaving home on the caprices of the English summer, they'd come equipped with clothing which would have given them heatstroke even outside in the gardens. Inside in the kitchens they'd had to strip off to a stage just short of their underwear simply to stay alive; and they were all wandering around with armfuls of heavy topcoats, Arctic-resistant anoraks and sweaters so thick you could have used them as carpets. I stopped one man to ask if he knew the way to the lavatory but he was Polish or Hungarian or something and didn't understand a word I said. Or at least I think that was it – though I suppose it's just about possible he was an Englishman who'd lost the power of speech in the high temperatures.

I stopped someone else but he was scary – so close to heatstroke his deeply furrowed face appeared to be melting like candle wax. Eventually – becoming a little desperate now – I sought out a member of staff. That was a lot of use too. They were so caught up with throwing logs on fires I'd have needed an asbestos suit to get near enough to them to make myself heard above the roaring flames. Eventually I fled in despair. By then I'd lost my bearings and didn't know how to get out of the place, being confronted at every turn by visitors as frazzled as I was and trying to do the same thing.

My concern now wasn't so much needing a toilet as exactly the opposite. I felt if I didn't get a drink soon I'd be collapsing with dehydration. Everyone else was reacting the same way, though while the English visitors seemed content to keel over and die quietly, the foreign contingent were at least making a fight of it and sending their kids on sorties to search out bottles of water and cans of Coke. I attached myself to a pair of Korean 12-year-olds who, in the absence of any official signage, appeared to have reverted to Google Maps to find their way about. After following them surreptitiously for a few minutes, nervous that at any moment I might get apprehended by some burly policeman accusing me of heinous crimes, I eventually found myself in another part of the palace where, to my relief, I just happened to find Em standing with Dave in a queue for a cafe. Fed up with waiting for me, they'd apparently gone off for a cup of tea.

At the counter, while I was waiting to order, I knocked back two or three glasses of iced water from the jug they provide free for those having lunch. Then I knocked back a couple more, emptying the jug completely. I suddenly felt very bloated. And very uncomfortable too. I found myself crossing my legs.

'I'm going to have to go to the loo,' I whispered to Em.

'What? Again?' she said, arching her eyebrows.

***

I'm convinced that if ever explorers were to stumble across some undiscovered part of the Amazonian rainforest, or scientists involved in the Antarctic Survey happened to locate a hitherto unknown ice sheet, they would almost certainly meet a cheery dog walker, holding back some canine straining at a leash with one hand while clearing up its oozing effluents with the other.

Dog walkers get everywhere. You can be on what you might think is the most isolated section of an isolated canal, but I warrant that before long a dog walker will appear round the bend. Maybe it'll be a tiny lady with blue-rinse hair and an aura of perfume around her you could choke on, maybe a young man in jeans with nothing but a flimsy T-shirt emblazoned with the legend of some esoteric rock band to protect him from the rigours of the vile winter. But believe me, they'll be there.

Trotting along with their toy poodles trailing behind them, or hanging on to their mastiffs for dear life as they gouge ridges in the towpath with their heels trying to hold them back. It's the same away from the canals too. You can be trekking across some uphill moorland half a day from anywhere, and still there'll be dog walkers up there wishing you a jolly good morning while their animals hare off through the bracken in pursuit of some breath of wind or rustle in the undergrowth which has momentarily caught their attention. Find me a local park in any town in the country too and it'll be heaving with dog walkers. Even parks where the poor things can't be let off their leads. Even parks where they have to be marched around the perimeters like prisoners in some Russian gulag on exercise hour.

The British are renowned for their relationship with their pets but as far as I know no one has studied this phenomenon of dog walking which, to a cat owner like myself, seems such an extraordinary thing. I mean to say, to a cat owner the equivalent process is opening the door and then... er, well, that's it, actually. Cats hate doors. And they're not that keen on being inside when they want to be out either. Open the door and they're off as if they've just escaped from hell, with your only concern whether or not you're ever going to see them again.

Dog walking on the other hand requires real commitment. You have to actually *do* something to walk a dog. You have to put the thing on a lead, and put your shoes on and get yourself a coat. At the very least you have to walk yourself and though this might be pleasant enough in the summer months, I've seen enough dog walkers returning home looking like they've been swimming in mud to know that it ain't always a bundle of fun in the winter. And then there's the dogs themselves. Of course, there are dogs that as a result of training or disposition trot alongside their owners with military precision. Most of them don't though, do they? Or at least not all the time. And why should they? They're sentient creatures with minds of their own. They are free spirits whose senses haven't yet been totally deadened to the call of the wild – though I admit that when they start squirming about on the carpet kicking their legs in the air and begging for biscuits that's a difficult concept to grasp.

Most of them out walking are likely to be either pulling up front and yanking off your arm because you won't move fast enough for them, or dragging along behind you and sniffing at lampposts with various levels of enthusiasm, or worse spraying them, marking out their territories with the studied determination of canine Hitlers resolved to establish a series of thousand-year Reichs down every high street in the country.

The size or breed of the dog doesn't seem to have anything to do with it either. The big dogs – the Alsatians, the retrievers, the Labradors – can be the worst dawdlers, especially in later years when their hips begin to go. But they can be some of the worst pullers too, at any age. Terriers or spaniels can be the same, throttling themselves on the lead one moment, challenging you to drag them like fur-covered sledges the next. Often they'll do both on the same walk.

Off the lead they can be even worse, as I know from a dog I had as a kid. They can trip along beside you, tucking themselves neatly into your heels, as if nothing in the world could tempt them to break ranks. And then suddenly they'll be off heading for the great beyond with their tails held so provocatively high I've often thought it's a doggy finger they're giving you. Take my brother's dog. He's got a cocker, good as gold off the lead usually. But take her into the country and give her a whiff of a pheasant and she's off and all the shouting and whistling in the world won't get her back.

I mention all this because the day after Dave visited was a Saturday, and since we were by now happily settled in our moorings, we decided we might as well spend the weekend there. We'd moved from the first spot we'd stopped at and were now in one of the best berths on offer: directly outside Jean Tijou's famous gilded gates, which stand at the south end of the palace in front of the baroque additions built by Christopher Wren in the late seventeenth century. Kit loved it. On the basis that a cat may look at a king (and if it can't, it doesn't care anyhow), she slunk off from the boat every night as soon as it got dark, slipping under the ornate ironwork to spend the night doing whatever it is cats do in royal flower beds.

At least it kept her out of the way of the dogs. The place was teeming with them day and night, such a constant stream of them passing along the path on the bank above us we began to wonder whether there was something happening. A show maybe, or perhaps an audition for those cute dog clips which are forever appearing on Facebook – you know the sort of thing, the sort that always promise to make your heart melt and finish making you want to throw up. We finally discovered where all the dogs were going when we went for a walk through Hampton Court Park, known also as Home Park. Along with the adjoining Bushy Park, this comprises an open space of some 1,800 acres, and on weekends it surely has to be one of the biggest dog-exercise areas in Europe. Actually the dogs are a bit of a problem in Bushy, where there's a herd of more than 300 deer which can react badly in the rutting and birthing seasons.

We walked past the Long Water, a bleak three-quarters-of-a-mile-long canal, 150 feet wide, which cuts across the park and is something of a barrier if, like us, you're walking into Kingston from the river. It was another of those blistering hot days when your face feels less sun-kissed and more as if it's been in a passionate embrace with a three-bar electric fire. But it was a gorgeous walk all the same. The park's rarely explored by those haring down the river on some schedule or another, and they miss a lot as a result. Kingston's worth an hour or two of anyone's life as well. It was the Westminster Abbey of Saxon times and half a dozen kings were crowned on the King's Stone which gave the town its name. The stone – more of a big boulder, really – is still there, open to the elements outside the current Guildhall, but don't expect a lot if you go to see it. It sits on a plinth surrounded by cast-iron railings, like something they might be trying to flog you in a garden centre.

East Molesey, on the other side of the river directly opposite Hampton Court, doesn't get much of a look-in from those cruising the Thames either. It's another well-to-do area, if lacking the same history as its noble neighbour. East Molesey's problem is that it sounds too much like East Cheam – that fictional encapsulation of everything that is dull and most monotonous about the outer London suburbs made famous years ago by the comedian Tony Hancock. You may never have heard of it, and never have heard of Tony Hancock either, but the faceless East Cheam is still rooted somewhere in the national psyche.

It's a shame East Molesey should have to suffer from such an accident of name. On a Sunday it's a buzzy little place with stylish restaurants and trendy bric-a-brac shops. It's also got one of the most upmarket pet shops I've ever seen, selling – honestly, believe me – ice cream for dogs.

We went into a pub and fell into a conversation with a bloke at the bar about new breeds of dog appearing on the street. 'Designer dogs,' he called them. The best known is probably the labradoodle, a mixture of poodle and Labrador. But there are others, like schnoodles, a combination of poodle and schnauzer. Or chiweenies, a cross between a chihuahua and a dachshund.

'What do you call a cross between a bull terrier and a shih-tzu?' the guy at the bar asked. But before we could say a word he answered his own question. 'A bullshit,' he said, breaking down in laughter at his own joke.

'And a Jack Russell and a shih-tzu?' Again he broke down in gales of laughter. 'A jack shit.'

'And what about a poodle and a shih-tzu?' Now he was almost rolling about on the floor like a four-year-old. 'A shit poo,' he spluttered, scarcely able to get the words out.

All of which would have been a good deal more amusing if earlier that year The Westminster Kennel Club hadn't opened an event to mixed-breed dogs, as a result of which some strangely named but genuine breeds began to emerge from the woodwork. One of them was a mix between a Siberian husky and a poodle known as a siberpoo. Another, a cross between a Yorkshire terrier and a poodle, is called a yo-yopoo.

They say that sometimes life imitates fiction. Now it seems to be imitating jokes.

CHAPTER FOURTEEN
Capital Pains

Teddington is the point at which the Thames becomes tidal. Some say that's why it's called Teddington – a corruption of Tide-turn-town. For a boater a tidal river presents a totally different set of challenges to a non-tidal one. Non-tidal rivers are pussycats by comparison. But a tidal river's a tiger river; and in the same way you'd never have a tiger on your lap tickling it under the chin, so you'd be careful how you navigated a tidal stretch of water, wherever it is. They have a life of their own, tidal rivers: they have undercurrents and eddies and flows which can get you into trouble faster than you believe possible. And, of course, they rise and fall twice a day, sometimes a great distance. You moor at your peril on a tidal river. You cruise at your own risk.

As tidal rivers go, the Thames isn't the worst there is. Over the years it's been channelled, dredged and controlled so much that it's had the life almost throttled out of it. The tidal Trent after rain is a far more intimidating river; after a storm it can flow torrentially. It's hazardous at other times too, even when the water's low. Em and I ran a boat aground on a submerged island cruising down it in a drought once and were stranded for weeks. The River Ribble in Lancashire can be a bit temperamental that way too, and the River Severn as it gets close to the Bristol Channel is potentially lethal, with some of the highest tide falls in the world.

No, what makes the Thames tricky for a boat is other boats. From Teddington Lock there are two ways into central London, both of which get you back on to the canal system. The first and most obvious is to go straight down the river, past the Houses of Parliament, the London Eye and the Tower of London, after which you can turn into Limehouse Dock to connect to the Grand Union Canal. This takes you past Camden Lock and right through the middle of London Zoo to Little Venice, where it sweeps across the western suburbs before veering off at Bull's Bridge Junction to the north.

To see these national landmarks from a vessel under your control is a terrific experience and if you own a boat you should do it at least once in your life. But it can be a bit nerve-wracking. There are some heavy-duty tourist boats plying their trade on the Thames around London, and some of them – like the multi-hulled clippers that fly between the Tate Gallery at Millbank and Woolwich – travel at unspeakable speeds and can cause a wash which is fearful from the deck of a narrowboat.

Most narrowboats heading for the capital tend to take the easier option and head down the river only as far as Brentford, a short trip from Teddington. From here they travel into central London along the Grand Union Canal from the west, which is almost a back route. This is what Em and I did that day after taking the 1.30 p.m. tide. It's not as scary a passage but, even so, in the wrong conditions the river section can still be alarming. I've been down this reach when the wind's been kicking up as if it was the North Sea, throwing spray across the stern deck; and worse still, when it's created a gentle, stomach-churning swell in which I've almost lost sight of the bow of the boat as it's dipped in the water. It's disquieting when this happens, take it from me: you feel as if you're in a lift with no ground floor. Your head tells you not to panic, that you'll rise again as naturally as you've fallen. But your gut tells you a different story altogether and it can easily convince you that you're facing imminent oblivion, about to nosedive to the bottom, the next stop eternity and mind the gap, please.

That day, however, it was calm and tranquil without even a breath of wind rippling the water. The river seemed to be barely moving, more like a sheet of glass than a river, more like a mirror than a sheet of glass with all the reflections of the trees along the bank shimmering on its surface in the sunshine. We passed Eel Pie Island at Twickenham where, in a dilapidated hotel converted to a jazz club, many iconic bands and musicians of the 1960s and 1970s learned their trade, from The Who to Rod Stewart, from Eric Clapton to the Stones. Afterwards we cruised along the outstandingly beautiful reach below Richmond Hill, which remains the only view in England protected by an Act of Parliament.

The turn-off from the Thames into the narrow neck of the River Brent for the short trip to Brentford where you join the Grand Union Canal can sometimes be awkward if you're on a boat travelling alone. The problem is that it's not always immediately obvious where the turning is, especially on a murky morning or a darkening evening when you're perhaps not paying as much attention as you should. That day, though, Em and I had come out of Teddington in a flotilla with half a dozen other craft and it was simply a matter of following the two or three of them going in our direction and breasting up temporarily against them in the lock approach, a little way along, until the duty lock-keeper could work us through.

The brief delay gave us pause to muse on the fact we were finally leaving the Thames, something we both felt unaccountably sad about, as if our departure might somehow break the spell of the summer which had been so unforgettable. It had been a unique trip, most memorable for us because we'd had the time to enjoy it properly at our own pace – something which we'd never done before on any waterway. Paradoxically, living on the boat had allowed us to get off the boat and explore more of the surrounding countryside and villages than we'd normally have been able to just holidaying. This had given us a different perspective on areas, which we'd therefore seen in a totally different way.

The beautiful weather, of course, had been the defining factor. It had been like one of those remembered summers of childhood, when all summers were long and hot and endless. But how many summers like this can you say you experience as an adult? And how many of the ones you experience do you have the opportunity to really appreciate as we'd been privileged to appreciate this one? It had been – it still was – an ephemeral summer yet it was lasting what seemed a lifetime. We're not used to this sort of thing in England. We don't like our seasons getting inside our heads and messing with them. In fact we don't like our seasons much at all, if truth were told. We're not keen on it when our summers are too extreme, either too warm like this or too cold as they have been recently. And we don't like our winters to be excessive either; we prefer them middling and mediocre. Given the choice most of us would opt for a prosaic, average type of climate that never went below freezing and never got much higher than the mid 70s Fahrenheit.

But this hadn't been a prosaic summer: it had been a poetic one filled with all the possibilities that offers. It had been an ice-cream summer melting in our mouths, a champagne summer tickling our tongues; it had been a summer of heady fragrances, of honeysuckle in the hedgerows and cloying oilseed rape in the fields; a summer of bruised grass in the midday sunshine and earthiness seeping from the river bank. It had been a summer of songbirds, exultant blackbirds and thrushes, and the low ululation of contented woodpigeons in the cool evenings; a summer of insistent bees and the far-off droning of mowers shaving suburban lawns; a summer of scalding evening sunsets and sweltering velvet nights. Now, leaving the river and heading towards the dark heart of the metropolis, we couldn't help but feel it was all over. Neither of us could avoid a sense of regret as the gates of the lock lifting us to the canal closed behind us. Cruising the Thames during such an idyllic period had been a bewitching experience. On the river the water had been bright and clear. When it caught the sun it had exploded on the tips of our propeller blades like starbursts in the sky. Back on the canal you couldn't help but notice how thick and oily was the water, streams of noxious bubbles rising to the surface as the boat disturbed the sedentary mud on the bottom. Occasionally the canal would eruct, making a sound like ketchup escaping from the bottle. From time to time it would send out a stench like a sewer, turning your stomach and making you want to retch.

This all makes Brentford sound dreadful, but this once-bustling old inland port has undergone startling changes over the past ten years and, as new developments go, it's not unpleasant

– though sometimes I feel I'll scream if I see another block of contemporary flats in the 'warehouse style'. For heaven's sake, do architects think they're being innovative designing them this way? Or does the fault lie with the developers who think they're on to a good thing churning out this old favourite for popular consumption as if it was a chocolate bar?

We started the ascent of the ten locks of the Hanwell flight with Peter and Jackie, a couple from Devon who we'd briefly got to know when they'd moored next to us at Hampton Court. They were lovely people and running into them again was typical of what happens when you're cruising; for you'll often find yourself repeatedly thrown together with the crew of another boat simply because you're both travelling in the same direction. These casual meetings and shared time together can be the basis for long and enduring friendships as we can attest ourselves, still having friends we met on the towpath decades ago.

Getting back to the canals after so long on the Thames was a culture shock. On the Thames the locks are worked for you by lock-keepers, so that all you have to do is stand around holding your rope and looking decorative, basking in the jealous admiration of the crowds who inevitably gravitate to locks on the river in the summer. On a canal – especially a city canal – your passage is likely to be met with a wall of indifference from the people you meet on the towpath who've got far better things to do and don't mind letting you know it if you get in their way. This is probably just as well, since in these circumstances if anyone were to start casting jealous glances in your direction you'd be well advised to secure your doors as quickly as you could.

The locks on canals are hard work too, which you forget when you haven't worked through any for a while. The

Hanwell flight consists of wide 'double' locks built to take Thames barges, so you can comfortably fit two narrowboats into them side by side. Working through big locks in company with another boat as a pair certainly makes life easier, but even so there's still a lot of hauling and heaving and pushing and pulling to be done. We'd agreed between us that we'd get to the top of the flight that night, but we'd barely got started before we came to the conclusion that we'd had enough that day and that we'd rather go off to The Fox, a lovely local pub just a step away from the canal.

There, after a couple of pints and a lot of inconsequential chat about life, death and the meaning of the universe, we got on to the serious topic of weed hatches which – like lavatory design and sewage disposal – is one of those subjects boaters always talk about incessantly when they're gathered together. Weed hatches are the boxes built inside narrowboats to allow you to get to the propeller to clear the rubbish it attracts. For obvious reasons they can only be accessed above the waterline even though they extend below it; and so to ensure they don't leak while the boat is underway they're secured by a heavy cover to keep them watertight.

There is folklore about weed hatches on the cut, or at least folklore about what you find in them. I forget the number of times people have told me about mattresses that have spaghettied themselves around their prop, or agricultural fertilizer bags they've dredged up from the mud which have taken hours to clear, or supermarket trolleys which they've driven over under bridges and which have trapped them for days. Supermarket trolleys have an emblematic place in the canon of stories about the stuff you find in a weed hatch. Today wherever two or three boaters sit together in pubs around great log fires cradling pints of ale they talk of supermarket trolleys that welded themselves to their propeller shaft with the heat of friction from the engine, or supermarket trolleys which have wound around their propellers in an embrace of death, or supermarket trolleys which emerged from the water in the shape of savage dragons, flying off towards the dark horizon.

Peter had a great story to tell about weed hatches. It happened to someone he knew – but then, don't all the best stories happen to people we know? Apparently this person, whoever he was, had his engine stop dead in the middle of the cut after his propeller jammed against something. After he'd struggled his way down to the weed hatch (they're never easy to get to) he hauled off the lid. There he was confronted by a severed head, the eyes staring at him from the murky depths below like something out of a horror movie…

We left him and Jackie at Bull's Bridge Junction. They only cruise in the spring and summer and were heading up the Grand Union to a boatyard where they'd arranged to moor for the winter. We, meanwhile, were detouring down the Paddington Arm of the canal into central London.

It's a tedious cruise from Bull's Bridge, a lockless length of 13 miles through the endless suburbs of Southall, Perivale and Park Royal. I mean, it comes to something when the highlight of a canal journey is passing over the North Circular on an aqueduct – even though it is always profoundly satisfying to see six lanes of belching traffic gridlocked while you fly over it all as if on a magic carpet. I couldn't be hassled with it and I went inside to read, leaving Em on the tiller. It was only when I could see the foliage of the trees in Kensal Green cemetery, a couple of miles before Little Venice, that I emerged again. I hadn't been back on deck for more than a few moments than we were welcomed to London by a volley of stones thrown by a gang of kids that we couldn't even see, let alone identify.

I gave them a piece of my mind, which is always a mistake. On the cut in a narrowboat you're only ever a foot or two of water off being a beached whale. You're vulnerable and you're best keeping your head down, both literally and metaphorically. Besides, you can never get the better of the oiks: slip off the boat and try and chase them and they'll either run off or they'll turn on you and you'll be the one doing the running. My futile bluster had the effect only of provoking another fusillade of missiles causing a few more chips to our new paintwork. But at least our portholes survived.

That night we sat in a restaurant with my godson and his girlfriend on the busy Edgware Road, drinking thick black coffee and eating baklava and pistachio cake after a huge (and ridiculously inexpensive) meal of kebabs and koftas and minty salads sprinkled with chick peas and aubergines. It was a Monday, past midnight, and though London can't claim as New York does that it's a city that never sleeps, it does go to bed awfully late a lot of the time. Outside it was as hectic as it would be in most British cities on a Saturday afternoon. Not just the restaurants were open but the halal butchers and food shops too, displaying their wares to the world on market stalls opening to the street. Along the road the clamorous traffic crawled along bumper to bumper while kamikaze cycle rickshaws hung with huge speakers blaring out Arabic music attempted to weave about plying for trade in what space they could find. It was night but it was as bright as day, the crowded street lit by the gaudy neon frontages of the shops and restaurants. Ours was Lebanese, I think. Or maybe it was Yemeni or Iranian. One way or another it sold no alcohol; few restaurants do in this part of town. Even so, along the pavement where clutches of outside tables added to the Middle Eastern feel, men of all ages sat sucking at hookah pipes, exhaling great clouds of sweet-flavoured tobaccos into the balmy night.

We were moored maybe ten minutes' walk from all this in the relative calm of Paddington Basin. This is a cul-de-sac off the main canal, just down from Browning's Pool at Little Venice, where a small island stands at the junction. Here we were sheltered from the commotion of the city by the skyscrapers that tower above the canal, enfolding it like a protective arm. Many of these buildings are the headquarters of big corporations like EE and Marks & Spencer and during the day their futuristic design seems totally at odds with the waterway underneath. At night, however, their lights reflecting on the surface of the dark water impart to it the colour and consistency of mercury, so that suddenly – somehow – the whole complex appears completely harmonious, as if the canal had been built as a water feature to enhance the architecture.

This is one of the great delights of the waterways: to be able to moor in the middle of the still countryside one day and then sleep in the beating heart of the city the next. We spent a week catching up with friends and being tourists. We went to the latest exhibitions. We saw the latest films. We were ravenous for culture and couldn't get enough of it. But this return to London was something of a test for us. How would we, Londoners, respond to London now we were living away from it on a boat. Would it make us homesick? Would we suddenly realise how much we missed it. Would it make us ask if we missed it at all? Actually, the answer wasn't long in coming, for after a couple of days back we both realised urban life was beginning to irk us again. After all, we'd left London to get away from all this and search for something new.

I soon began to feel the thousand petty inconveniences of the place starting to wear me down, as they had when I'd lived here. And one morning I got to the end of my tether. I'd been out to buy a pint of milk or something and I'd been jostled in the queue by a querulous woman who hadn't had the civility to apologise. But I could see it from her point of view. Why should she apologise? After all, what had happened wasn't an accident. What she'd done pushing me or standing on my toe or elbowing me – whatever – she had fully intended to do. She was just in a bad mood and taking it out on the first sucker she saw. You don't apologise after doing that. Apologising's for losers.

And then at the checkout whatever bar code should have been on whatever I was buying wasn't there, and with a queue building up behind me the guy on the till had to go back into the shop to get another one he could scan. I think he must have taken the opportunity to take a tea break at the same time. He seemed to take forever. As the minutes ticked by I could feel the mood of the queue changing. They blamed me for the hold-up; it was my fault and they were damned if they were going to stand in the queue much longer quietly waiting for me. Luckily the till guy got back into position before things turned ugly, but it was clear he was pissed off with me too. Well, of course, why wouldn't he be? It was my fault there was no bar code on the item I'd brought to the checkout, any fool could see that. He scanned in the price now as if he was raking my nose across a cheese grater.

It was only after I left I realised that, bar code or not, the plonker had overcharged me.

That afternoon Em and I upped and bolted from the city and before long we were back at Bull's Bridge where we'd left Peter and Jackie. We tied up that night past Cowley Peachey in the Uxbridge suburbs, 16 miles away; and the night after that we stopped near Watford, pressing on the following day to Berkhamsted, 40 miles and nearly as many locks from London. There we paused for breath, London finally behind us and the imperious architecture of Paddington Basin replaced by a towpath, its peace disturbed only by a familiar dog walker or a courting couple out for a stroll.

There are a lot of good reasons for stopping at Berkhamsted, or 'Berko' as the old boat people called it. For a start it has an outstanding butcher so close to the canal you can almost see it from your boat. He sells high-quality, properly reared meat and will throw in a few bones for stock if you ask him, which I reckon is always the measure of a decent butcher. Berkhamsted also has some terrific pubs – though I don't intend saying anything about them for fear that if I mention one it will reflect badly on the others. Go on a pub crawl is what I advise if you're passing through Berko on a boat. See how far you can get before you pass out drunk. Or before you lose the will to go on another step and decide that the pub you're sitting in can't be bettered so you might as well settle down there for the rest of the evening and mine's a pint please, hic!

The jewel in the crown of Berko – a rather hidden jewel since surprisingly few boaters passing through the place seem to know about it – is the Rex Cinema just off the High Street. It's been described more than once as the most beautiful cinema in the country, a wonderfully preserved and sumptuously decorated art deco building erected in the late

1930s on the site of a house once occupied by the Llewelyn Davies family. That's the same Llewelyn Davies family whose son Michael drowned in the suicide pact with his lover in Sandford Pool, which we'd passed months before on the Thames just outside Oxford.

By the 1970s, like so many other cinemas up and down the country, the Rex was on its last legs. It had been bought up by a football pools company, who filled it with fruit machines and made half of it into a bingo hall and the rest into a couple of 'studio' cinemas showing *Confessions of a Window Cleaner* and the like. Even then it didn't make money and it was sold to a property developer who planned to demolish it for flats. And that would have been the end of the story except for some enthusiastic locals with a good eye for publicity who conscripted film buff Barry Norman to head their campaign to maintain it as a cinema and restore it to its former glory.

After a lot of hard work it was reopened in 2004 and today the original foyer of the building has been transformed into a 1930s-themed restaurant which makes excellent use of the floral friezes and embossed cornices which somehow survived the neglect of the past. The cinema itself is approached from the side, underneath a remarkable projection booth which seems to have been tacked on to the side of the building as an afterthought. Actually, it was designed to maximise space but it also had a safety function in separating customers from the highly flammable nitrate film stock used in the past, which was so unstable it could explode spontaneously with fatal effects.

The cinema itself is gorgeous, one of the most luxurious you'll ever visit. Downstairs in the stalls is a bar with lush swivel chairs arranged around tables where you can socialise before swinging around to watch the film. Upstairs in the circle it's no less lavish, the red velvet seats so much wider and softer and plusher than you normally find in even the most plush of modern cinemas. But it's the screen and what surrounds it that's the star of this show, whatever's showing on the night. The proscenium arch is edged by a rim of ornate bronze, which stands around it like an old-fashioned bonnet, and at the side, playing the part of earrings, are scallop-shell lights set into the wall. The whole effect is to make the screen seem like a face, drawing your eyes inwards as if searching for features that aren't there, preparing them for the film to follow.

Still not entirely sated of culture, Em and I took the opportunity of seeing a few more pictures, including the remastered version of the 1953 classic *Roman Holiday* starring Audrey Hepburn, which left us light-headed as we walked back to the boat along the towpath. Perhaps it was Audrey Hepburn's loveliness which is almost too much to bear on the large screen, perhaps it was the beauty of Rome itself in the days before the traffic finally did for it, or perhaps it was just the elation of the frothy rom-com plot which celebrates personal reinvention in a way that we'd come to understand since creating new lives for ourselves on the boat. We felt frivolous and playful, intoxicated by the heady combination of the film and summer.

But it was then, while we were at the height of our good humour, chatting mindlessly about fifties fashion or Italian food or whether Gregory Peck was handsome enough as a leading man, that I stopped dead sensing something on my face.

'Did you feel that?' I asked Em.

She nodded. 'Rain,' she said. 'No mistaking it.'

Before the night was out it was hammering down, drumming on the boat in a way that it hadn't since we'd left Banbury. Before the week was out it had turned cold enough for us to light the fire again.

It looked like summer might be over.

CHAPTER FIFTEEN
Secret Worlds

I'd got involved with some humourless old bat on Facebook who'd accused me of being spiteful to the canal restoration pioneer Robert Aickman in one of my books. I'd spent too long arguing my case with her.

'Why, oh why, do I let myself get drawn into this sort of nonsense?' I asked myself in frustration. 'You never get anywhere with these people.'

Over lunch, Em could see I was grumpy. 'Why do you let yourself get drawn into this sort of nonsense? You never get anywhere with these people.'

'Oh, thanks for the support,' I said.

'You're welcome,' she replied. 'Another cup of tea?'

I'd been in a bad mood all morning and it wasn't anything to do with the old bat on Facebook. In fact, the only reason I'd got involved with the old bat on Facebook in the first place was because I was in a bad mood. But why can't I be in a bad mood? Does being on a boat living the dream disqualify you from ever being in a bad mood? It certainly doesn't disqualify you from quarrelling. Em and I were always quarrelling. We quarrelled all the time. We quarrelled about everything: what we were going to eat, what we were going to do, where we were going to go. I swear if we saw two dogs coming down the towpath we'd quarrel about which of them would get to us first.

You wouldn't know it reading this book, which tends towards Arcadian romanticism and sometimes glosses over the harsh realities of life afloat, but coming down the Thames we quarrelled all the way from Abingdon to Wallingford. On one occasion we started quarrelling over breakfast and didn't finish until bedtime – and that despite the fact we'd visited some stately old pile, done the weekly shopping and travelled 12 miles in the interim. Indeed, when I showed Em this chapter before sending it off to the publishers I have to report that we even finished up quarrelling about the quarrels we'd had – which must represent some sort of first in the history of the sex war.

Maybe it's not surprising: being shoehorned into a small space 24/7 is a recipe for disaster. When you're spending that amount of time together the potential for an argument is always there, lingering below the surface like a corroded landmine.

And it can explode anytime. When you live together so closely, it can be detonated by something as small and insignificant as one of you deciding, say, to sit on one chair when the other had been thinking – mark me, just thinking – of sitting on the same one. Or by one of you wanting to move to another part of the boat, thereby disturbing the other who'd just got comfortable with a book. Or by one of you (for the very best of reasons, you understand) not wanting to bother the other with a request to pass a cup of tea, or a magazine, or an apple from the fruit bowl, and instead of stepping around them, or squeezing over their legs, or edging behind them – thus causing double the inconvenience it would have been if you'd just asked in the first place. Even in a house there's potential for conflict between any couple, however long they've lived together and however well they get on. But at least in a house there's room to breathe. At least in a house you can get away from each other. On a boat you're trapped together and if, like us, you've had your own careers and are used to living your own lives, it can sometimes be hard going.

At first we thought it was just us, but as we began to talk to other couples we met along the way we realised that everyone felt more or less the same. On a boat, life for any couple is a constant war of attrition over limited space, fought with the same bitter commitment that nations fight for continents.

We soon realised we needed a strategy; we needed rules for moving about the boat. Firstly, there was to be no pushing or jostling for position under any circumstances. In the fight for space the narrowest parts of the boat became designated 'no-go' areas because dawdling there blocked any through passage. Places that were wider, like the bathroom, were natural crossing points when we were moving in opposite directions. Before long we found ourselves tripping around the boat in an intricately choreographed pas de deux, our stomachs tightened, our arms extended or held in the air like performers on stage in a ballet.

Even so, it didn't take much for all the carefully formulated rules of engagement to blow up in our faces. It happened a lot when we began to shift stuff around to save precious space, which we did all the time. The process usually involved moving some insignificant object from a drawer or shelf to another position, where something would have to be shunted away to make room for it. This in turn would mean relocating something else, which meant that yet more objects would have to be repositioned. And so on ad infinitum. Believe me, this pass-the-parcel stuff could take a morning and lead to complete upheaval in the boat.

OK, if everything went according to plan it could lead to space being miraculously saved. But that was only if everything *did* go according to plan. If it didn't then every relocation of an object would be accompanied by acrimonious negotiation depending on who the object belonged to and if its owner, guardian or appointed protector thought it was being relegated in importance. If one of us valued an object more highly than the other and thought it was not being sufficiently cherished, there could be much bad-tempered squabbling and throwing of hissy fits.

Nothing epitomised us at our worst so much as the incident of the oak magazine rack. I accept I was to blame buying the thing in the first place. I picked it up at a charity shop which makes new furniture from rehabilitated wood. But I didn't consult Em, which is not a clever thing to do when there are only two of you living in such limited space. I mean, it's not as if on a boat you can forget you're living with another person, is it? It's not as if you can wake up in the morning surprised to have company. Not when you're treading on each other's toes every five minutes.

The magazine rack was a couple of feet long and about the same height, and as soon as I saw it I could see that it would make a perfect replacement for one which had broken. Because of its design it had the added benefit of providing us with a low table for morning coffee or afternoon tea or whatever. I'm not a great one for shopping, but when I found it I was like a kid waking up on Christmas morning. I brought it back to the boat convinced that Em would love it as much as I did. I was wrong.

'You paid how much for it?' she asked. Her face looked like I'd put too much lemon juice in the salad dressing.

'It was from a drugs rehab centre,' I said, appealing to her charitable side. 'They make stuff in their own workshop.'

'I don't care. It's ugly. And it's too big. We've only just got rid of all that junk at home. The last thing we need is someone else's discarded tat. It doesn't fit in anyway.'

'How can it not fit in? It's made of oak, isn't it? The floor in here's oak, the boat's lined in oak...'

There followed a spat about domestic design, then another about functionality because Em thought it would be too heavy and difficult to move around. After that we were back to how much it had cost and how Em didn't think it would go with anything on the boat. This quarrel looked like going the way of all our arguments, cyclically and repetitively.

'Steve, it's ugly,' she said again, as if this statement of personal taste resolved everything when actually it only resolved one thing: and that was what the offending magazine rack was now to be called. Henceforward it would always be referred to between us as 'The Ugly'.

Arguments over it lasted a week on and off until eventually boredom as much as good sense forced us into a compromise. We would cover The Ugly with a piece of woven Mexican cloth we had, and if after a month we decided we couldn't live with it (i.e. if Em decided she wasn't prepared to live with it) we'd get rid of it. It was a close-run thing. A week from deadline day she was feeling as ill-disposed towards it as ever and I was considering my options for when she gave it the thumbs down.

Em, I knew, would be in favour of me donating it to another charity shop in the hope they could find it a loving home. I was more inclined to chop it up for the fire. At least this way I'd get something for the money I'd paid – and I don't just mean warmth either. The way I saw it, there wasn't a better way of me making my point at the same time as making her feel uncomfortable than by chopping it up in front of her and feeding it into the fire bit by bit. She might get her victory but I could ensure it was Pyrrhic.

It never happened that way, though. A couple of days before we were due to make the decision The Ugly won a reprieve after some friends came for lunch and the magazine rack that was also a table found itself conscripted into use as an emergency chair too. After that even Em couldn't find it in her heart to get rid of the thing, and so I'm pleased to report that The Ugly is still on the boat, still in use and still as ugly as it ever was.

Well, that's what Em still thinks anyhow.

***

Somehow or another, without either of us being aware of it, September had crept up on us. Mercifully the weather had improved since the cold snap at Berkhamsted. The rain had stopped and it had become warmer; the sun had even begun to show its face again, though it seemed more remote and detached now, without the warm smile it had worn throughout the summer. Mind you, we weren't complaining: by anyone's standards it was a lovely autumn, and autumn's a season that in its own way can match the attractions of summer.

We continued our journey north through Hertfordshire to Cowroast Lock, 42 miles and 42 locks from London, where the

Grand Union rises to its 3-mile-long summit level. It's fed here from four reservoirs at Tring, which have been nature reserves since the mid 1950s and are renowned for the variety of their birdlife. It's a beautiful walking area, which Em and I decided to take advantage of. We planned to have a late breakfast at a canalside cafe nearby, and after that maybe use our bikes to cycle up to Aylesbury on the towpath, along a short arm that branches off from the main line, too shallow for *Justice*. We keep the bikes mainly for practical tasks like getting milk when the shops are miles away, but occasionally they do have a recreational use too.

We weren't the only ones enjoying the day. Along the banks of the reservoirs and on the narrow causeways that divide them, fishermen were out in force; and as we were passing, one of them happened to land a 14-pound carp. We watched the whole process with fascination, since we'd never seen anyone catch a fish this size. It put up a good fight, and though in terms of national records it was probably a mere bagatelle, a thing of meagre and average proportion, to us it looked monstrous. Either way, it was deemed impressive enough to merit its own photo shoot, with other fishermen walking up the bank to snap it on their camera phones as if they'd been paparazzi and the fish some delinquent celebrity.

There have been problems with fishing around here, as we learnt when we fell into conversation with one of the local bailiffs. You'd have thought being a bailiff on a stretch of water around a nature reserve would be the most restful and relaxing job out. But apparently not. Fish – especially carp, which are eaten widely in eastern Europe – have become a target for organised criminals who have been known to use violence against bailiffs trying to prevent them poaching, something which in some places is happening on an industrial scale. Incidents have happened so regularly that emergency lines to report thefts have been established and some wardens have even taken to wearing stab-proof vests.

We stopped that night in the scattered village of Marsworth, where we moored underneath a canopy of laden damson trees. Tangled between them were countless blackberry bushes, so heavy with fruit that it only took us 10 or 15 minutes to pick ourselves huge bowlfuls of each, saturating the boat with the most delicious seasonal fragrances. That evening, sitting opposite the old village stocks outside the Red Lion, I spotted a Bramley tree in the front garden of an adjoining cottage. It was so loaded with apples they were kissing the lawn underneath, its boughs in danger of snapping off with the weight. I had a sudden image flash before me of blackberry and apple pie, the crust baked to a golden brown and glistening with sugar. I could picture pots of damson and apple jam too, and imagine it melting into hot buttered toast. It fair put me off my pint working out how I could do a bit of scrumping without the embarrassment of getting caught.

Eventually, in the absence of a criminal master plan, I decided honesty might be the best policy so I knocked on the door and asked if I could have a few. 'Take as many as you like, I'll get you a bag,' the householder said. 'It makes me so annoyed when people just help themselves. It's a pleasure to meet someone who has the courtesy to ask.'

'See,' Em said when I got back with them. 'More apples than you can use – and the moral high ground too.'

***

The trouble is that once you know summer's over, you become aware of the signs of autumn appearing around you all over the place. All these fruits of the bounteous countryside – like the indifferent, oddly unwarming sun – were a sign that the season was changing. But there were other signs too. We couldn't really see them as we went through Leighton Buzzard, which is a sizeable market town, but in the remote countryside beyond the suburbs we could make out a slight change of colour in the foliage of faraway woods and copses. From that distance you couldn't swear that the leaves were turning brown, yet they'd lost that translucent summer green and were darker than they had been.

However, the hawthorn leaves in the hedges were definitely yellowing, and the horse chestnut trees, which were shedding their conkers, were tanned with autumn too; although you can never tell with horse chestnuts nowadays because their leaf colour can be as much to do with disease as autumn. They've had a rough old time of it lately, what with bleeding canker and the recently arrived leaf miner moth, both of which can turn them brown in the dog days of July.

It was a long day's cruising but a glorious one too, and we moored up that night at Fenny Stratford on the edge of the fusion of once-small villages that make up modern Milton Keynes. The town gets a bad press in my book. I know that, from a car, its confusion of ring roads and endless roundabouts can be a nightmare; but from a boat you can cruise through it for hours without ever being aware that you're in such a major conurbation. The towpath is kept tidy, the water is relatively litter-free and the bridges are remarkably short of graffiti for a place that's a city in everything but name.

Milton Keynes cherishes its canal and it's made a lot of it, using it as a link between its many parks and open spaces. The canal also acts as a unifying feature to connect the many disparate architectural styles of the town, though if you asked people living there if they'd noticed this, they'd probably look at you as if you'd just beamed down from planet Zog. Even so, people respond to this sort of thing on a visceral level. They'll tell you that they think the canal's nice-looking, or attractive, or pretty; they'll say they find it calming, or relaxing, or comforting. On a half-decent day you'll see streams of people enjoying it, walking the towpath with their kids or their dogs; or if they've got houses or flats that overlook the canal, you'll see them sitting in their gardens or on their balconies, or just even looking out of their windows enjoying the view.

We'd stopped because we planned to visit what was once the government's Code and Cypher School in Bletchley, one of those rural villages which have been incorporated into Milton Keynes. Known variously as London Signals Intelligence Centre, Station X, and even HMS Pembroke V to the Wrens – the Women's Royal Naval Service – who were stationed here in the Second World War, it's best known today as Bletchley Park, where the most extraordinary combination of mathematicians, linguists, academics and crossword experts ever assembled spent the war decoding messages generated through the German Enigma machine – work said to have shortened the war by up to two years.

After decades of being designated 'ultra secret' – the highest category in Britain's hierarchy of security classifications – Bletchley Park has been opened to the public as a museum of computing. We've all heard so much about the place through books, films and TV documentaries that we feel we know it intimately. Even so, actually seeing it – in the flesh, as it were – is powerfully evocative and not at all the anticlimax it could be. Located among a predictable tangle of Milton Keynes roads, difficult enough for us to negotiate even on bikes, it's in an unprepossessing estate of wooden huts and prefabs, at the centre of which lies a lake and an over-decorative mansion house built in an ugly mishmash of styles. All the same, the complex has a dignified sense of the past about it.

We visited on a quiet midweek when it wasn't overrun with crowds, and at a time when the museum was more of a work-in-progress than a completed project, with many of the old buildings still clad in scaffolding awaiting restoration. I preferred it that way. Some of those famous wooden huts were much as they had been when the codebreakers left after the war and the estate became a teacher training college. They were derelict and their wooden clapboard exteriors were rotting, the white distemper flaking and discoloured. Even though you were prevented from going inside you could get close enough to smell that heady mix of damp, mildewed official papers and stale dust that speak of another age. This, for me, was paradoxically much more conducive to imagining what Bletchley Park must have been like in its heyday than the restored parts, which looked too unweathered to be authentic.

The star turn at Bletchley Park is of course the famous bombe, which took 13 years to rebuild and get back in working order. Bombes were the early part-electric/part-mechanical proto-computers designed by the famous Alan Turing to allow the codebreakers to decipher Enigma messages. At the height of the war there were scores of these complex machines at Bletchley working around the clock.

Knowing how important the bombes were to the achievement of the codebreakers, I've spent many long hours over the years unsuccessfully puzzling to understand them. Not properly understand them, that would be beyond me. No, all I wanted was to get a general idea of how they worked. I'd not been able to do it on my own. I was hoping a visit to Bletchley Park, with someone explaining it to me in front of an actual working machine, would do the trick.

Not a hope. The staff did their best to guide me through the complexities of it. They give demonstrations of the bombe at set times, and I went to one and struggled to understand the use of the wheel arms on the spindles and the relationship of the alphabet ring's turnover notch to the rotors. But it went completely over my head. So later in the afternoon I attended another – but that didn't get me any further either. I tried, believe me, I tried. I wrestled with the concept of wheel orders and scrambler positions until my head was spinning. But could I grasp it? Could I heck. Sitting an A Level in quantum mechanics would have been easier.

Eventually I gave up the struggle and let my mind fix on to something it could understand. Mainly that was the sound of the bombe. I couldn't get beyond how noisy the thing was. And how big and clunky. OK, I was expecting a machine, but not something that would look more at home on a factory floor. If that thing hadn't been breaking codes in the war it could have been stitching army boots. Or weaving uniforms. Or stamping out gun parts.

I realise I must have been about the worst type of visitor to the place there could be: one that wants to learn but isn't quite up to it, however much it's simplified. I walked back to the boat chastened at how slow on the uptake I was, and how bright the rest of the world was compared to me.

* * *

The next day it was early when we let go – as the old boatmen used to say. We were heading for Stoke Bruerne, the tiny but exquisite Northamptonshire village which lies on a flight of seven locks just short of the 3,057-yard Blisworth tunnel, the third longest in the country. This takes the canal under Blisworth Hill and towards Birmingham, where we'd decided to stop for a while on our way north.

There's only a handful of houses in Stoke Bruerne, but even so it's probably one of the best-known spots on the canal system, home to a canal museum and The Boat Inn, one of the most authentic and welcoming pubs on the waterways. The Boat's been in the same family since the 1870s and the landlord's got a macabre sense of humour. If he likes the look of you he'll invite you to 'have a drink on my old dad'. Sadly this won't mean getting a free pint on the house, but you will be invited to stand on a memorial plaque set in the flagstones of the bar where his father is buried, and drink one you've paid for yourself.

Opposite the thatched and honeystone pub is a short row of terraced houses, one at the end now an Indian restaurant. It was in this building that Sister Mary Ward, an icon of the canals, worked until her retirement in 1965 ministering to the health and well-being of working boaters and their children. Anyone who's ever talked to an old boater can testify to the reverence in which Sister Mary was held by the boating community. Boat people – who were more often than not illiterate – felt themselves outside the society in which they lived, spurned by people 'on the land'. Sister Mary was their lifeline to the world of modern medicine and though she wasn't trained, she used to care for them as a nurse, looking after the women during confinements, dressing the men's wounds and providing basic healthcare for the kids, as well as being a point of contact with doctors and hospitals for more serious illness. But she was also a friend and confidante, a much-loved and much-trusted member of the community who once said, 'You can't take me away from boat people. There isn't one of them wouldn't die for me, or one I wouldn't die for.'

In 1959 Sister Mary was the subject of a *This is Your Life* programme on BBC TV, which featured a large number of boat people who were brought to London to celebrate her life. Some 20 years later Em and I were moored at Charity Dock in Bedworth near Coventry, where many working boaters had been rehoused after British Waterways resolved almost overnight to get out of canal-carrying for good, leaving the boaters not just without a job but without a home too. This followed the Big Freeze of 1963, which had iced up the canals for months on end, and the decision effectively marked the end of centuries of canal transport in this country.

Charity Dock was a focal point for some of these old working boatmen who couldn't keep away from the cut and you'd often find them standing misty-eyed on the water's edge watching these newfangled leisure craft which had taken over the canals. At least one of the boatmen – John Saxon, from a very old boating family – had bought a leisure boat of his own. We became friends and since I was working at that time for the BBC he asked if I could get him a copy of the *This is Your Life* programme in which both his parents had appeared.

I searched the corporation high and low for that programme, and though I managed to dig out the paperwork that still survived from those years, including a rough script, I couldn't find the programme itself. In those days most BBC output, if it was recorded at all, was recorded on 2-inch-wide videotapes kept in enormous cassettes so heavy they had a built-in handle for carrying. They were expensive and had to be reused, which is what had happened here. A unique record of a lost way of life, and a very special woman who had a part in it, had been wiped.

CHAPTER SIXTEEN
Tunnel Vision

The image of English canals is bound up in the public imagination with a mental picture of the gentle English countryside through which they wind, but it's as well to remind ourselves from time to time just how much they cost in terms of the blood of the navigators – the navvies – who dug them out by hand. I doubt there's a mile of canal in the country where someone's not died, either buried under tons of earth in a landslip, or crushed in a tunnel collapse, or drowned bricking up the inside of a culvert. There's probably no better example of the human cost of canals than Blisworth Tunnel, which was a problem from the first and continues to be a problem to this day.

Yet looking north-west from Stoke Bruerne over the lush meadows that lead up to Blisworth Hill you couldn't image a more bucolic scene, with sheep grazing hedge-lined fields and fine old trees ascending to the horizon.

The problem with Blisworth lies not on the surface, but 150 feet below, where marine limestones, shales and marls (known collectively as Lias clays) lie on top of sandstone. This is not a hill you'd choose to tunnel through. Sandstone's a soft rock at the best of times; at its worst it can be little more than loose sand. Lias clays are soft too, prone to shrinking and swelling according to their water content, and the limestones within them transmit water easily, weakening the geological integrity of the hill.

Unfortunately when the navvies started digging Blisworth Tunnel in 1793 neither surveyors nor engineers knew this. Neither were they aware of the extent to which Blisworth Hill is threaded with underground streams, some of them very powerful. The result was that three years into the excavation the tunnel collapsed when the clays liquefied, blowing out the shafts and the tunnel lining and killing 14 men. The incident was enough of a tragedy for engineers to be cautious of attempting to dig under the hill too soon afterwards, and it was another five years before they turned their minds to the project again. By this time Blisworth remained almost the only section of the canal between London and Braunston, 18 miles to the north of Blisworth, which wasn't finished; and so a horse-drawn tramway had to be built across the hill as a temporary measure to move freight from one side to the other.

Eventually the navvies began digging another tunnel along a different line, which had been drawn up by the famous canal engineer William Jessop – though a couple of other unsuccessful starts are rumoured to have been abandoned before this. Jessop's proposal for the tunnel was to build 21 shafts from the top of the hill to the line of the canal from which excavations could take place in each direction. With digging taking place from the tunnel ends at the same time this meant there could be a total of 44 working faces in operation at any one time.

Surprisingly, given the fatalities of these early major civil engineering projects, the number of deaths on the second Blisworth tunnel wasn't particularly high by the standards of the day. A young man called Benjamin Ludlow, whose brother had been killed on the canal a couple of years before, died when he was overcome by gas, or what in those days they called 'the damps'. Two other navvies lost their lives when a basket pulling them up one of the shafts came off its hook. Others almost certainly died too, though history hasn't done them the courtesy of remembering their names. But why should it? These casualties were par for the course, the price demanded for progress.

But the problems at Blisworth didn't stop even after the tunnel finally opened in March 1805. There were other fatal incidents, one dreadful one in 1861 when the canal companies were experimenting with steam-driven boats and the crew of a vessel called the *Bee* was overcome with smoke and asphyxiated. A carpenter named William Webb and the steerer Edward Broadbent suffocated to death and two others on board collapsed insensible against the boiler, which caused horrific injuries.

The tunnel itself was never entirely stable and within 20 years of its opening, further geological problems led to the brickwork rising in the central third of the tunnel, which was always its weakest spot. The problems remained fundamentally unresolved for the next century and a half until the late 1970s when the brick lining failed once again in the same area, and for a while temporary timber supports had to be installed to prop up the tunnel until a full survey could be completed. This revealed the extent of the damage, which was far worse than anyone was expecting. The clays around the tunnel had absorbed water, leading to ground heave in several places; in addition, in the troublesome central third of the tunnel, iron-rich water had eroded the brickwork mortar, weakening the tunnel lining. If all this wasn't bad enough the construction shafts, which had been filled in after the tunnel was built, had let water percolate into the soil at the rear of the tunnel linings too, making it an odds-on bet that sooner or later sections of them would collapse.

There was nothing for it but to close the tunnel indefinitely pending repairs; and so between April 1982 and September 1984 – nearly two and a half years – the canal system in the UK was effectively sliced in half while Blisworth was drained for a major rebuild. Most work was to that vulnerable central third where the brick lining was removed and replaced by a new lining of precast concrete segments bolted together and faced with a secondary concrete lining for good measure – a technique that anticipated the construction of the Channel Tunnel.

With all this high-end contemporary engineering expertise being brought to bear, you'd think the problems with Blisworth Tunnel were now finally solved. And maybe they are. It's just that knowing all this about its history I still don't entirely trust it. Its problems have left it with a kink in the middle so you can't see all the way through it. When I get to this point – dark and claustrophobic with water dripping from the roof – I can't help thinking about the inherent geological weaknesses of Blisworth Hill. And I can't help remembering too those who were killed building the tunnel; though maybe this – the memory of them – is their ultimate epitaph, one far more resilient in the long run than any stone, gravestones included.

Em and I left Stoke Bruerne after two days. We'd have stayed longer except that deadheads from the Canal & River Trust were trialling a new mooring system aimed at controlling the number of boats visiting the village in summer. When we'd first moored up a couple of locks short of the tunnel we'd been greeted by ugly and unwelcoming 6-foot-high signs outlining some complex system of zoning regulation and threatening a £25-a-night 'extended stay charge' for any transgression thereof. True, there were a couple of week-long moorings where we could have stayed but they were further away from the pub and close to the busy A508, the noisiest and most unpleasant moorings in the whole village. We couldn't be bothered with it. Rules of this sort might be OK in July and August when Stoke Bruerne can be teeming with boats, but in the autumn when there's barely anyone around they're futile and completely contrary to the go-as-you-please spirit of the waterways.

It makes me wonder what these visionless bureaucrats in their sequestered offices think they're achieving by introducing them. It makes me marvel at how little they must know about the culture and past of the waterways. Using a sledgehammer to crack a nut doesn't even begin to describe it. Have they seriously considered the effects on local businesses of continuing these restrictions so late into the year? On pubs like The Boat, which have always attracted a lively trade from the canal? Have they thought of the consequences for Stoke Bruerne itself and the visitors it attracts all the year round, who come to the place as much to see boats as buildings?

During the couple of days Em and I stayed in the village there were just two boats in the restricted mooring zone, which stretches from the bottom lock to the tunnel end – a distance of a mile or so. There was us and there was Pat and Graham, who we'd last seen sunning themselves at Godalming at the top of the Wey. It was lovely to see them. We spent an evening together in The Boat. But after they'd gone and we'd left, Stoke Bruerne – one of the biggest canal centres in the country – was entirely devoid of cruising craft.

***

We stopped for two or three nights in Weedon, beyond Gayton Junction where an arm of the Grand Union branches off to Northampton, the River Nene and the flatlands of East Anglia. We tied up the first night on the embankment which overlooks the village of Lower Weedon, on a level with the Norman tower of the parish church of Saints Peter and Paul.

This was not a clever thing to do. It was bell-ringing night. We'd just poured ourselves a beer when, without warning, the chiming began. I was so startled I threw half of mine over my shoulder. Even Em, who has hearing problems, jumped like a startled rabbit when the first quarter peal, or whatever, began. Once we'd readjusted to the sound level it wasn't too bad. Even so close and so loud there's something about church bells that's reassuring. Maybe it's because if you had to identify one single sound that encapsulates rural England, then it would surely be this: a call to prayer which over the centuries has also been used to warn of invading armies, celebrate great victories and acclaim the births of princes – as well as commemorate the commonplace rituals of love. Admit it, you hard-hearted cynics out there, there's nothing to get the old tear ducts working as much as a young bride and groom emerging from a church with the bells ringing out behind them, is there?

The next day we went for a stroll round the village, a lovely place dotted with thatched honeystone houses and graced with a stylish, though severe, Congregational Chapel built in 1792. We were walking round by the greengrocers on our way back to the boat when one of us saw the facade of a building which we hadn't noticed on previous visits. At first it looked no more than an interesting house, but when we detoured to have a look, it left both of us staring in amazement. What lay concealed behind was a complex of buildings so unusual that had they been in London or Manchester or any other big city they would surely have been a major tourist attraction.

What we'd first noticed was a square-fronted Georgian warehouse topped by a cupola and faced with a huge portcullis constructed to block off an arm of the canal which at one time had run underneath it. Trust me, this was no frivolous bit of decoration such as you might see on a Victorian folly: this was a serious bit of kit, a key component of what had obviously been an important military installation. Behind the portcullis, the canal which once connected to the main line was now stagnant and choked with green algae. It continued for about a quarter of a mile, past eight other Georgian warehouses, arranged symmetrically four on either bank, until eventually it passed through another portcullis on the far side. These buildings were immense: 160 feet long and 35 feet wide, we discovered later. Each of them was two storeys high with an arched door and ten arched windows at ground-floor level; on the first floor, positioned to be in perfect harmony, were ten matching rectangular windows and a rectangular loading gate.

We managed to get inside to have a look around the complex. Despite its grandeur and the elegance of its architecture, it was looking decidedly the worse for wear and whatever it once had been, it seemed to be functioning now as an untidy storage depot for various local businesses. I had a smartphone with me and did a quick Google search. The place turned out to be Weedon Barracks and Ordnance Depot, built more than 200 years ago at the height of the Napoleonic Wars when Britain faced the threat of an invasion every bit as dangerous as the one it was to confront fighting Hitler in 1940. The depot was built by the canal as a similar complex today might be built near a motorway. With convenient transport links on the doorstep, Weedon could store huge amounts of military equipment, distributing it efficiently as and when required.

Eventually the depot had expanded to cover 150 acres. As well as the warehouses in which small arms and field artillery had been kept, there were four large magazines beyond the second portcullis where gunpowder had been stockpiled in a separate walled enclosure. The place had been big enough to have its own church, its own prison and barracks for 500 men. This was such a large number of troops to defend a supply centre even of this scale that there have been persistent rumours that Weedon had a secondary function as an emergency sanctuary for George III if ever he'd had to flee Napoleon's advance on London.

All I can say is that the large, elegant house called The Pavilion, which stands on the site, looked to me more like the sort of country house you'd see in the middle of a rural estate rather than anything you'd expect to find in a military garrison. It struck me as far too grand to be officers' quarters, which we are asked to believe.

At the back of the cupola in the main warehouse was a clock which, astonishingly, was still in full working order and showing the correct time. Its steady, purposeful tick made it seem, paradoxically, not as if time was moving on, but as if it had stopped, frozen at a particular moment of history. We clambered up the creaking wooden steps inside to see its workings, which someone obviously continued to look after. The device was mounted inside a cast-iron frame – a set-up both functional and beautiful. It was meticulously maintained, its complex mechanism of variously shaped brass cogs carefully greased. Presumably, because grease attracts flies which can clog up the mechanism, the whole contraption had been protected by regular spraying. Aerosol cans littered the floor along with unsavoury heaps of dead flies.

The complex had been built to do a functional job, but the warehouses flanking the canal had a symmetry and grace about them which, like the clock, transcended their function. The place was deserted and you could hear the echoing sound of birds singing to one another across the courtyard. It was as if a little slice of Regency England had survived the centuries; and you didn't need much imagination to picture a detail of red-coated troops marching up the concourse in their breeches and high boots, like supporting extras in the film of a Jane Austen novel, one of them – who knows? – some dashing officer who'd just eloped with the youngest daughter of a Bath family...

It seemed strange that Em and I hadn't seen this before. I'm sure many boaters will be horrified that we didn't know of its existence. On the other hand, I warrant there will be as many again who still haven't seen it.

But that's one of the delights of living on the canals and having the opportunity to explore them in a way you normally wouldn't have time to do. There's always something to discover.

* * *

We pressed on towards Long Buckby, accompanied by the increasingly noticeable M1. It comes so close to the canal at this stage that, if the wind's in the wrong direction, the noise can make you feel as if you're cruising up the hard shoulder. It was a blustery cold day, the quarrelsome squalls ripping the leaves off the trees and tossing them into the air like clouds of black confetti. The seven locks on the Buckby flight are always hard-going and that day they were as stiff and unyielding as ever. I was steering the boat but with stormy gusts sometimes catching the gates just at the point they were ready to be opened, there were one or two which no one could have managed without help and I had to get off and give Em a hand.

The flight, like the rest of the cut, was deserted, not even a recalcitrant dog walker to relieve the ceaseless solitude of the day. Above the top lock at Norton Junction where the Grand Union branches off to Leicester, taking the motorway with it, one or two boats had called it a day, moored up and lit their fires, the wood smoke dancing from their chimneys, the only cheering sight on what had become a gloomy and overcast afternoon. Other boats seemed to have settled in for the winter, even though it was only early October. They had supplies of coal in black plastic bags heaped along the towpath, stacks of logs neatly piled up on their roofs.

We carried on to Braunston, making our way through the damp embankment which leads to the 2,042-yard Braunston Tunnel. This is another tunnel that had problems during its construction and as a result it's been left with a curious S-bend in the middle. Needing to stretch my legs, I left Em to take over the tiller while I stepped on to the towpath for a short walk before we got to the entrance.

On my own and away from the boat, the day seemed even more melancholy than before. In the cutting the canal water shone an oily black and was thick with more fallen leaves than I'd seen so far this autumn, which made it seem even darker yet. It had started raining too, a thin drizzle you'd hardly notice in the open, but under the trees it gathered on the black branches overhead and fell into the water in huge droplets as startling as pebbles falling from the sky. Underfoot fallen acorns made the going tricky, rolling around under my boots like marbles before giving way with a crunch under my weight. I hopped back on to the boat at the last bridge before the tunnel, but as we edged into the blackness even the approach to the village and the prospect of a few pints before a raging pub fire didn't brighten my mood any.

We tied up a couple of locks down from the tunnel in the middle of the flight at the attractive moorings just down from The Admiral Nelson. We never did go for a drink that night, though. We had every intention but just as we were about to leave the boat, the rain, which hadn't let up all afternoon, suddenly exploded into an immense storm. It hammered on the roof and cannoned into the canal with the force of a machine gun strafing the water. Before long the towpath was sodden, reduced to a quagmire of mud and puddles. Even Kit, who'd been waiting at the front door for darkness to fall before she made her nightly escape from the boat, wasn't having any of it. For a while she stood on the step, balanced on her back legs, her tiny nose pressed against the window watching the deluge. Finally she turned back into the cabin for a period of desultory grooming before looking up at us with a haughty sweep of her tail as if to say, 'You expect me – ME? – Queen of the Cut – to go out in THAT?'

***

Braunston is often called the capital of England's canal system and it's not hard to see why. Positioned centrally on the system, with convenient access south via the Grand Union and the Oxford Canal, and north via Coventry and Birmingham, it's a place that's within easy reach of the greater part of the cruising network. As well as this it's got a couple of long-established boatyards, more marinas than you can comfortably count, a couple of decent chandlers and a wide selection of good shops, including one of the best butchers in the Midlands in the village and one of the best canal bookshops in the country at the Bottom Lock.

So why have I never really warmed to the place? I mean, it's not as if I've had bad experiences there, is it?

Well, maybe I did once when the British Waterways Board served me with a warning notice for not having the name of the boat prominently displayed on both sides. The fact that the name was displayed on the licences we are obliged to display on both sides of the boat didn't seem to matter. Neither did the fact the name was clearly displayed on the front of the boat in letters 6 inches high – so we could hardly be accused of travelling anonymously.

Then there was the time the boat was broken into just outside the former Toll House, one of the most prominent buildings along the canal frontage – the first and only time we've ever been broken into anywhere on the canal system. And there was the occasion we took a boat there for a repaint and came back to find that without any consultation the people doing the job had replaced the hearts on our hatches with diamonds. And then there was that incident when, without any provocation, some muppet with a moustache and a posh voice who I didn't know from Adam accused me of letting the side down (or something like that) by not polishing my brasses. And there was the time that… oh, sod it, I can't be bothered going through all this. I just never feel comfortable in Braunston, that's what it comes down to. I never feel I can relax there. We have too much history, Braunston and I.

Mind you, having said all that, the times I've had things happen in Braunston have always been in the summer, and walking around the day after our arrival on this trip, I have to confess that the autumn vibes seemed totally different and the place much more laid-back. It was still busy, as it always is, but it didn't seem as frenetic as normal and not as ostentatious as it can be with everyone feverishly polishing their brasses and buffing their paintwork to ever more lustrous radiance, which as I've noticed before is something of a local sport around here. Part of the mood music of Braunston on that trip was, I guess, that everything was winding up for the year and everyone was feeling relaxed about things.

We'd stopped in Braunston because I'd been nurturing plans with some old workmates to go for Sunday lunch that coming weekend. Two were travelling up from London for the occasion and one coming over from nearby Rugby. It meant that Em and I needed to stay longer than the 48 hours allowed on the mooring where we'd tied; but rather than just ignore the rules I had words with a lock-keeper I'd noticed patrolling the area – a retired copper, as it happened. He waved away my concerns. Despite the incomprehensible regulations in Stoke Bruerne, the rule in Braunston was that in the autumn all the 48-hour mooring restrictions revert to longer periods. Or maybe that wasn't the rule and the lock-keeper was just applying some old-fashioned common sense to the situation. In which case, all power to his arm, I say. A man on the ground with common sense will always act more reasonably than a bureaucrat in an office churning out rules and regulations.

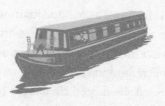

CHAPTER SEVENTEEN
Westward Woe

*W*e were having coffee on *Justice* with my old workmates after coming back from Sunday lunch at The Admiral Nelson. There'd been a lot of light-hearted banter all afternoon about some of the things we'd got up to when we were trainee journalists with a local newspaper group in south-east London and drinking more than was good for us. Did I really climb across the roof of Sidcup police station for a dare one night? Me? With my head for heights so bad I can barely climb a stepladder?

Now, as darkness fell and we switched on the lamps in the boat, conversation became more sombre. These are difficult times for people our age. A couple of us had retired already; a couple were on the verge of retirement. One of us, for reasons of her own, was intending to work for as long as she could. We began to talk about our plans for the future and in the course of the conversation someone asked Em and me where we were proposing to spend the winter.

This innocuous question was more difficult to answer than you'd have believed possible and we both shot nervous glances at each other and simultaneously screwed our faces into grimaces. It wasn't that we hadn't thought about the encroaching winter and how we were going to deal with it. On the contrary, I'd been thinking about it for weeks, and knowing Em as I did, I guessed she'd been chewing it over herself too. It was just that we'd kept our opinions on the matter to ourselves: where we were going to spend winter was one of those difficult subjects we might disagree about. It was best not to fret about it too much until it was absolutely necessary.

Insomuch as there'd been any arrangement at all between us about what we were going to do, we'd agreed we didn't want to spend winter in the south. We'd more or less agreed too – through some process of telepathy – that we were going to keep cruising, dodging around the various stoppages that take place between October and March when the authorities use the opportunity of reduced traffic to catch up on maintenance. But we'd arrived at this understanding, such as it was, in the middle of summer during a heatwave when the reality of winter wasn't exactly at the forefront of our minds. It wasn't as if at any point we'd ever actually sat down and discussed the pros and cons of cruising through the winter and arrived at any sort of rational decision. Indeed, watching the season rapidly approach, the 'decision' we'd somehow arrived at seemed increasingly absurd.

For heaven's sake, we hadn't even looked at the stoppage list yet; we had no idea which canals were going to be open or which closed. We were just cruising merrily north without a care in the world or a thought for the future. And official maintenance stoppages weren't the only problem either. The weather was getting colder by the week; soon the canals could begin to freeze over and if that happened it would make cruising almost impossible – as we knew from bitter experience. Not only are you unable to move through the ice, but taps freeze up so that even getting an adequate water supply becomes a challenge. Finding a place to empty lavatory cassettes is a nightmare too: pipes in service points burst, cisterns crack.

I was beginning to think that what we needed was a permanent winter mooring with facilities we could depend on, somewhere we could hole up until the weather improved. But how was I going to raise this with Em who would probably think I was wimping out now the going was getting tough?

After everyone had left for home we sat listening to the rain beating on to the roof. I threw another log on the fire and Kit shifted position against the hearth to take maximum advantage of the warmth. *What is it with long-haired cats? I thought. Is there any limit to the amount of heat they can take?* I took to idly speculating whether, if I actually put her on top of the stove, she'd jump off or just curl up and make herself comfortable.

I was still lost in frivolous thought of this ilk when, apropos of nothing at all, Em suddenly made an announcement. It was as if she'd been reading my mind. Well, reading it before it had gone to pieces with trivial fancies about the heat conductivity of domestic long-haired cats.

'I have to be frank,' she said, 'I've been thinking about it, and I don't fancy cruising full-time through the winter…'

* * *

The rain in Braunston continued unrelentingly for the remainder of our stay, but it did at least give us the opportunity to talk to each other seriously about our plans. And it gave us the chance of researching the options open to us. If we weren't going to cruise continuously through winter, what were we going to do? And more to the point, where were we going to go? There was talk about heading down to the Fens, which was an idea I'd always been keen on, and after some phoning around I managed to find a mooring near Cambridge through some people I knew. But Em was unenthusiastic. She'd got her heart set on the north and the hills. We looked at the possibilities of going to York, or Skipton, or maybe even Marsden on the Huddersfield Narrow Canal. But none of these suggestions was going to work for us. They are all lovely places but they all have their drawbacks as a winter base.

'York's been flooded for the last three years,' I said. 'And Skipton's been frozen solid. As for Marsden, there are always problems with water.'

Em was crestfallen but far from disheartened. The next day after breakfast she settled down to the task she'd set herself to find a place she'd like, browsing through our canal guides and surfing the net for information with an attention to detail that's typical of her. After a couple of hours I could see she was on to something. She became more excited the longer she went on. After a while she began poring over a canal map and scribbling on a sheet of paper. Eventually, and somewhat triumphantly, she tossed both in my direction.

On the paper she'd written a list of all the facilities we'd discussed the previous day as being ideal for a winter mooring. I couldn't help noticing that every one she'd identified had a large tick next to it. There was 'water', of course, and 'lavatory disposal', even 'electricity'. But she'd added a lot of other things too, like 'decent shopping', 'reasonable internet connection', 'good library', 'lovely walks'.

The place she'd homed in on was Llangollen in north Wales.

'And, remember, it's got to be really, really cold for the canal to freeze there,' she said, a reminder that the Llangollen Canal is a water feeder from the River Dee to Hurleston Reservoir near Nantwich in Cheshire. It was moving water, almost a river itself. The chances of us getting iced up there were so low as to be non-existent.

It was a terrific suggestion, and not just because of the amenities the mooring offered. The Llangollen Canal is 44 miles long and the most popular canal in the country, an accolade it's won for good reason. It takes boats from the heart of rural Cheshire to the town of Llangollen in Denbighshire, passing through the beautiful Shropshire Lake District and across an ancient peat bog before crossing Thomas Telford's extraordinary Pontcysyllte Aqueduct over the River Dee – the longest and highest aqueduct in Britain, a UNESCO World Heritage Site and a Grade I listed structure to boot. In fact the only problem with the Llangollen Canal is that because it offers so much to visitors it's too popular for its own good and most of the time it's uncomfortably overcrowded, heaving with hire boats from a dozen or so companies which start renting craft out when the snowdrops force their way above the ground and don't stop until the first frosts appear.

Wintering on the canal offered us the chance of experiencing another side of the Llangollen – a side we had seen once before when we'd travelled along it one Christmas with Em's mum 25 years earlier. That year it was almost as if the canal had been abandoned, so little traffic was there. It seemed remote and hauntingly secluded in a way I could hardly believe possible after the madness we'd experienced on it more recently. That year they had drained the last 5 miles of the canal and were digging it up from the aqueduct to Llangollen. After years of stoppages caused by landslips they'd grasped the bull by the horns and were lining the canal bed with concrete.

Em's suggestion offered us the chance of spending more time in Llangollen itself than would normally be possible. Because the canal is so busy, and the place itself so pretty, nowadays there's a limit of 48 hours on mooring there in summer – a constraint which is rigidly policed to give everyone a fair chance of seeing the place. Spending winter in the town meant we could stay for an extended period and explore the countryside around the Dee Valley where there are some of the most attractive hill-walks in Wales. True, we would have to rent a mooring and that would cost us an arm and a leg since, after London, Llangollen is about the most expensive winter mooring you can buy. But in terms of what we were looking for it suited us down to the ground. I couldn't help feeling excited at the prospect.

This time, though, Em was the one to sound a note of caution. The problem was those maintenance stoppages which had already started to kick in. Closures had started and were coming into force by the week. One, she had discovered, had already cut off a possible route to Wales along an easterly itinerary up the Trent and Mersey Canal; another was now threatening to block the remaining and more direct western route along the Shropshire Union Canal where a flight of locks at Adderley, 90 miles away, was due to shut for repairs in less than a week's time. If we were going to get to Llangollen then we were going to have to clear Adderley by the cut-off date and that meant putting our foot down.

We looked at the map again and did some calculations. 'It's not an impossible target,' Em said.

'No, not impossible at all,' I agreed. 'But it's tight. There's very little wiggle room and if we encounter any problems we're in trouble. It'll be hard-going too, there're more than a hundred locks...'

We looked at each other as if seeking validation for pressing on with this journey, which I suppose we both knew wasn't strictly necessary. I mean, we didn't *have* to go to Llangollen; we could have gone somewhere else for winter. We could have even stayed where we were in Braunston. But by then we both knew what we wanted and that was to go to Wales. We welcomed the challenge of it. We'd been pottering along the waterways for so long we'd become lethargic. We both needed a test like this to snap us out of our inactivity.

The fact is that although you're only moving slowly on a canal, you can travel a surprisingly long distance in a short period if you put your mind to it. Three or four miles an hour may not sound much compared to the speed of a car, but you can still travel 15–20 miles comfortably in a day, even allowing for locks. Over a week the mileage builds up. Ninety miles to Adderley in under seven days wasn't an unfeasible target; we'd have done it without thinking when we were younger.

So we decided to give it a go.

The next morning we were up and away at first light, our path lit by the menacing flame of a fiery red sunrise. We negotiated the remaining couple of locks in the flight and pottered through Braunston on tick-over, trying not to disturb the few other boats moored there, none of which had stirred yet as far as we could see. Turning off under one of the arches of the iconic double-span bridge built by the renowned Horseley Iron Works in 1830, we set a course towards Oxford before branching off near the village of Napton-on-the-Hill, where a famous windmill stands on the summit overlooking four counties. At this point the Grand Union veers north to Birmingham and it changes character immediately, the result of the modernisation programme that followed the merger of various original canal companies into the unified Grand Union Canal Company in the early 1930s.

The locks along this length used to be narrow, single chambers but after upgrading they were rebuilt to accommodate pairs of boats travelling together, and as a result they were constructed to a much larger scale than normal double locks. The paddle gear is distinctive too. The cog and ratchet mechanism of the older locks was supplanted by what was at the time a cutting-edge hydraulic system, the mechanism of which looks like an upturned cannon on each gate. This new system was supposed to make the paddles easier to wind by making them lighter; the reality was that you had to wind them twice as many times to get them open – an inconvenience which is still the case today. It makes the locks along this section hard-going, and allied with the weight of the gates, which are massive, makes progress slow and exhausting.

We went through the three locks at Calcutt, and after a mile or two's cruising through open countryside we were soon dropping down the flight at Stockton, where a further ten locks took us past the village of Long Itchington. The locks were coming thick and fast now as we descended towards Leamington Spa and into the valley of the River Avon at Warwick. After that the canal starts rising again, ascending the long hill leading towards Birmingham by way of the Hatton flight which is among the damnedest and most cussed lock flights on the whole system. The old boatmen called Hatton the 'twenty-one steps to heaven' long before Led Zeppelin nicked the idea for a song. It consists, as the name suggests, of 21 of these monstrous hydraulic locks, one after the other, with barely a break between them. Looking at them rising up the hill is a fearsome sight, like watching a troop of soldiers on the march. It's enough to make you go weak at the knees. Even at the best of times and in the best of conditions – in the summer, say, with a full crew – they're a swine to get through, although usually at that time of the year you can find another crew going in your direction to share the work with.

But this was the autumn. Nothing else was moving on the canal. We were worried we might have to work the flight on our own. You can imagine our delight then, as we were passing the now-derelict back of what used to be the old Queen's Head in Leamington, to run across Pat and Graham who we'd last seen in Stoke Bruerne after our night in The Boat. It was perfect timing. They were planning their assault on Hatton too. We arranged to meet them the following morning outside the house of a couple of our friends, Bob and Judy, who live by the side of the canal just around the corner from the bottom lock.

We've known Bob and Judy for years, from the time before they moved to the land when they lived on a boat with their young daughters. Not seeing them as often as we should, we tend to have a few drinks for old times' sake when we meet up – which is just a polite way of saying that we all get blind drunk together, trying to pretend that we can still knock it back the way we did 30-odd years ago. So the next day when Pat and Graham pulled up alongside us ready to begin the ascent of Hatton, hangovers were the order of the day on *Justice*. My head was ringing and my mouth felt like I'd been eating cat-litter. Em wasn't at her fragrant best either. She looked as if she might throw up at any moment.

Mind you, Pat and Graham didn't look too good themselves. The weather was filthy, a thin film of rain shrouding the canal in mist. This sort of rain – 'growing rain' as farmers call it – is dreadful for getting you wet. It seems to cling to your clothes and then somehow percolate through whatever you're wearing so that sooner or later you feel it caressing your back like the clammy hand of a stranger. Pat and Graham had already been cruising for an hour and done two locks. They looked like drowned rats. They looked cold too – but then it *was* cold, colder than I remembered it being for months. Frankly, if we hadn't made the arrangement with them I'd have been inclined to suggest we give the whole thing a miss and all go back to bed for the day.

But a deal is a deal. We made up the fire, we pulled on our wet-weather gear – anoraks, waterproofs and the rest – and we started the engine. Em and Pat had volunteered to do the paddles and gates while Graham and I steered the boats. This wasn't as sexist an arrangement as it seems: the two women knew that in these conditions you're better to keep moving than stand around on a boat which won't give you much shelter anyhow when you're constantly having to get on or off to lend a hand with the grunt work.

It was 11 a.m. when we finally got underway. I was still feeling a bit shaky and immediately hit the wall of the first lock. 'Rain on my glasses,' I shouted over to Graham who was cruising at the side of me. 'Blinded by it. Couldn't see a thing.' He looked at me oddly. Later I realised that was because I hadn't got my glasses on. Mercifully the locks were in our favour over the first part of the flight and we made decent progress despite the towpath having turned into one long, muddy puddle. The rain didn't let up; in fact it got worse, hammering down like stair rods now with such grim malice that by the time we'd got to lock nine or ten, where the ascent becomes steeper and the locks more frequent, none of us could have gone on a moment longer without getting dried off and changing our clothes.

We tied against the bollards in the next lock, which is totally contrary to the rules. You're not supposed to stop in locks. You can't block them for other boats. But who was going to be coming up or down Hatton on a day like this except idiots like us? We had tea and cake in Pat and Graham's saloon attempting to get warm. Me, I could have murdered a whisky as well – which says a lot considering the delicate state of my physiology first thing that morning. It also says a lot for cruising in bad weather, which is a cracking hangover cure.

It was then we heard the familiar beat of the engine of another boat approaching up the locks with a crew of idiots like us. It had been following us all morning, we discovered, though none of us had been aware of it because it had been so far behind and there was such poor visibility that day. We were mortified to be holding them up, but the crew waved away our apologies. They'd been stopping in locks on the way up too. They'd have stopped in this one as well if we hadn't been in it.

The rain finally eased off and we managed to struggle up to the top in pale sunshine which highlighted a superb view down the hill and over the locks we'd just ascended to the tower of Warwick Cathedral in the distance. Pat and Graham were drained by their exertions and moored for the night straightaway.

'Blimey,' Graham said as we passed him. 'If we hadn't agreed with you to do that I don't think you'd have got us out of bed today.'

I looked at him blankly. What could I say?

We decided to press on a mile or two, beyond the short Shrewley Tunnel where I had a vague recollection of a wonderful mooring on an embankment with a spectacular view over the countryside. But it was a mistake to go on, a dangerous mistake. We were both feeling better now the rain had stopped, but we were exhausted. Em was particularly tired, which was no surprise given that she and Pat had been the ones walking up and down the locks, hauling open the gates and opening and closing the paddles, each of which had to be turned 30 times to lift it and another 30 to drop it again. Feeling as we did, we should have packed it in for the day. We should have been sensible like Pat and Graham.

Em made us a cup of tea but walking back along the gunnels with two mugs clutched in her hand, she missed her footing and slid down the side of the boat into the canal. The shock was how deep the water was. Her head disappeared under the surface and she couldn't stand on the bottom. I saw her making panicky attempts to get to the side, and I became aware that the boots and waterproof trousers she was wearing were filling with water and dragging her down. She was splashing around trying to get to the side but at the same time trying to keep away from the boat until she could be sure I'd put the engine into neutral. She knew, as I did, that there was a danger of getting drawn towards the propeller – a potentially fatal scenario.

Falling in is an occupational hazard of boating, and anyone who hasn't done it can't really call themselves a boater. But there's falling in and there's falling in. In safe conditions and good weather, one of you taking a tumble into the cut can be hilarious: indeed, I've sometimes been known to disappear into the boat for the camera before I've helped pull Em out of the water. But on occasions like this it's far more perilous. People panic. They don't always act in the way you expect them to. *You* don't always act in the way you'd expect.

The boat had drifted past Em by now and she'd somehow managed to get to the bank. I engaged gear again and brought *Justice* into the side, expecting to see her hauling herself out of the water. But as I glanced behind I could see she couldn't get out. She was clinging to the side for dear life, her sodden clothing too heavy and the concrete banks of this canal too high for her to clamber out on her own. I couldn't leave the boat to itself, so I had to moor before I could get back to her and drag her out. By the time I got to her she was shivering with a combination of cold and shock, barely able to speak.

But she was still clutching two empty mugs as if her life depended on it.

I moored the boat single-handed in the first convenient place I could find while Em got under a hot shower.

***

The next morning we made another early start. The misfortune of one of us falling in couldn't be allowed to interfere with our schedule. If we were going to clear Adderley Locks in time we had to get a certain mileage under our belts each day. That night, day three out of Braunston, we moored at Cambrian Wharf in the centre of Birmingham under the shadow of the city's wonderful new library. It had been a heavy day's cruising, a trip of 17 miles and 29 locks, including three long flights.

We were so late cruising that when we came to negotiate the last of them at Farmer's Bridge in the city centre, night had fallen. It wasn't the first time we'd gone up these locks at night so we were chilled about it. There's something about Farmer's Bridge in darkness: edgy, yes, peppered with drunks and druggies. But exhilarating too. And visually striking, surprisingly so. A lot of the flight's floodlit and the colour and shadows of the light against the bridges makes it seem at points like a Mondrian painting with vertical black lines and horizontal splashes of primary colours.

I love Birmingham from the canal – which is some admission for me to make because I was brought up in the East Midlands where we were taught to hate everything about the West Midlands with a vengeance, particularly Birmingham. I used to think it a grubby, unsightly place, full of aloof, unsociable people speaking in an incomprehensible accent. This prejudice was, I suspect, more to do with Tom Coyne on *Midlands Today* feeding me news stories I didn't want to hear than any objective appraisal of the city, which in truth I didn't know at all, only ever having visited it once in my life on a school trip.

But I probably did get it right about Birmingham being an ugly city back then, something I can say now without fear of contradiction because Brummies finally came to that conclusion themselves and totally rebuilt the place. What they've achieved is remarkable. The canal at Brindleyplace, and around the new Mailbox development near where we were moored, is nothing less than a new quarter of the town, youthful, vibrant and animated. For a commercial centre the Bullring development is impressive too, and unrecognisable from the old Bull Ring Centre – that brutalist concrete monstrosity dominated by the Rotunda which for so long shaped the public perception of the city. This new Birmingham seems to have managed finally to come to terms with its Victorian inheritance, neither cowed by it as it was in the 1950s nor trying to obliterate it as it attempted to do in the 1960s. Yes, there's still work to be done, of course, but past and present seem finally to have integrated, creating a city which seems more comfortable with itself than it ever did.

We'd made such good time getting to Birmingham that we became overconfident: we decided we'd got enough time in hand and that we'd rest up the next day. There were reasons we wanted to do this. We had friends who lived locally; one was having a birthday party. She'd booked a table in an Italian restaurant and invited us for a meal. It was a celebration we didn't want to miss – though we promised ourselves that, since we had to make an early start the following morning, there had to be no repeat of the alcoholic excesses that had preceded Hatton.

Not that we need have worried. The birthday party proved to be a lot of fun, and next day we woke bright and clear-headed, relaxed and tranquil from our day chilling out.

The problem was that when we turned on the boat engine it wouldn't start.

CHAPTER EIGHTEEN
Racing Uncertainty

Compared with petrol engines in cars, narrowboat diesel engines don't break down that often, especially engines like the one in *Justice*, which was built in 1931 and was celebrating its eighty-third birthday that year. It may seem counter-intuitive but these older engines tend to be more reliable than their modern counterparts: they are unsophisticated and so basic that there's not that much that can go wrong with them. As long as you keep them supplied with fuel and change their oil from time to time they'll keep ticking over quite happily for years on end.

This is particularly true of our Lister JP3 because it didn't do much work in the early part of its life. In fact it's never done much work, if truth be told. Before we installed it in the boat, it belonged to the old General Post Office in the days when the GPO ran the telephone service as well as delivering letters. It was linked to three emergency generators, which kicked in when there was a power cut. We like to think it might have been used a bit during the Second World War for powering searchlights and perhaps during the Three Day Week too –

though that's just conjecture. More likely it was never used in anger at all and probably only ran for an hour or two a year during its annual service.

JP3s are powerful beasts, robust enough to push Thames tugs – the ones you see punching the tide when you're walking up the South Bank, the ones pulling half a dozen rubbish barges behind them. By comparison, for most of its life in *Justice*, this one's been pootling up and down the still waters of canals at walking pace, sometimes for only a week or two a year. The rest of the time it's sat in a dry and insulated engine room doing absolutely nothing. Work? This engine doesn't know the meaning of work. It's done so little it ought to be in the Cabinet.

I wasn't in the best of moods that morning when I went down below to see what the problem was. I am very fond of that engine but our relationship at that point was at a low ebb. I felt betrayed that it had let me down at such a crucial moment when we were chasing the Adderley deadline. We needed a Relate session. However – and doesn't this happen so often in close relationships? – I soon became aware that my unhappiness was all based on a big misunderstanding. It wasn't the engine that was stopping us going, but an electrical fault that was failing to start it.

Knowing this didn't make me feel any happier. It was a version of the good news/bad news joke except it was bad news/worse news. The bad news was that the engine wouldn't go; the worse news was that it was an electrical fault. (Pause while I scream and tear out my hair.) I know nothing about electrics, not a blind thing. To me electricity is magic, black magic at that, and what is worse, black magic conjured up by men in white coats. I remember teachers at school vainly trying to explain voltage and amps to me in terms of plumbing pipes which I didn't understand either. They were always going on about the 'flow' of electrons as if they were tiny Smurfs fighting for their lives as they got washed along the wires. As a result I was hopelessly confused. I was hopelessly confused now. I needed an electrician. And if we were going to get past Adderley before the flight closed, I needed one now.

This was easier said than done. Time was in Birmingham when you could stand in the Bull Ring and shout the name of the first manufacturing trade that came into your head and within minutes you'd be surrounded by a crowd of people asking you what your rates were. Nowadays, you start announcing publicly that you want a brazier, or someone to cast you a bearing, or heat-seal a ring, and you'll finish up in care. Electricians survive because their main work today is domestic not industrial. But even so they aren't ten a penny in the new Britain. I spent a morning on the phone only to find that every boat electrician for miles around was booked for weeks. I'd have still been ringing around now except that someone moored in a boat close to me realised I had a problem and suggested a bloke they thought might be able to help. He wasn't an electrician, just a boater who did odd jobs for other boaters. Good thing too, really. Otherwise he wouldn't have been able to squeeze me into his diary until June.

As it was he popped in later that afternoon with one of those boxes of tricks which measures current and resistance and probably the presence of nearby ghosts too for all I know. Someone with one of these things always reassures me: it makes me think they're in control, like a doctor with a stethoscope. I've often thought about buying one myself to keep my spirits up when I'm down – the electrical thingy, I mean, not a stethoscope, though I suppose either would do the job equally well. The problem turned out to be a simple one: the main switch from the battery to the starting motor had become disconnected. It was the job of moments to fix, but by the time we'd finished drinking tea and yarning about the waterways the way boaters do whenever they're thrown together it was dark and Em and I had to face the fact we'd lost a day.

Time now was even tighter; we had two days left for a journey that should take three. I'd said to Em in Braunston when we were talking about the feasibility of getting to Wales that we couldn't afford any hold-ups if we were going to get through Adderley Locks before the flight closed. Well, we'd had one and we certainly couldn't afford another one. The next day we set off before first light. It was a fine, dry morning and soon a pale dawn broke over the city, revealing patches of shifting mist hanging over the water. We were cruising roughly north-west, along what is called the New Main Line built by Thomas Telford in the early nineteenth century to replace the Old Main Line, which snaked around so much it was 7 miles longer. In those days there were 160 miles of waterway in the Birmingham Canal Navigations – the BCN, as us canal folk call them. Today, depending on how you count them – and that depends on how you define the boundaries of Birmingham – there are either more than 100 remaining, or 35. Either way, it's more than Venice, which is what counts to the Birmingham City Tourist Office bosses, who are determined that if there's one statistic about the city that everyone remembers it's this.

Telford's canal is wide, deep and straight, characterised by odd loops of the old canal which branch off from it, and by the many blocked-off old arms to long-derelict wharves. Hardly anyone was around at that time in the morning. There was the occasional cyclist making their way to work, and the odd dog walker as well, of course. One figure I remember particularly was a young lad in a pair of jeans and a thin sweater walking up the towpath hugging himself for warmth. It was eerily silent, the engine performing so quietly it was like a sewing machine. JP3s like these damp, cold mornings; they like deep canals. Or perhaps this one was trying to make amends after the previous day's shenanigans. Perhaps it blamed itself and was being apologetic.

The morning wore on. We drank tea together standing at the tiller and we took turns to eat breakfast in the saloon. As it got later we could make out the sound of trains in the distance and the far-off clamour of the city behind us waking up to another grey autumn day. But barring that, ours was a silent and solitary journey, slipping through a landscape that was peopled by the ghosts of our industrial past, a past so vivid in our imagination we could almost hear the din of the lathes and presses of factories we were passing, which had closed long ago and were now no more than derelict shells or flat, featureless plots of vacant land.

From time to time we passed islands where the canal narrowed to the width of a boat on either side. These were once toll islands where the canal companies collected fees from craft, based on the weight and the type of goods they were carrying. Millions of tons of goods every year in hundreds of thousands of boats. Eight and a half million tons a year at its peak, and as much as a million even as late as 1950. That morning there wasn't a boat of any sort to be seen, let alone a commercial boat. The hexagonal booths which once stood on the toll islands had been levelled long ago and now the islands themselves had reverted to nature, overgrown with weeds and tangled brambles.

In Smethwick we cruised under the delicate filigree of Telford's Galton Bridge soaring high above us, another product of the Horseley Iron Works and now a Grade I listed structure. Later we passed through the three Factory Locks at Tipton, which took us towards Wolverhampton, where an arduous flight of 21 locks drop down the other side of the hill on which Birmingham's built.

As we arrived there a boat was emerging from the top lock. Normally this would be a cause for celebration since it means you're likely to have the locks set for you all the way down. That day it threw us into turmoil. It was already past lunchtime and after such an early start we badly needed a break. But taking time out in those circumstances was a risk. Another boat might arrive and steal our place. We couldn't make up our minds what to do. Part of us wanted to ride our luck; part of us just wanted a sit-down and a sandwich. Eventually we rationalised that since we hadn't seen a boat all day it would be a stroke of bad fortune beggaring belief if one should turn up now.

Of course, the minute we sat down, one did. It meant that now every lock in the flight was likely to be against us, which would make progress doubly difficult on a day when we could have really done without it. Em, who had agreed to do the grunt work, set off on the bike to set the locks, leaving me to finish my tea, ruefully contemplating what might have been.

I love the Wolverhampton 21. They're not a particularly pretty flight of locks and they're not historically important either, but they are a critical link in the canal system as a result of their geography. They start uncompromisingly, wedged between the city's ring road and its railway station, and the first couple are dominated by the railway, which runs so close that you could, if you were so minded, hop off the boat and catch the 11.43 to Euston. But then they begin to spread out a bit, and gradually you find yourself in the suburbs; eventually it's something of a surprise to discover you're adjacent to the racecourse, where you catch tantalising glimpses of the countryside beyond. It's this I like about them: that the gradual progress from town to country, which you're so aware of on a narrowboat, happens so swiftly as you descend the flight. One minute you're as near as damn it in Wolverhampton city centre, the next you're cruising through a landscape that was probably busier under the Romans when the old Watling Street passed nearby.

Halfway down the flight we were disturbed in our labours at one lock by a shriek of delight from a girl of about 12 or 13, who happened to be coming up the towpath with her friend. 'Ohhhhhhh! I've never seen anything like this before,' she screamed, watching with some concern as I squeezed *Justice* into a lock with an inch or two to spare on either side. 'Wow!' she gasped, clutching herself in excitement and jumping up and down on the spot. 'That was so cool – really, really cool. Do you live on it?'

It turned out she was staying with her friend while visiting Wolverhampton 'to see me mum'. Though what sort of family fissure had caused the separation between them; and what sort of mother couldn't find a bed for her daughter when she visited; or what sort of a daughter didn't want to stay with her mother – these were things we were destined never to know. I just got a sense that at the core of this relationship was some tragedy and that the pain it had caused was still raw.

The two youngsters were curious about *Justice* and wanted to see inside. I'd have liked to show them because young people are fascinated with the small spaces of boats – which, when you think about it, are just houses built to their scale. Some of them are unashamed about asking you if they can have a look around; most of them are cagier. Either way, it makes no odds. We don't live in that sort of world any more, do we? We have to be guarded towards the young and they have to be cautious of us adults. Even so, I always feel sad on their behalf when I see the look of disappointment in their eyes. I could see it in the eyes of these two – disappointment and a certain amount of resentment too. It was obvious they thought they'd got the measure of us now. They could see we'd got so much and they'd got so little. As far as they were concerned we were just posh wankers up from London and full of ourselves. And they might have been right.

At the bottom of the flight we turned right, northwards, joining the canal connecting Staffordshire and Worcestershire. Soon afterwards we turned again, this time swinging a sharp left to the west on to the Shropshire Union Canal, the route to Wales. Here there's what's called a stop lock. This is a lock with a rise and fall of only an inch or two, the purpose of which in the past was to prevent water belonging to one canal leeching into another. There was an unexpected and surprising hold-up here with half a dozen or so boats queuing to get through. They were all going in the direction from which we'd come, most of them heading to Smethwick where the BCN Society was having a fund-raising bonfire-night party in a few days' time. We fell into conversation with a couple and their son in a small fibreglass cruiser. The young lad can't have been more than about five or six and he was already so excited about the fireworks he couldn't stop talking about them; and this got us all talking, chatting about nothing in particular. It was the sort of thing that happens on the cut every day.

But in front of them, heading the queue, waiting to get into the lock after we vacated it, was one man and a narrowboat. He was on his own, in his sixties, I guess, with a shock of white hair and prominent black eyebrows that were running wild on his face. You could just tell he wasn't going to be friendly: maybe it was something in his face, maybe his body language. As I left the lock he lurched into it. 'Hi there,' I said as we passed, observing the due proprieties of the cut. He said nothing.

Em closed the gate for him, which she needn't have done. 'Hi there,' she said. Still he said nothing 'Hi there,' she said again, raising her voice slightly. Still nothing.

By now I'd begun to realise that his failure to return our greeting wasn't just an oversight, or a result of a hearing problem, but a direct snub. Perhaps he thought we'd spent too long chatting, perhaps he was in a hurry. Perhaps, who knows, he'd been offended by something I'd written. My guess is that he was just one of those bad-tempered Victor Meldrew sorts who's always looking for an excuse to rail against the world. I've noticed there seem to be rather a lot of them cruising around the canals recently. I mentioned it to Em, once we were underway again. She agreed. She mumbled something about taking one to know one.

We pressed on up the Shropshire Union – the Shroppie, as it's generally known. At this time of the year it gets darker much earlier and it looked like we wouldn't be able to go on much longer, even though we hadn't yet reached our target of miles for the day. But then, without warning, the clouds that had been hanging over us all day suddenly parted like theatre curtains across a stage. Behind them, the sun was just dropping below the horizon, sending out a fan of blood-red rays across the countryside, illuminating part of the landscape as if in a spotlight and plunging the rest into darkness with that effect the Italians call *chiaroscuro*.

That night we moored in the countryside near the Staffordshire village of Brewood. As soon as we'd eaten we went to bed and the next morning we rose early for another long day's cruising. Still 25 miles and ten locks from Adderley, there was no time to be wasted. At first light we slipped our moorings, and were soon beyond the small hamlet of Wheaton Aston and heading over embankments and through cuttings in the long, lockless pound leading to Norbury Junction, so called because it was where the now-derelict Shrewsbury Canal once branched off to the south-west. We'd set ourselves a relentless pace, too demanding to be able to stop for any reason, so we were eating on the hoof and taking it in turns to rest. This was travelling with a purpose, which couldn't have been further removed from the gentle ambling which had passed for travelling on the Thames earlier in the year. *We have to get to Adderley, we have to get there*. It was a single-minded mantra, echoing through our brains, a rhythm as pervading as the rhythm of the engine. *We have to get to Adderley, we have to get there before tomorrow*.

The villages we were passing, the features of the canal, the very landscape through which we were travelling became irrelevant to us. All that mattered now was to keep moving. All that mattered was to get past Adderley Locks before they closed. It all became a blur. We must have gone through the famous Grub Street cutting where the embankments on either side become deeper and deeper, and the bridges across the canal become higher and higher. The cutting is one of the landmarks of the Shropshire Union Canal and it appears in a thousand holiday snaps, especially at High Bridge where no one going through ever fails to take a photograph of a strainer arch on which is positioned what's claimed to be the smallest telegraph pole in the country. But I was inside making sandwiches. I didn't even notice it.

It was the same passing The Anchor at High Offley. This is one of my favourite pubs on the whole canal system. Normally I don't do passing where this pub's concerned. On the contrary, I plan lunchtime stops around it. Or overnight stays. Or even, sometimes, complete holidays. That day as we cruised by I barely glanced in its direction. We were making good time, but not good enough; we couldn't afford to stop. The mantra had become a pulse to us, it had become the cadence of our hearts. *We have to get to Adderley, we have to get there.*

After some miles we arrived at the short flight of five locks at Tyrley, some of which are hacked out of solid sandstone so they lie beneath low, moss-covered rock faces shaded by a canopy of trees, which in the summer makes for a pretty sight. Late on a grey autumn afternoon like this, however, with dusk about to fall and the trees bare and their branches straining from a wind that has just blown up, it is a different scene entirely. The locks then are strangely sinister: the boughs of the trees swaying in the wind create shadows like moving figures and the creaking of the branches sounds like voices. You can't stop looking around you. You can't help feeling uneasy.

We'd hoped not to be delayed too long here: we were, after all, just a short distance from our destination, and like marathon runners entering the final mile all we wanted to do was get to the finishing line. But it wasn't to be as easy as that. Although there was barely another boat moving on the canal, one of them had somehow contrived to let all of the water out of the flight. This had drained the pounds – the short lengths of canal separating the locks – so that they were mudbanks, far too shallow to navigate. It meant we had to fill them all up from the canal above. This was an irksome and time-consuming process involving a lot of walking and a lot of waiting and a lot of work that we could have done without at that time of day. It was pitch black when we finished, so late that we had to limp into the town of Market Drayton a mile or so further on under headlights.

We decided to call it a day and moor there overnight. We were exhausted and figured that with Adderley so close we could leave early the next morning and be there before they closed the flight. The workmen were hardly likely to start at the crack of dawn, after all. They'd have to unload their tools and materials and that was going to take half a morning.

There was to be one further heart-stopping moment in this race to clear Adderley. The next morning when I turned on the engine it had gone dead again and wouldn't start. Em gulped down a sharp intake of breath. She had a look of despair on her face, a look that seemed to ask why, why after all these early mornings and late nights were we going to be held up here, just a mile or so short of our destination. I hastened to reassure her. It was just the connection again, the same as at Birmingham; I could tighten it easily now as a stop-gap measure. All it needed to solve the problem completely was a new switch. I'd buy one at the next boatyard we passed.

***

After Em closed the last of the lock gates at Adderley behind *Justice*, a feeling of relief swept over us both. The last week had been unusual cruising, but it had been a salutary lesson experiencing the canals as the old boatmen experienced them, constantly having to travel against the clock regardless of the weather, their livelihood dependent on these early starts and late finishes. We'd had a bellyful of it now, though. We were all for getting back to our normal sedate cruising pace where we didn't cruise at all. As a celebration we decided to stay for a while in Audlem, a village just on from Adderley, which we know well and are fond of.

Audlem is another of these lovely canal villages that seem almost too picturesque to be true. Set on a flight of 15 beautifully manicured locks that lower the canal from Shropshire to the Cheshire Plain, the canal skirts the village by way of a small complex of buildings incorporating a mill – now a shop and craft centre – and a pub, outside which sits a much-photographed crane once worked by a crank handle. This used to be in a railway coalyard somewhere or another until it was relocated here, and although it's got nothing to do with the canals it's somehow become emblematic of them. Despite it not being completely authentic to Audlem either, it appears in any number of photographs in books and magazine articles. But then little canalside in Audlem is particularly genuine. The pub, for instance, the Shroppie Fly, used to be an old warehouse and only dates back to the 1970s. The mill was built in 1916 during the First Word War. Architecturally, however, the place hangs together well and is very pleasing to the eye – and I doubt one visitor in a thousand thinks that they're looking at anything other than a traditional canal settlement that's been there for centuries.

But here, once again, we were brought face to face with the senseless mooring regulations that had plagued us since Stoke Bruerne.

We'd tied up at a signposted 48-hour mooring which – though there were no other boats moored in the whole flight – we were supposed to vacate within the stipulated time. Meanwhile, Canal & River Trust volunteers, who are all local people with the interests of the village at heart, descended on us handing out leaflets advertising Audlem's shops. You wouldn't credit it, would you? C&RT volunteers trying to drum up trade on the one hand; C&RT regulations moving on trade with the other.

We couldn't be bothered with the red tape. Bad regulation engenders bad behaviour. It undermines its own authority.

We stayed on the moorings a week. C&RT can sue us if they want.

CHAPTER NINETEEN
Christmas Is Coming (and the Geese Are Getting Out)

Christmas was coming; you couldn't miss it. On the way to Hurleston, where four locks and a large reservoir mark the start of the Llangollen Canal, we stopped off briefly at the old salt town of Nantwich to stock up with essentials. The supermarkets were piping out carols and most of the shops were already bedecked with twinkling lights, their windows festooned with tinsel. Christmas suits Nantwich. It's one of those places that look like a Christmas card whatever the time of the year. It's all narrow streets and wonky half-timbered houses, short only of an inch or two of snow to put the finishing touches to the place.

On the canal you didn't have to look far to see signs of the impending season. Some of the houses we cruised past had already put up decorations in their living rooms; one or two had laced lights across outside trees or under their eaves to create illuminations as impressive as you'd find in many villages. Even on the boats we passed – almost all of them moored for the winter now – fairy lights were appearing in windows. More than one had a Christmas tree, though given the limitations of space they were little more than table decorations.

The countryside too seemed to be dressed for the occasion. On our first day on the Llangollen Canal the sun was streaming down through a sky so clear that the light was as sharp as cut glass. When you get days like this on the canals they are breathtaking. The water reflects the colour of the landscape, amplifying it, so it's as if there's been some sort of explosion in the bowels of the earth and its viscera have spilled out in a chaos of burnished crimsons, browns and yellows. In light this powerful the hedgerows are a riot of reds and scarlets from rose hips, hawthorn and holly, whose berries glow like hot coals against its dark glossy leaves. There was another plant we kept coming across, a plant that we didn't know, with vibrant golden-ochre foliage and berries of a darker and richer and more intense colour than anything else around. I looked it up and I'm pretty sure it was a guelder rose. We picked some of the berries for decoration and they lasted forever.

The days were getting shorter now, and the year was flashing by like some unstoppable metaphysical truck on the way, literally, to God knows where. At this time in November it didn't get light until 7 a.m. and it was dark by about 4.30 p.m., pitch black half an hour later. A day of less than ten hours – and that's assuming you were up at first light and not, like us, stewing in bed until 10 a.m, sometimes even later.

The problem was we didn't set the alarm or wake each other; we weren't living the sort of life that justified it. Which is why it was unusual for Em to wake me the next morning, especially as early as she did. We had moored in the middle of nowhere; some spot with flat fields on either side as far as the eye could see. We were tied under an oak tree where the acorns hadn't properly fallen yet and kept dropping randomly on the roof all night, which is what I learnt later had woken her. She gently shook my shoulder to draw me out of my dreams. Then she put her finger to her lips and led me from bed to the front of the boat where she threw open the curtains.

I was greeted with a blaze of light as intense as the one in Spielberg's *Close Encounters*. It was the morning sun flooding into the boat – blinding enough on its own, except that morning it was intensified by the frost-encrusted landscape, frozen white to the horizon on all sides and fading in the distance to the ghostly hue of an undeveloped photographic print.

We put on coats over our nightclothes and stood on the deck hugging each other for warmth as we contemplated the quietness of this strange day that seemed to have silenced the birds and stilled the earth. The air was so cold it stung your lungs to breathe, and when we exhaled our breath came out in blasts, bursting like the smoke from a steam engine. The cat followed us to see what we were getting up to. With her genetic links to an American breed that was raised for the rigours of a New England winter, she even has fur growing between the pads of her feet for insulation against the cold. Even so, she wasn't having any of this sort of outside nonsense. She didn't do outside. Not in this weather, at least. She sniffed the air, twitched her whiskers and went back indoors to the fire.

We soon followed her.

* * *

The 'Big Idea' of the Georgian period was to link the four major rivers of England. It dominated the canal engineers. There was already a workable coastal shipping system, but if you could somehow join up the Thames, the Trent, the Severn and the Mersey you'd have an internal transport system too. You'd be able to move goods around the country; you'd be able to get stuff to the sea and export it all over the world. Most of all you'd be able to make some big bucks, as the Trent & Mersey Canal Company had proved in 1777 when it had opened its new waterway to general acclaim and heavy traffic.

The Ellesmere Canal Company wanted a slice of the action too. It proposed its own canal to connect the Mersey to the River Severn at Shrewsbury. In addition there would be branches and arms built: to the town of Whitchurch and the village of Prees, to the coalfields of Ruabon and the limestone quarries at Llanymynech.

Everybody got terribly excited about the project but, unlike the Trent and Mersey, this canal never happened. It got bogged down in detail as Big Ideas often do. In 1797 the company built a link to connect Chester to the small fishing village of Netherpool on the Mersey, and to commemorate it they changed the name of the place to Ellesmere Port. An 18-mile section from Trevor towards Shrewsbury was built too. But the two sections were never connected, separated by the engineering problems posed by the valley of the river Dee. When this obstacle was finally overcome by the construction of Telford's extraordinary aqueduct in 1805 it was too late, as it was impossible to raise enough money to make the link. By then Britain was fast approaching the Railway Age when the focus of the country's transport system would leave canals a thing of the past.

Meanwhile, in a desperate attempt to connect itself to the rest of the canal system, the company extended an arm past the towns of Ellesmere and Whitchurch to connect with the Chester Canal at Hurleston.

Today, the canal from Chester to Ellesmere Port survives; but like some Ozymandias of a lost age, the only other bit of the ambitious Ellesmere Canal Company undertaking which is properly navigable is the section between Hurleston and Trevor, along which Em and I were cruising. It's come to be called the Llangollen Canal – though no one ever intended it should go to Llangollen, which at that time was a tiny drovers' settlement. But canals need water and the top end of the current canal at Llangollen is actually not a proper canal at all but a navigable 'feeder' built to tap into the limitless supply of water percolating from the surrounding mountains to the young River Dee.

***

We moored that night at Wrenbury, where there are a couple of nice pubs on the canal which we've used in the past. On this occasion, however, we were planning to go further afield and eat at a place called the Bhurtpore Inn, which had been recommended to us by a boater in Nantwich. It was a good couple of miles from the canal and we walked there along dark country lanes without footpaths where the traffic drove by so close and so fast you could feel the wind of it in your face as it was passing. It was such a hair-raising hike that the first chance we got afterwards we bought ourselves high-visibility tabards in case we ever had to do anything similar again. By the time we got to the pub we were wondering if it was all worth it. Going for a drink is one thing; having to risk your life for one is a different matter entirely.

OK, I know I'm one of those well-off retired the Department of Health is always banging on about as being at risk from alcohol abuse, but there are limits even for me. Around about four pints generally, since you ask. But don't go running away with the idea that I can't do without it, especially if I have to risk being mown down by a car. I don't want to be mown down by a car. I want to have my chance of catching Alzheimer's like everyone else.

Judging by its name you'd think the Bhurtpore was an Indian restaurant of the sort you'll find all over the place in contemporary Britain. In fact it's a long established local in the tiny Cheshire hamlet of Aston, otherwise known as Aston in Wrenbury, or Aston by Wrenbury, or sometimes Aston near Audlem, or occasionally Aston in Newhall. This is not to be confused with other Cheshire villages like Aston Vale Royal, Aston by Budworth and Aston juxta Mondrum. Aston, you feel, is a village that is somewhat unconfident of its place in the world.

The unusual name of the pub originates from the exploits of one of the local gentry, Field Marshal Sir Stapleton Cotton, a close associate of the Duke of Wellington. In 1826 Cotton led the successful siege of the Rajasthani town of Bhurtpore (now Bharatpur), which was thought to be impregnable. For this he was made Viscount Combermere of Bhurtpore, one of that select bunch of soldier-peers like Mountbatten of Burma and Montgomery of Alamein whose military achievements became incorporated into their titles.

There's an interesting story told in Cheshire about Combermere who, in advance of the siege, ordered the main canal feeding the defensive ditches in the fortress to be blocked off. Make of the story what you will, but it's claimed locally that this fulfilled an ancient Brahmin prophecy that the city would never fall until a crocodile drank the moat dry, the Sanskrit word for crocodile being transcribed as *combeer*.

Except that I couldn't find a Sanskrit word *combeer* meaning crocodile. Mind you, I did dig one up on Google transcribed as *kumbhira*, which I guess with a posh accent and enough regimental claret might just about be made to sound like Combermere. However, I'd feel more confident with the story if, in this ancient and rich language of classical India, there weren't at least 20 other words for crocodile, most of which sound nothing like Combermere. Still, who am I to rain on the parade – especially when it's a military one?

The food at the pub was as good as we'd been told it would be, and the selection of beers was outstanding. But in terms of personal customer service, what stood out for me was the kindness of the landlord who heard of our perilous journey along the local roads and insisted on driving us back to the boat in his car.

It's just not the sort of thing that happens a lot back home in London. If you're driven home there it's generally in a black car. And you have to pay through the nose for it.

***

One of the most remarkable things about the Llangollen Canal is that, though it begins in the flat Cheshire Plain and ends in the Welsh mountains 44 miles away, it only has 21 locks. When you consider that other canals going into the hills – like some of those across the Pennines, for example – are almost like continuous lock flights, this demonstrates how much this canal is a triumph of the surveyor's art. As a result it's not a hard canal to cruise. It doesn't leave you on your knees exhausted after a holiday, needing another holiday to get over your exertions. This is another of those features that attract visitors. But it has its downside. With so few locks to delay progress many hire boats hare up the canal and back again in a week, fixed on the idea of crossing the aqueduct and seeing Llangollen and missing most else of what it has to offer.

We moved the next day a couple of miles further up the canal to Marbury, which is one of the places that tends to get overlooked by a lot of holiday boaters. This is a great shame. The place is a hidden gem, and if that sounds too much like a cliché, then you'll just have to get used to it because everything about Marbury is a cliché.

It's a tiny hamlet with just a handful of houses and farms scattered around two lakes – or meres, as they're known in this neck of the woods. The focus is the village green, which is shaded by a 100-year-old spreading oak tree with a seat encircling its trunk. Facing it are a couple of half-timbered houses and a pub, the Swan Inn, which was rebuilt in 1880, but originally used to be a farmhouse until some far-sighted tenant in the past realised the way British agriculture was going and decided to get out early.

Predictably, because Christianity and alcohol always seem to go hand in hand in England, just around the corner is the fifteenth-century village church of St Michael's, a red sandstone building with a squat tower, and a lych gate built as a memorial to those who fell in the First World War and inscribed with one of John Maxwell Edmonds' poignant epigrams:

Ye who live on, mid English pastures green.
Remember us and think what might have been.

The church sits on a hill commanding a fine view of the larger of the two lakes, known as Big Mere. If you're not expecting it – and Em and I weren't expecting it when we first visited many years ago – the prospect comes as a complete surprise. One minute you're walking around the side of the church looking at the gravestones; the next you're faced with this extraordinary vista stretching out before you. You seem to be much higher up than you actually are, looking across a landscape of copses and gently undulating farmland. In the summer it has a unique tranquillity that's drawn us back to it whenever we've travelled the canal; but even in the winter it has a rugged charm of its own that's equally attractive.

You can scarcely credit that places like Marbury exist in the twenty-first century. It's so far removed from the contemporary world that it didn't get a water or electricity supply until the 1930s; until then it was candles and the village pump.

We walked along the edge of the mere, no easy job when the path stops halfway round and the rest of the route this time of the year is across fields with mud up to your knees. If you know what you're looking for, you can see from the other side of the mere that the church tower sits awkwardly on the church, as if it's leaning slightly. That's because it *is* leaning slightly. Well, more than slightly, actually. It's out of true by more than 2 feet, Cheshire's answer to Pisa.

We made our way back to the boat while above us flocks of birds too far away to identify danced in the sky like ashes rising from a bonfire. There must have been a thousand of them, maybe more, how could you tell? They dipped, they dropped, they splayed outwards in sweeping layers before they regrouped, impelled by some common purpose beyond our understanding. Watching them, they became less a group of individual birds and more a constantly changing inanimate pattern, strangely hypnotic to watch.

What on earth were they doing? What was this incomprehensible aerial game they were playing? Were they just doing it for the heady thrill of flight itself, just to experience the lift and fall of the wind? Or was this some winter ritual of their own invention, some adjunct to their own identity as a group? We hadn't got time to puzzle it out. During the afternoon it had clouded over, and now it was beginning to rain. It was getting dark too, darker than it had been yesterday and darker than it was a week before. It made us feel like primitives, like early man who could only watch and fear the passing of the seasons without any scientific explanation of its cause. We began to doubt the drift into darkness would ever stop. We began to think we'd be cast into eternal night.

And of course, taking the pessimistic view, we will be soon enough, as we all will in time. But on the bright side the Swan would be open soon and we could have a walk back there after dinner.

* * *

We went on to Whitchurch by way of Grindley Brook on the border of Shropshire and Cheshire, where six locks – almost a third of the locks on the whole canal – are concentrated. Three are ordinary locks, three are in a staircase, and in total they lift the canal another 40 feet closer to Wales. These staircases can be fun if you know what you're doing. They can be fun even if you don't, as long as you're not on a boat. The front gates of one are the back gates of the next, which is a nice break to the routine if you're an experienced boater, but which is a nightmare if you're on a hire boat early on in your holiday and have only just got used to normal locks. Generally there's a lock-keeper around to prevent you swamping the adjacent A41 and killing yourself, because if you get it wrong the staircase can quickly turn into a waterfall, as I can attest since I once made a film here and was allowed to flood it.

But people don't always take any notice of the lock-keeper. They get impatient. They try and jump the queue. He can't be in two places at the same time and so sometimes when he's helping a boat come up the staircase, another boat at the top will attempt to come down it at the same time.

There's a convenient cafe at Grindley Brook where you can sit with a pot of tea and a toasted teacake and see exactly why that's impossible, and what chaos can ensue when some idiot thinks it isn't. But even if you're not privileged to see a full-on face-off in the staircase, you'd be unlucky in the summer not to see some form of altercation since up to a hundred boats a day can pass through the locks and waits of two and three hours are not uncommon. People tend to get a bit tetchy after that time, especially when the kids are griping and the boat's due back in two days and it's a three-day trip back to the hire base. By then they're asking themselves why they came on a canal holiday at all...

When we passed through the locks, the canal was almost deserted – as it had been for most of our journey so far. Because a number of stoppages were scheduled on the Llangollen for the new year, including one at these locks, the only boats moving apart from us were those few travelling in the opposite direction away from Llangollen, trying to avoid getting trapped for the rest of the winter.

We slipped through the locks in under an hour, which many people with experience of summers at Grindley Brook may find completely implausible. But they'll have to take my word for it, it *is* possible.

***

Whitchurch is one of my favourite places on the Llangollen Canal. I can't help but have a soft spot for a town named after a white church when its parish church, St Alkmund's, is actually a lurid shade of red sandstone. That's because the original white one collapsed suddenly in 1711, which – if I was the vicar of St Michael's in Marbury with its leaning tower – might give me pause for thought about the competence of Shropshire builders.

The town's not generally popular among boaters except as an emergency supply point when food and drink are running low. It's too far from the canal, and although it used to have an arm that went to a terminus closer to the centre, that was closed in 1939 and not reopened when the main canal was resurrected in 1955 by the Mid & South East Cheshire Water Board as a feeder to their reservoir at Hurleston. Now boaters have to walk a mile or so to the pubs and shops and they can be a lazy bunch so many of them prefer to go on to Ellesmere, further up the canal, where there's a supermarket on the water's edge.

Well, let them go, I say. Good riddance. It leaves Whitchurch more of a genuine Salopian market town living on its own resources rather that dependent on passing tourist trade. There's been a scheme for years to attract people by restoring the arm all the way back to its old terminus, and who knows, one day this might happen. In the interim, the Whitchurch

Waterways Trust, which is heading the restoration, has set its sights on a more modest plan to extend it a hundred yards or so under a bridge where it hopes to be able to build a new basin with moorings.

Until then the route from the canal to Whitchurch is through an attractive country park where you can still see endangered water voles. The path to town brings you out near St Alkmund's, which dominates the hill on which this part of the town is built. From here you drop down the sloping High Street to the centre, past a series of buildings dating from every era since Tudor times. And extraordinarily – with just one exception – they all seem to fit together organically, as if someone had sat down and planned it that way.

The exception, predictably, is the new town hall built in our own times, which is an unsympathetic mess of an eyesore, totally out of character with its surroundings. As if the design of the building wasn't bad enough, it's partly raised and set back slightly from the street, which emphasises its ugly blockishness. There was improvement work going on while we were there, which was just throwing good money after bad as far as I could see. In this area where agriculture is the most important industry, the council should know that however much lipstick you put on a pig it will still be a pig.

The new town hall notwithstanding, Whitchurch looked a picture at this time of year. The shop windows were twinkling with seasonal decorations and there was a general air of affluence about the place. Even on midweek days, when a lot of similar-sized places are so empty they're like ghost towns, Whitchurch was busy, its shops buzzing.

Even so, there's a vein of poverty in these small rural towns which you'd be blind not to see. In Whitchurch one afternoon we almost got knocked over by a thief running out of a supermarket with a bottle of spirits in each hand. There were food banks inside the supermarkets and one in the church too. In other towns you find pawnbrokers and shops offering payday loans. Some places are so impoverished there are more charity shops than commercial businesses.

We stayed in Whitchurch a week and on the Saturday the town had its Christmas Fayre, with a stage set up underneath the town clock where bands played and choirs sang throughout the day. The clock was made up the road by a company called W. B. Joyce. Once one of the most famous companies in the country, it made tower clocks for such impressive public buildings across the globe as Worcester Cathedral, the Shanghai Customs House and the beautiful General Post Office in Sydney. The factory's closed now, of course, like so many of these places where our reputation as a craft nation resided. But at least it was sold to another British company, which is about as much as you can hope for nowadays.

The day of the Christmas Fayre was also the day of the formal switch-on of the town lights. The High Street had been closed off to traffic and down its whole length were stalls on either side selling Christmas food and drink, toys and gifts. People milled about, browsing, chatting with the stallholders or gossiping with friends. There was a real sense of community about the event, a feeling of neighbourliness in the air that didn't exclude us as visitors. People wanted to know where we were from and what we were doing and what we thought of their town. Eventually, as soon as twilight settled, the mayor or whoever it was flicked a switch and the town burst into light, arcs of illumination across the High

Street suddenly transforming it into a glowing arcade up the hill to the floodlit church.

* * *

Whitchurch has a train station and we used it to go to the town of Wem, where we wanted to check out a cattery in case we had to leave Kit for a day or two over Christmas. It was early closing day. Well, no; strictly speaking, as we discovered, every day is early closing day in Wem. It was a little after 3 p.m. when we finished our business, and we were gagging for a cup of tea. The first place we tried was a bijou shop selling smelly candles and glassware which had a cafe attached. The shop was open; it had a sign on the door saying it was open and I didn't doubt for one moment that it was. It was open until five, six some nights, apparently. Even longer now it was getting towards Christmas.

The problem, however, was that although the shop was open the cafe wasn't. The owner was a chirpy young woman with a warm smile and a steely way about her. 'We're closed,' she said. 'Until tomorrow,' she added, with a rhetorical flourish you'd expect from someone in Wem where the eloquent literary essayist William Hazlitt lived for two years.

I couldn't understand what she meant by closed. I mean, there she was standing in front of us, dressed in an apron and her smile, leaning on a glass-fronted counter that contained a selection of biscuits and delicious-looking cakes. Behind her was a small kitchen where there was probably a wide variety of teas, coffees and herbal infusions. There was doubtless a kettle there too, in all probability water as well. If this was closed, I couldn't see what open was. Maybe open was when the band started playing. Perhaps it was when the clowns appeared and the acrobats began performing.

'We're closed,' she said once more with that precise economy of style Hazlitt had pioneered. 'Try over the road.'

Over the road turned out to be open too, the door so open it was swinging on its hinges. This wasn't as nice a cafe, all Formica tables and the smell of chips in the air. Not that it mattered to us, as long as we could get some tea. But before we could get inside our way was blocked by a bossy harridan sporting a mop. 'We're closed,' she said. 'But we only want a cup of tea,' I protested, 'and it is tea time.' 'Sorry,' she said when she obviously wasn't.

We finally managed to get tea inside the civic centre, but when we decided halfway through the pot that we'd have a slice of cake to go with it, they'd shut up shop and wouldn't serve us either.

We caught the early train back to Whitchurch.

The next morning, a dull and grey day, we slipped our moorings early, passing Prees Junction and a short arm that leads to a boatyard built around a disused pit where clay was once dug to make the canal watertight. We were soon crossing the melancholy wastes of Whixall Moss, one of the last remaining peat bogs in England. When we first visited the canal, peat was still being extracted commercially for horticulture; but in 1996 it was declared a national nature reserve and after that the silver birches which colonised it were steadily cut back so that now, from the canal, you look over a bleak and desolate topography that doesn't invite you to linger long though a walk across it is well worth the effort. Before long the canal begins its approach to Ellesmere. It skirts Cole Mere and afterwards almost touches Blake Mere, where just a narrow strip of towpath separates it from the lake. Here we moored for a few nights with water on either side of us, our only company a few noisy geese plucking up the courage to migrate before someone came looking for a cheap Christmas dinner.

CHAPTER TWENTY
Transnational, or Home from Home

Once, in an unguarded moment, I said I wouldn't mind living in Ellesmere. Since then, threatened even hypothetically with the prospect of me as a resident, Ellesmere set about changing a lot of what I liked about it.

In particular it set about redeveloping its short canal arm leading into the town from Beech House, the imposing mansion at the junction, which was once the canal company HQ. At first they demolished the dairy that had been at the end since the 1920s, replacing it with a supermarket. Other buildings nearby were pulled down and bland retirement homes soon began to spring up in their place. Like so many of these old canal wharves, the Ellesmere Arm used to be a hidden place, part of the town, yet somehow separate from it. Now it's like a building site that isn't being built on. The redevelopment seems to have stopped dead and what charm the arm once had has evaporated.

There's a warehouse at the same end the dairy used to be, the last vestige of the town's industrial past. It looks more derelict every time I see it, fenced off and overgrown, its windows and loading bays boarded up. Vegetation's got into its guttering, which is hanging precariously off the wall, and makes you think that inside it must be crumbling away with damp. Everybody on the canals knows the warehouse, even if they've never been to Ellesmere. Indeed, they come to Ellesmere to see it. For us on the canals, this modest warehouse at the end of the Ellesmere Arm *is* Ellesmere. It features in magazines, guides and books, and is more distinctive than any other building in the town, including Beech House.

This is mainly because it's got a huge company legend across its gable end. Painted artlessly on to the brickwork in blockish black letters a foot high, it's a constant reminder of when the canal was important to the town and when Ellesmere sat at the centre of a nationally important communications network.

SHROPSHIRE UNION
RAILWAYS AND CANAL COMPANY

GENERAL CARRIERS
TO
CHESTER, LIVERPOOL,
MANCHESTER
NORTH AND SOUTH STAFFORDSHIRE
AND
NORTH WALES

Ellesmere has such potential – that's why I could once see myself living in the place. It sits adjacent to The Mere, a substantial lake which covers almost 120 acres – the size of more than 70 football pitches – and there are eight other meres close by, making it the natural capital of what's called the Shropshire Lake District. The town itself is pleasing too, with modest, harmonious streets of two- and three-storey red-brick terraces interspersed with the odd imposing building, like the old Town Hall with its grand pediment reminiscent of the Pantheon in Rome. Ellesmere is on the up and despite the supermarket, it's still rich with small, independently run shops which have managed to survive despite the recession.

Perhaps that's because Ellesmere has traditionally been an enterprising town with an energy and vitality of its own. It was here, after all, that the canal was launched on 10 September 1792 at the Royal Oak Hotel. It is said that, though the books weren't open until noon, almost £1 million was pledged that day to the Ellesmere Canal by eager investors chasing the profit which could be made from a new waterway. The hotel's been renamed the Ellesmere Hotel and a plaque outside commemorates the event. Today, Ellesmere seems to be rediscovering the self-confidence that made it what it was, and it seems to have a new civic vision and a belief in its future.

Meanwhile the canal arm, which is always jammed with moored boats in the winter, is still a mess and the warehouse looks as if it'll fall down soon if something isn't done to it. Which – who knows – might be the intention. But why has it been allowed to get into this state? Does no one in Ellesmere care, or have they just stopped seeing it? Surely this emblem of Ellesmere should be the first thing to be spruced up as the town attempts to rebrand itself. Like you'd paint the outside of your house first if you were doing it up.

I like Ellesmere, though, I can't help it. I still have a sweet spot for the place, like you have a sweet spot for lovers from the past. Thirty-odd years ago Em and I spent New Year in the town with her mother. It's hard to believe it now, but that year we were the only boat in the arm. Once we'd tied up – adjacent to the warehouse, as it happens – we marched off to one of the local pubs, desperate for a drink. It was only after we'd ordered whiskies, and sat down, that we noticed three blokes on a table next to us. Apart from the fact that their beards were like birds' nests and could have done with trimming, they were otherwise unremarkable. Except that they were all dolled up in short skirts with what looked suspiciously like suspenders and stockings underneath.

'Evening,' I said to one whose eye I happened to catch.

'Evening,' said he. 'Chilly out, eh?' I felt like telling him that if he felt that way he'd be best adjusting his underwear. But I was distracted by another couple of blokes I'd seen near the bar. They were in dresses.

Now don't get me wrong here: the only way I'm narrow-minded is about boats. If a bloke wants to walk around in a dress that's fine with me as long as he doesn't feel he has to become a priest to justify it. But cut me some slack here; this was my mother-in-law I was with. I hurried her and Em to finish their drinks so as to move them to more salubrious surroundings, though this proved a waste of time. Outside it was apparent that something was happening in Ellesmere that New Year. Perhaps it was something they'd put into the water, or more likely something they'd put into the beer. Either way, the streets and pubs were milling with lady-blokes.

We soon got into the swing of things, however, and with a few drinks inside her, Em's mother quickly found herself dispensing style advice, which, in my opinion, some of them were taking rather too seriously for comfort. By the time the bells rang midnight heralding the onset of 1980-something or another, everyone in Ellesmere was the best of friends: we knew everyone in town and they all knew us and we were being invited to move on from the pub to people's houses for drinks and parties. It was hospitality we didn't want to refuse but which, at that time of night, having entered too literally (and too liberally) into the spirit of things, we were in no real state to accept.

We made our excuses and left. Staggered off, might be a better way of putting it.

It had been an odd evening, but in its own way arriving back in Ellesmere on a boat, like Em and I were doing now, was odder yet. Because, of course, now I *was* living in Ellesmere as I said I wanted to all those years ago. OK. I might not be living there permanently. I might not have a house there. I might not have long-term commitments to the place. Even so, for the time I was there, it was my home as much as I've ever had a home anywhere.

It was, as Marvin Gaye put it, where I had chosen to lay my hat.

* * *

At Frankton Junction, beyond Ellesmere, the canal changes course and homes in on Wales like a guided missile. Welsh Frankton, as it's also known, is a sleepy, nowhere sort of place today, just a couple of houses on either side of a bridge; but in the past it was the hub of the Ellesmere Canal and the point at which it swung off to Shrewsbury. Today, a restored flight of locks leads down to what was once an arm taking boats to the limestone quarries at Llanymynech, now being made navigable under its new name: the Montgomery Canal.

After you've negotiated the last two locks on the canal at New Marton it's an easy run through gentle and unexpectedly flat farmland towards the border at Chirk. The Berwyn Hills rise in the distance to your left but at this stage they seem too faraway and remote to be real. Besides, the thunderous A5 passing over your head at Rhoswiel keeps in check any romantic delusions about Cymru you might be harbouring. For the moment at least the noise of the traffic keeps you firmly rooted in the realities of contemporary England.

That all changes at Chirk, Y Waun in Welsh, which you skirt on a bank built around the side of a sizeable hill. You're in UNESCO World Heritage territory now, and the landscape is visibly hillier. Even so, it's still a surprise to turn a corner and come face to face with the first of the two great aqueducts on this canal spanning the valley of the River Ceiriog. The river marks the border between England and Wales and the aqueduct sits 70 feet above it. It's more than 700 feet long, an iron trough supported by ten masonry arches; and uniquely it's also got a railway viaduct running parallel to it, 30 feet higher and so close you could almost stretch out your arm and touch the supporting piers. On most other canals the unusual juxtaposition of two imposing structures like this would be its major feature, but here on the Llangollen Canal, Telford's Pontcysyllte – the second of the two aqueducts you cross – so dominates that Chirk gets nothing like the attention it deserves from boaters.

Photographers, however, are a different breed and there always seem to be one or two of them hanging around the aqueduct waiting for the classic picture of a boat going one way and a train the other. There were a couple of them that day and though it was bitterly cold I suspect they'd been waiting there for hours, with trains passing regularly on the busy Chester to Shrewsbury line but nothing at all passing the canal. It wasn't surprising really. For all intents and purposes the canal was closed now. The locks at Hurleston were shut, and soon the aqueduct itself would be drained for repairs. In fact, they were lucky to see us on the move and a part of them must have known it for as soon as we appeared there was a flurry of activity and the flickering sound of shutter apertures on auto drive.

But sadly no train passed at the same time to give them the shot they'd been waiting for. Now they'd be lucky to see another boat for two or three months.

Bit of a bitch sometimes, Life, isn't it?

***

There's a short tunnel immediately after the aqueduct. It leads into a cutting which is remarkably secluded given that immediately above it are two huge industrial sites, one of them a chipboard manufacturer and the other a former Cadbury's chocolate factory, now part of the multinational Mondelez group, a sister plant to the one familiar to us from Banbury. The canal passes a boatyard and a marina, and then enters an even shorter tunnel just a couple of hundred yards long.

We hadn't gone far into it before we began to slow down. Soon we were barely moving. Eventually we ground to a halt. I revved up the engine but we didn't shift. I revved up the engine some more. Still we didn't budge.

We were stuck, completely trapped.

To be honest, this problem wasn't altogether unexpected. The Llangollen Canal only exists today because it was an important water feeder to the rest of the canal system; and after it stopped being used commercially it only survived because it was used to supply Hurleston Reservoir at the bottom with drinking water, which it still does. Today the canal carries around 14 million gallons a day from the River Dee, a figure which has been gradually rising from the 6.25 million gallons it was permitted to extract in 1944 – an indication, if one were needed, of how demand for water has increased in modern times. No one travelling the canal can overlook the effects of it: cruising towards Llangollen you're constantly fighting the flow, which makes progress drawn-out and laborious. You slow under bridges and get buffeted in weirs approaching locks. And there's always the risk of getting stuck in tunnels – especially if you're deep-drafted like us and autumn leaves are beginning to clog up the channel.

We got off the boat, leaving it in forward gear to hold it against the current. It's futile trying to power your way out of these situations: the propeller just digs you into the canal so you finish up worse off than you were before. Best is to use as little forward power as possible – none at all if you can manage it – and haul the boat through manually. We attached two ropes, one fixed to the bow, which I took, the other for Em secured to the centre. From now it was just brute force, dragging the boat through as best we could.

At first *Justice* didn't respond: it was as if she was stuck to the bottom or as if we were pulling against some fixed object like a wall or a tree which we had no hope of moving. We strained more, leaning against the ropes to get greater leverage. Still there was no response. We were gasping for breath now, arching so far forward on the ropes we were almost touching the ground. Finally, almost imperceptibly, she began to edge forward, and though this movement was so slight anyone watching would scarcely have noticed it, it meant that at least we'd got some momentum. Now we just had to keep it going. We had to ensure that we didn't stop, that we didn't have to get this 20-tonne Leviathan moving from a standing start again.

I found myself talking to the boat, cursing at it to relieve my frustration as I heaved on the rope. 'Come on, you little shit, come on. Don't stop now. Move!' I found myself talking to Em to encourage her. 'Come on, love, not far now, just a little further.' Sometimes I found myself talking to Em thinking she was the boat, 'Come on, put your back into it, you bastard, don't let me down now...' Luckily for me (though not her) she's got hearing problems and didn't catch what I was saying.

Step by step, inch by inch, we crept forward, but 191 yards under these conditions is an immense distance and it took us more than an hour to cover it. When we finally emerged we were hot, sweaty and exhausted, but too keyed up to stop even for a cup of tea. We were approaching Telford's aqueduct now – we could see it through the trees, a certain majesty to it even at this distance.

However, before I go on, there's the question of the name of this aqueduct. Every year some four or five thousand boats travel up the canal and without exception they nearly all refer to the aqueduct as... well, as the aqueduct. Some might call it *the* aqueduct, the stress made not to distinguish it from Chirk so much as to acknowledge its grandeur. Some, recognising that it has a name and that it is disrespectful to a unique Grade I listed structure like this not to use it, will attempt something that comes out sounding like they're choking on their morning cornflakes. Pontiskilt, or Puntyskylight, or Pantisulty. A few will just give up the challenge and call it the Pontywhatnot, which is worse than useless.

For heaven's sake, why can't boaters behave? This is Welsh, it's not a foreign language. They wouldn't go through Slaithwaite in Yorkshire calling it that when everyone knows it's pronounced Slawit. They wouldn't cruise through Loughborough calling it Loogerborooger. They'd get laughed at. The same as the Welsh would laugh if they weren't too polite to do it.

So let's get this right, once and for all: Pontcysyllte can be broken down as if it had four syllables. The first, 'Pont', is simple, pronounced as it looks (except that in this context you'll find yourself swallowing the 't' off the end as you say it). The second, pronounced to rhyme with 'bus', is 'cus'. The third is 'uth' (imagine someone with a lisp trying to say 'us'). Finally, there's a bit on the end which shouldn't cause you any problems at all. Just pronounce it 'te' as in 'ten' or 'television' or 'tension'.

Now put them all together, say it in a Welsh accent and let's have no more of this nonsense:

'Pont-cus-uth-te.'

See. Easy peasy.

Whatever you call it, nothing quite prepares you for it. You'll have seen photographs and videos and TV programmes until they're coming out your ears, but the reality of the Pontcysyllte Aqueduct is that, even in today's world of towering office blocks and bridges like knife blades, it's a wondrous creation that defies belief. Completed in 1805, the year of the Battle of Trafalgar, it's a cast-iron trough more than a thousand feet long which towers nearly 130 feet above the River Dee, supported on 18 precipitous stone columns.

By boat, you approach it along an embankment from which you seem to launch into the air abruptly, like a bird taking off from the edge of a cliff. This impression of flying is amplified by the fact that, though the aqueduct has a towpath with railings on one side, on the other there's nothing except a sheer drop to the ground. In canal-carrying days some horses wouldn't cross it. Today I won't. Or not on the back of the boat, at least. We have what's called a 'traditional' stern deck where just a cant – a narrow, inch-high ledge of steel at foot level – prevents you falling off. So I leave the steering over the aqueduct to Em, or if Em's not around and I'm single-handing, I set the boat to bump itself across on its own in forward gear while I take to the towpath and wait for it on the other side.

I'm not exaggerating. If, like me, you have no head for heights, even walking over the aqueduct on the towpath is an ordeal. A friend of mine won't do it. Crossing on a boat, where the only thing which prevents you plunging over the edge to eternity is the side of the trough, the feeling it engenders in us acrophobics is close to terror. You can walk over the Pontcysyllte aqueduct on the towpath a thousand times but you won't experience the half of it until you've been over it on the water.

If you can find a space, it's worth mooring up and having a look at it from below. A steep, well-marked path leads down from the Llangollen side to the river; alternatively there's a narrow packhorse bridge that crosses the river further down and which is just a short walk by road from the boatyard at the end. From either of these vantage points you can see how the aqueduct dominates the wide valley and how gracefully it spans it, the individual piers tapering elegantly towards the top, giving the impression of the structure being a lot more insubstantial than it is.

Or putting it another way, it looks as precarious as it feels.

The aqueduct is too narrow for boats to pass each other, but even so there's no rule governing right of way except that if you see that it's clear, you go for it. This works OK, sort of, except at certain times of the week in the summer when there's such a prevalence of hire boats going in the opposite direction to you that you just have to wait. Mind you, if you've come this far up the canal in the summer this should be something you're used to by now. Occasionally you do get some impatient lamebrain who ventures on to the aqueduct when it's obvious there are boats coming in the opposite direction. We witnessed a stunning example of it once when a boat in front of us decided to mix it with a flotilla of canoes coming towards us. They were already on the aqueduct and they weren't intimidated. He was forced into a humiliating climb-down and had to reverse.

The same rule about right of way applies turning the 90-degree bend at Trevor that takes you off the main line of the canal and on to the water feeder to Llangollen – though this is a trickier manoeuvre altogether. At least on the aqueduct it's self-evident who has right of way. On the bend it's far from clear. It doesn't matter from which direction you're approaching, you don't have a clear view; and though the sensible thing would be for boaters to send a crew member to see if anything's coming, you'd be surprised how many don't bother. And if I'm frank, even when they do it makes no odds. Even if they don't collide with another boat, turning a 90-degree bend in a boat more than 60-feet long is a task beyond many of them, and they either go crashing into the concrete wall of the towpath or, if they realise that's what about to happen, they'll throw their engines into reverse at the last moment and fling their boats all over the place uncontrollably. By which stage, even if they had the right of way in the first place, there'll be another boat coming in the opposite direction and they won't have it now...

The Trevor turn is like Grindley Brook in this respect. There are places to sit and a cafe to hand and lots of laughs to be had watching everyone make a balls-up of it.

You'd expect that after all the fun and games coming over Pontcysyllte and turning into the water feeder that the remaining few miles into Llangollen would at least be a bit quieter. Yet you'd be wrong. This is a beautiful section of canal – some say the most beautiful in the whole country – but it's also the narrowest. There are pinch points where boats can't pass, and lay-bys where approaching craft have to moor temporarily to wait their turn to go through. In high summer, as in so many places on this overused, abused waterway, it can be chaos. People are in a rush to get to Llangollen; they're in a rush to get away; they're just in a rush, full stop. It means queues and more queues, and sometimes a tiresome and bad-tempered crawl to the basin at the end, which is the terminus. But hey, if you choose to cruise in high season it's what you have to expect.

For us, boating at this time of the year with Christmas getting closer by the day, the canal was empty, cut off from the rest of the waterways by the stoppages. It was ours and ours alone now: a seasonal gift to us from providence, which seemed to have been so generous to us already over the course of our year's travelling. It meant we were able to enjoy the Vale of Llangollen in tranquillity. To the right the limestone plateau of Eglwyseg and Trevor Rocks was like a huge wall towering over us, while to the left the constantly narrowing valley of the Dee, bordered by misty meadows and hills, began to enclose us like a welcoming arm. Ahead, marking our destination was the thousand-foot peak of Castell Dinas Bran, an Iron Age hill fort crowned with the ruins of a medieval castle built in the thirteenth century when princes of Powys ruled this land.

This part of our journey gave us the chance for some quiet reflection on our period living on the boat. Looked at one way, we hadn't really travelled very far – 400 miles, maybe, perhaps a bit more. But looked at another way, our voyage had been an odyssey of great distance. It had been a distance of the mind, a psychological distance. And what is distance anyhow but a psychological phenomenon?

In the past they understood this better than we do now. In those days the relationship between places wasn't measured by the mathematics of mileage: it was measured by how long it took to get between them. A village might be a day or a week away – and that determined how you felt about it. Most places were a long way off; some were so far as to be fantasies, scarcely existing in the real world at all.

But then came the railway and somewhere that had been days or even weeks from a large city now became hours. Things like that change the way you see the world. The distances didn't alter; what altered was the way we felt about distance. Soon there were planes littering the skies. Before long it was feasible to go to New York for the weekend.

People who didn't understand what we were doing on the canals asked us how we could call what we did travelling. Except they didn't put it that way because that would have been too rude. Instead, they'd make some facetious comment like, 'It took you how long to get there? I could have done that in an hour in the car.' We'd given up responding eventually. We knew what we were doing even if they didn't. Travelling at a snail's pace with our home around us, covering 10 or

12 miles a day, often less, we were redefining our relationship to distance, going back to how it had been a couple of generations ago. That way we could see the world rather than just pass through it.

'But how can you manage in the space?' people would ask. 'How can you fit things in?' Things? I'll tell you about things. We only had one small crockery cupboard in which we kept four glasses, two for us and two for anyone who happened to visit. They were basic wine glasses, the sort you can buy in a pound shop. I call them wine glasses but they were actually quite tall and looked a bit like champagne glasses if you squinted, though actually, when you did that, they didn't look like champagne glasses at all because they were wide and bulbous at the bottom like port glasses. Except they weren't really port glasses because if you were in a fix, and didn't want to neck it out of the bottle, you could drink beer out of them too.

And you know what? For a lot of our time on the boat, until we smashed them to bits on the River Wey after our altercation with the lock gate, we drank wine and champagne and port and beer out of those glasses and it all tasted just as good, and got us just as tipsy, as it would have in the best crystal.

'But how do you pass the time?' people asked. 'What do you do with yourselves?' This was a more difficult question to answer. After all, what did we do with our time? I don't think either of us knew where it went except it was the morning and then, by some process of which we were barely aware, it was dark again and we were going to bed.

Of course, you spend time on a boat doing a lot of basic things that in a house you'd take for granted: you have to empty your lavatory and fill up with water and ensure you've always got enough gas and diesel. But that still leaves a lot of time over. We spent a fair amount of it looking at birds – by which I don't mean we spent time birdwatching. I mean we spent a lot of time looking at birds – mainly big ones – geese, ducks, chickens in people's gardens. Just watching them. For no reason at all. Because they were interesting, I guess. Well, we thought they were interesting. They were never interested in us, though. They got bored very quickly and walked off.

We spent a lot of time reading notices pinned to trees too. About planning applications or killer shrimps in the cut, or missing dogs. We found them totally engrossing. We found the windows of village shops absorbing too, filled with ads for gardeners or local car repairers or retired teachers offering conversational French; and announcements from the WI who were having a crochet evening on the 18th and the Mothers' Union who were making a quilt and wanted volunteers...

What did we do, people kept asking. Well, I'll tell you what we did. We did so much that however much we did we never had time to do it all; and we were both left puzzling how short was a day, a week, a month. A lifetime.

The canal arrives in Llangollen on a high embankment on the north side of the town, so that the first time you're aware of it is when grey slate roofs and the painted white walls of buildings start appearing through the trees below and it reveals itself like a bud gently blossoming. It was evening by now and the town was lit up with Christmas decorations. The bridge crossing the crashing white waters of the River Dee was strung with lights which continued up the main street; and further over, the tower of the church of St Collen, which gives Llangollen its name, was topped by a glowing Christmas cross. Even the stars sparkling in the frosty firmament seemed part of the ornamentation: they hung over the town like a glistening crown from one side of the valley to the other, from peak to snow-covered peak.

There were already a few craft along the towpath tied up for winter, one of them, extraordinarily, the boat we'd seen so long ago on the River Stort in Hertfordshire – the boat which had revived the plans we'd had for living afloat. The coincidence of this seemed like a good omen and we tucked ourselves into a nearby mooring spot.

It was strange. We hadn't planned to come here; neither of us had nursed a burning desire to be in Wales. In fact, it was only chance that had brought us here at all, chance and the opportunity of spending time in a place that was comfortable and about as far removed from London as it was possible to be. But now we'd arrived we knew immediately that we'd done the right thing. There was something about Llangollen we both warmed to immediately. There was something about its quiet, ordered streets, its turreted Royal Hotel and its library which had once been a chapel. There was something about its people, their quiet and undemanding friendliness. There was something about the sound of the town too, the unceasing clamour of the river crashing over the rocks and the resonance of steam trains echoing around the valley from its heritage railway.

Yes, it was odd. It was almost as if, for the first time since we'd left Blackheath all those months ago, we'd found somewhere that felt like home.

ACKNOWLEDGEMENTS

Firstly, many thanks as usual to my friend and former colleague Miles Hedley who, along with my long-suffering editor Jennifer Barclay, managed somehow to make a book out of my grammatically illiterate, chaotically organised manuscript. I owe more to them both than I am willing to admit publically. Thanks are due too to my copy-editor Ray Hamilton who at an alarmingly late stage picked up so many of my mistakes that I'm embarrassed to think what an idiot I'd have looked otherwise.

Before, during and after the journey I took down the River Thames, which I describe here, I read a large number of books for research. One I kept coming back to time and time again was Christopher Winn's *I Never Knew That About the River Thames*, which is a delightful repository of all that is most unusual in this most unusual of waterways. I'd recommend it to anyone planning on exploring the river, whether by boat or foot. I'd also recommend The Wey Valley website (www.weyriver.co.uk/theriver) for anyone interested in finding out more about the beautiful River Wey. This website is everything that a volunteer website should be: it's packed with information, anecdotes, gossip and history. Most of all it's entertaining and it's quirky.

ACKNOWLEDGEMENTS

Last but not least, my thanks to the staff at Llangollen Library, where most of this book was written. As soon as they identified me as a writer they showed interest in this project and offered me encouragement and support however they could. In this era when libraries seem to be closing by the week, I can only thank Denbighshire County Council for their pig-headed and very Welsh determination to buck the trend and strike a blow for the old-fashioned values of literacy, education, knowledge, community and scholarship which libraries represent.

NARROWBOAT
DREAMS

*A Journey
North by
England's
Waterways*

 ## STEVE
HAYWOOD

NARROWBOAT DREAMS

A Journey North by England's Waterways

Steve Haywood

£8.99

Paperback

ISBN: 978-1-84024-670-4

At home, I'm a cantankerous old git. On the boat, after a week's cruising, I'm just a cantankerous old git with dirty hair.

Steve Haywood has a problem. He doesn't know where he comes from. In the south, people think he's a northerner; in the north, they think he's from the south. Judged against global warming and the sad demise of *Celebrity Big Brother*, this hardly registers highly on the Richter scale of world disasters. But it's enough to worry Steve. And it's enough of an excuse for him to escape his long-suffering partner Em for a voyage of discovery along England's inland waterways.

Travelling by traditional narrowboat, he heads north along two newly opened Pennine canals, a trip that takes him from Banbury in deepest Oxfordshire, through the vibrant modernity of Manchester, to the trendy affluence of Hebden Bridge, West Yorkshire's answer to London's ciabatta belt.

With irrepressible humour he recounts the history of the waterways and stories of his encounters with characters along the way, and attempts to define the magic that makes England's waterways so appealing.

ONE MAN
— AND A —
NARROWBOAT

*Slowing down time
on England's
waterways*

STEVE
HAYWOOD

ONE MAN AND A NARROWBOAT

Slowing Down Time on England's Waterways

Steve Haywood

£9.99

Paperback

ISBN: 978-1-84024-736-7

If I'd really been serious about getting to grips with my mid-life crisis, then I'd have been better opting for a course of therapy than going off travelling. Or if I had to travel, I'd have been better opting for somewhere warm with a beach...

In an attempt to get to grips with a BIG birthday, Steve sets out from Oxford to explore what makes the English... well, so English. His quirky humour is inspired by Tom Rolt, who took to the canals on a similar journey immortalised in the book *Narrow Boat*, kick-starting the revival of Britain's waterways. Prepare for a generous helping of mayhem, mishaps and the staple of every English summer: torrential rain.

'A quirky look at the English and English countryside... splendidly written'   CANAL BOAT magazine

'A very enjoyable book to read – light-hearted, interesting and informative. What a way to travel!'   David Suchet OBE, actor

TOO NARROW
-TO-
SWING A CAT

*Going Nowhere in
Particular on
the English Waterways*

❀ STEVE HAYWOOD ❀

TOO NARROW TO SWING A CAT

Going Nowhere in Particular on the English Waterways

Steve Haywood

£9.99

Paperback

ISBN: 978-1-84953-065-1

She was under the sink, curled up in the vegetable rack, her head cushioned by a large potato. She opened one eye and looked at me lazily.

Casting aside the road maps that show the country as a web of interlocking motorways, Steve escapes to a different England on his narrowboat and cruises slowly through a landscape unchanged for centuries, visiting picturesque towns and canal festivals. But the new member of his crew, Kit, is an untidy bundle of fur with all the attitude you would expect from a 'sarf Lunnun' cat, and determined to keep him on his toes.

'His quietly humorous style makes these books a joy to read'
TOWPATH TALK

Have you enjoyed this book?
If so, why not write a review on your favourite website?

If you're interested in finding out more about our books,
find us on Facebook at **Summersdale Publishers** and follow us
on Twitter at **@Summersdale**.

Thanks very much for buying this Summersdale book.

www.summersdale.com